T0265495

OCEANS RISE EMPIRES FALL

OCEANS RISE
EMPIRES FALL

WHY GEOPOLITICS HASTENS
CLIMATE CATASTROPHE

GERARD TOAL

OXFORD
UNIVERSITY PRESS

OXFORD
UNIVERSITY PRESS

Oxford University Press is a department of the University of Oxford. It furthers
the University's objective of excellence in research, scholarship, and education
by publishing worldwide. Oxford is a registered trade mark of Oxford University
Press in the UK and certain other countries.

Published in the United States of America by Oxford University Press
198 Madison Avenue, New York, NY 10016, United States of America.

© Oxford University Press 2024

All rights reserved. No part of this publication may be reproduced, stored in
a retrieval system, or transmitted, in any form or by any means, without the
prior permission in writing of Oxford University Press, or as expressly permitted
by law, by license, or under terms agreed with the appropriate reproduction
rights organization. Inquiries concerning reproduction outside the scope of the
above should be sent to the Rights Department, Oxford University Press, at the
address above.

You must not circulate this work in any other form
and you must impose this same condition on any acquirer.

Library of Congress Cataloging-in-Publication Data
Names: Toal, Gerard, author.
Title: Oceans rise empires fall : why geopolitics hastens climate catastrophe / Gerard Toal.
Description: New York, N.Y. : Oxford University Press, [2024] |
Includes bibliographical references and index.
Identifiers: LCCN 2023038585 (print) | LCCN 2023038586 (ebook) |
ISBN 9780197693261 (hardback) | ISBN 9780197693278 (epub)
Subjects: LCSH: Geopolitics—Environmental aspects. | Climatic changes. |
Environmental degradation. | Economic growth—Environmental aspects. |
Fossil fuels—Environmental aspects. | Fossil fuels—Economic aspects. |
Fossil fuels—Political aspects. | World politics—21st century.
Classification: LCC JC319 .T588 2024 (print) | LCC JC319 (ebook) |
DDC 320.1/2—dc23/eng/20231101
LC record available at https://lccn.loc.gov/2023038585
LC ebook record available at https://lccn.loc.gov/2023038586

DOI: 10.1093/oso/9780197693261.001.0001

Printed by Sheridan Books, Inc., United States of America

For Sabine

Contents

Introduction

Rising Threats

A decade ago, a threat rose from the ocean. By pumping vast amounts of sand onto living coral reefs and mixing cement to create concrete foundations, a fleet of dredging machines from China raised a string of artificial islands across the internationally disputed waters of the South China Sea.[1] Built upon the newly reclaimed land was a familiar island infrastructure: ports, hangars, towers, lighthouses, and housing. But there was more: large runways, radar installations, missile batteries, reinforced bunkers, and fortified point-defense systems. China was expanding.

Xi Jinping became the paramount leader of China in 2012. The following year, China built twenty artificial outposts on the Paracel Islands and seven on the Spratly Islands, reclaiming about 3,200 acres of land from the sea as new Chinese territory.[2] The strategy, dubbed "the Great Wall of Sand" by US Pacific Fleet Commander Admiral Harry Harris, created a chain of military infrastructures and fortifications that enabled the Chinese navy and air force to project hard power across the region.[3] These have also backed up more assertive ownership claims by China over the surrounding volumes of water and air.[4]

Before China's territorial moves in the South China Sea, the prevailing US perception of China was of a peacefully rising world power. China's creation of new territories for itself on the sea, however,

helped change that.[5] Strategists saw China's practices in the South
China Sea as a challenge to US dominance in the Pacific and, more
generally, to the rules of a liberal international order.[6] Did China seek
exclusive control of the South China Sea?[7] An estimated $2.5 trillion
worth of oil and gas reserves on the ocean floor, as well as control
of rich fishing resources, were said to be at stake.[8] The 1.4 million-
square-mile expanse of sea accounts for approximately 12% of the
total global fish catch.[9] The South China Sea also handles roughly
one-third of the world's oceangoing trade.[10] Old marine maps with
dashed lines showed, according to China, that it owned the South
China Sea. New island forts and aggressive territorial behavior now
backed up this spurious claim.[11] Surely, this was proof that China was
becoming a threat and that it wanted to replace the United States as
the most powerful country in the Pacific, if not the whole world?[12]

Amidst this wave of strategic anxiety, a few sharp-eyed analysts
noticed something more. The infrastructure that the Chinese navy
had so quickly and impressively constructed was not doing so well.
Rumors suggested that the concrete was crumbling and the foundations were turning to sponge.[13] Exposed metal was corroding quickly.
"An artillery gun," one researcher reported, "was put out of service in
just three months because of rust."[14]

Others noticed that China's hasty island construction had destroyed
many fragile coral ecosystems across the South China Sea. These supported rich fishing grounds which provided protein to millions in Asia.
Overfishing, especially by Chinese factory ships which bullied smaller
Vietnamese and Filipino fishing boats on the water, also threatened
the sustainability of the South China Sea's fishing stocks. Oceanic
pollution, particularly from plastics waste, was a serious problem too.[15]

Further issues were visible on the instruments of the scientific
community: rising ocean temperatures and acidity levels, increasing
storm intensities, and sea level rise. The latter was already threatening low-lying islands in other parts of the Pacific. Human habitation
on Pacific Island nations such as Vanuatu, Tuvalu, Fiji, Kiribati, and
the Marshall Islands is seriously jeopardized by rising seas, degraded

fishing, and more frequent storm surges connected to climate change. Would China's new island formations suffer the same fate? Was their construction an expression of power or of hubris?

The desire to capture untapped fossil fuel reserves on the ocean floor is a presumed motivation for Chinese island-building in the South China Sea.[16] But the climatic consequences of the fossil-fuel burning energy systems that have powered the capitalist global economy for more than a century threaten to overwhelm the entire endeavor. Indeed, unless modern civilization sharply reduces greenhouse gas emissions, the oceans are expected to swallow large swaths of land over the next quarter century.[17] According to current estimates, approximately 150 million people now live on land that will be below the high-tide line by 2050.[18] Shanghai and its surroundings, a vital hub in the global economy, will be submerged unless there is a massive engineering response. Bangkok in Thailand, Mumbai in India, Ho Chi Minh City in Vietnam, and many other cities around the world will follow suit. Southern Vietnam, once fought over with massive firepower and toxic chemicals to keep communism at bay, may also be lost to rising tides.

Climate change is shifting the earthly foundations of our geopolitics. World powers today face a fundamentally new question: Are rising Earth temperatures and sea levels a greater emergency than the rising power of rival states? The question is increasingly insistent, yet the trade-offs and choices it demands are not yet clearly grasped and debated in democratic societies. Some policymakers understand that climate breakdown is an unprecedented planetary emergency, one that demands a radically new collaborative international order. Most state security institutions and politicians, though, are fixated on economic and military competition against rival world powers. Few consider the deeper problem, namely that geopolitical practices themselves are a major structural driver of the climate crisis. In obsessively promoting their own security, mission, and military might, world powers have long played geopolitics against each other, at the expense of the planet. To understand the climate crisis fully, we need to see the practices of geopolitics geo-ecologically. We need, in other words, to "Earth" geopolitics.

Modernity Exposed

Chinese island-building in the South China Sea opens up much larger questions about territorial formation and modernity. Over the last six centuries, humans have dramatically increased their capacity to mold the Earth to their requirements. Terraformation, the making of land, the reworking of the natural environment to serve specific groups, is an enduring human drive.[19] Terra, while often equated with fixed dry land, actually encompasses all sorts of terrains, themselves never singular but interacting: lands and seas, rivers and fields, mountains and valleys, wetlands and plains, deserts and tundra.[20] All lands and seas, however, are not themselves without the planet's atmosphere, and the dynamic hydrological and atmospheric processes that are climate. In clearing forests, cultivating crops, and burning materials for energy, humans started altering its chemical composition. For most of our species' history, human societies developed their capacity for terraformation in very limited and localized ways. The development of a capitalist world economy anchored in Europe from the fifteenth century onward changed this, giving birth to a massive terraforming enterprise that is still working itself out across the vast spaces of the planet.[21] *Modernity* is a one-word name for this remarkable environmental engineering project, a connected flowing network of resources, commodities, states, peoples, technologies, and, importantly, pollution.

Modernity sought to harness the planet's dynamic geophysical processes and biospheres to serve the specific economic, social, and state interests associated with capitalism's global expansion as a mode of production and exchange. The project's crucible was initially Spain and Portugal, then the Dutch Republic, then the British Empire, and finally the United States.[22] Now the world economy is global, with just a few earthly spaces beyond its extractive imperatives. This global economy is configured along grooves established over hundreds of years, pathways for the flow of investments, peoples, and commodities that once coexisted with movements of soldiers, priests, weapons, and diseases, and still do in certain instances. Global cities are the organizational nodes of the vast system, sustaining dense concentrations of humanity while altering the Earth's geo-ecological systems with relentless extraction and pollution.

Capitalist modernity always had a great story to tell, of expansion and growth, of development and progress, as modern humans gradually acquired greater power over their surroundings and freed themselves from prior constraints. But these familiar stories of progress, of modernization, of inexorable growth on a bountiful Earth are no longer as persuasive as they once were. Modernity is a dream of making the world better, of providing further growth, superior technologies, and greater affluence for all. Yet it is perpetually thwarted by crises and crashes, wars and collapses. It demands the Earth and then some. Classical modernity saw the transformation of traditional societies into industrial societies, first through the adoption of steam power, then the widespread adoption of coal and later petroleum for energy.

Following World War II, industrial societies experienced a second wave of modernity associated with the adoption of new technoscientific forms of production and consumption. Proliferating infrastructures of hydrocarbon fuel extraction, transportation, and consumption were supplemented by nuclear power systems. Industrial societies became what the German sociologist Ulrich Beck in 1986 termed "world risk society" with abundance coexisting with more intrusive forms of pollution. This second modernity is a "reflexive modernization," one constantly striving to adjust to the success and excess—the "side effects" that are always much more than this—of classical modernity. But it is still modernity, a dream of endless growth.[23]

That dream has produced the ecological crises that are now surrounding us, and that claim the future. "The modes of common life that have arisen largely within the last one hundred years, and whose intensity has accelerated only since 1945," the historian Timothy Mitchell observes, "are shaping the planet for the next one thousand years, and perhaps the next 50,000."[24] Modernity's side effects are now taking center stage.

While many societies hold fast to the dream of modernization, updated to include solar panels and wind farms, the scientific findings on the current and likely future trajectory of global climate changes suggest that life on the human-dominated Earth created by modernity is going to be radically different from what it has been until now. Climate change is just one of an interconnected series of distressed Earth systems. Biosphere integrity is threatened by collapsing biodiversity, land system change, biogeochemical imbalances, disrupted hydrological systems, atmosphere aerosol loading, ozone depletion, ocean acidification, and endemic pollution from novel entities introduced by technoscientific modernity.[25] The latest round of Intergovernmental Panel on Climate Change (IPCC) reports makes it clear that Earth's surface temperatures are going to keep going up.[26] Each of the past four decades has been successively warmer than any decade that preceded it since 1850. The global surface temperature rise since then is approaching 1.5 degrees Celsius and will almost certainly exceed this in the next year or so.

Climate breakdown is radically changing oceans, as temperatures and acidity levels rise sharply. Around 90% of the energy trapped in the climate system by greenhouse gases goes into the ocean.[27] The hottest ocean temperatures in recorded history were in 2022, the seventh consecutive year this record was broken.[28] And 2023 has almost certainly surpassed this. Combined with acidification and pollution, these spikes in temperature have devastating effects on marine life and ocean ecosystems. Their effects on oceanic circulation systems are a matter of considerable concern.

Average sea levels are also rising at an unprecedented rate. The rate of global mean sea level rise, according to satellite data, has doubled between the first decade of observations (1993–2002 at 2.27 mm per year) and the latest (2013–2022 at 4.62 mm per year).[29] Massive sea level rise scenarios are on the horizon. The threshold of global temperature rise that would trigger irreversible melting on the planet's enormous ice sheets in Greenland and Antarctica is estimated to lie between 1.5 degrees and 2.0 degrees Celsius.[30] Current research suggests warmer tides are eroding the seafloor moorings of huge glaciers in both of these critical Earth system regions, rendering them increasingly unstable.[31] Geomorphological realities matter crucially: the West Antarctic Ice Sheet lies largely below current sea level and is thus particularly vulnerable to warmer ocean waters undermining it from below. A collapse of the Pine Island Glacier and Thwaites Glacier will raise global sea level by 1.2 meters (4 feet). This will undermine the West Antarctic Ice Sheet, and its disintegration would add another 3.3 meters (11 feet) in global mean sea level rise. Antarctica, as a whole, holds enough ice to raise sea levels by 60 meters (200 feet).[32] The tipping points here are uncertain, but it is entirely possible that global sea levels could rise by a meter or more by the end of this century.[33] Indeed, the recent IPCC Report noted that global sea level rise approaching two meters by 2100 and five meters by 2150 cannot be ruled out under its high emission scenario due to deep uncertainty about ice sheet disintegration processes.[34] No matter what the scenario, current 1-in-100 year extreme sea-level events are projected to occur at least annually in more than half of all tide gauge locations by 2100.[35]

The extent to which these trends continue depends on the interaction of multiple Earth system dynamics, but nonlinear change is expected as tipping points, cascade effects, and feedback loops work themselves out. The scale of recent changes across the climate system, as well as the current state of many aspects of this system, is unprecedented over the last 125,000 years.[36] The past nine years have been the hottest in recorded human history. The year 2023 was the first with all days over 1 degree Celsius hotter than the pre-industrial average; a third of its days were 1.5 above this. There is no future scenario that does not involve significant adaptation to higher temperatures, as this is already built in due to accumulated greenhouse gas emissions which can linger in the atmosphere for thousands of years. At the annual United Nations climate summits, the gap between the pledges of delegate states to reduce emissions and the material realities of actual emissions is increasingly stark. Even factoring in existing decarbonization pledges, the trajectory of emissions suggests that the planet is headed for a median 2.8 degrees Celsius temperature increase by the end of this century.[37]

Explaining Collective Failure

Clearly, modern civilization is headed for catastrophe if it continues to produce greenhouse gases at the rate it has for the past century, and especially the past few decades. The alarming trajectory of the Earth system is now well known. Newspapers cover the topic regularly with ever more alarming updates and summaries of scientific reports. It is crystal clear that modern human civilization is not acting in its collective best interest. Despite having abundant scientific evidence that humanity's future is imperiled and that climate catastrophe is a very real possibility, modern civilization continues to operate as "normal," meaning in a future-destroying manner. Corporate elites and state leaders, educated and knowing, still act in ways that sabotage the future of their children and their children's children. Climate change is an existential threat that is not treated as an emergency.

There are many theories that account for this indifference to looming catastrophe, a seeming civilizational death wish. Political economy explanations focus on the power structures that helped create the global environmental crisis. Marxist accounts focus on the historical development of capitalism as an extractive and environmentally degrading mode of production that favored monetary exchange value over non-monetary use value.[38] Political ecology details how market logics marginalize Indigenous people, convert land into property, ignore pollution, and discount the future.[39] Because it is a mode of production that has long prioritized short-term profits over the long-term sustainability of its extractive practices, capitalism is blamed both for the current environmental crisis and for an inability to do anything about it.[40] "It is easier to imagine the end of the world than the end of capitalism" is a popular summation of this sentiment.[41]

For some corporations, this was their actual working practice. Oil companies like Exxon Corporation (ExxonMobil after its merger with Mobil Oil in 1999) knew for decades that their business of extracting and selling fossil fuels would result in a significant global temperature rise. From the late 1970s and early 1980s, its scientists accurately modeled and skillfully predicted global warming from fossil fuel burning.[42] Yet the company's corporate strategy was to systematically deny and obscure this material reality. It made economic sense to pursue profits in the short term and discount the future consequences. In 2022, ExxonMobil earned a record $55.7 billion in profit, about $6.3 million every hour. Five of the West's largest energy companies—ExxonMobil, BP, Shell, TotalEnergies, and Chevron—reported a combined $195 billion in profit in 2022.[43] Saudi Aramco, largely controlled by Saudi Arabia, alone recorded a record profit of $161 billion, a figure described as "probably the highest net income ever reported in the corporate world."[44]

Philosophical explanations of the climate crisis examine the disenchantment of nature in modernity. This has been variously characterized as a shift from an organic to mechanical conception of land and from a vitalist to a calculative conception of the Earth. Early modern Christian theology justified human supremacy over nature and the expropriation of lands from non-Christian peoples ("pagans") in the name of a parochial faith declared universal.[45] Further, land was inanimate, a commodity that could be parceled and traded. The late French philosopher Bruno Latour argued that the modern worldview that separates nature from culture, or tries to at least, is a source of the environmental crisis. This cleavage leads to a devaluation of the natural world and a failure to recognize the actual material interconnectedness of things.[46]

Yet other explanations alight on the material dependencies of modernity. Modern human civilization is so reliant upon the consumption

of fossil fuels for energy and many other activities that this is pro-
foundly difficult to shift. Vaclav Smil identifies four pillars of modern
civilization: cement, steel, plastics, and ammonia.[47] The mass-scale
production of all of these heavily depends on hydrocarbon use.
Cement, steel, and plastics are indispensable materials in the construction of modern cities and infrastructures. Ammonia is vital in the
production of nitrogenous fertilizers that make it possible for agriculture to produce sufficient food to support billions of people. Indeed,
Smil suggests the modern world's most existential dependence on
fossil fuels is their direct and indirect use in the production of food.[48]
Decarbonizing modernity is next to impossible, many argue, and may
itself tempt catastrophe.

Yet other explanations focus on the psychological roots of the crisis
and the myriad of human "cognitive biases" that reward turning away
rather than confronting the crisis.[49] The satirical film *Don't Look Up*,
for example, is an indictment of the narcissism of contemporary culture and media.[50] Distraction and short-termism dominate. Humans
are reluctant to make major changes to their lives absent an extreme
and visible emergency. Even then, many would rather retreat into
fantasy or fatalism. The constituency for action is not overwhelming,
and it may never be. Indeed, it is almost inevitable that when global
heating comes to dominate, it will already be too late to reverse the
radical disruptions it will bring to human habitation across the Earth.

Clearly the coming climate catastrophe does not have a single cause,
but is rather a complex entanglement of many different factors. In any
explanatory framework, one powerful factor, nevertheless, cannot be
ignored: *geopolitics*. This book is an argument for why it is significant
and why it needs comprehensive critical analysis.

What is Geopolitics?

Geopolitics is an elastic term with many meanings. Today it is most
commonly associated with great power competition. A great power

is a country with a large territory, population, economy, and military capacity. A status construct in international society, the term can obscure major differences between states, though it usefully signifies a shared hubris for "greatness."[51] To certain state leaders and international relations scholars, great power competition is an endemic feature of the interstate system. Indeed, in recent years this notion has become an obsession in Western strategic circles. Great power competition is now a catchphrase used to justify new rounds of military spending, new industrial policies, and new strategic alliances.[52] A performative speech act that thinks itself merely descriptive, it has even earned its own Pentagon abbreviation: GPC.[53]

This new emphasis of great power competition is frequently cast in terms of a global clash of ideals and values, a struggle between democracy and authoritarianism. But the rivalry between the United States and China, and the United States and Russia, is also widely understood as a geostrategic struggle for relative power over the perceived material resources for future prosperity in world affairs. Though the United States and China are strongly connected by trade and investment networks, both states have become more explicit geo-economic rivals. Under President Biden the United States has restricted China's access to leading-edge technologies and has sought greater control over what it has deemed strategic supply chains and critical minerals. This has heightened frictions with China and has driven it into closer strategic alignment with Russia. Obscured in this discourse of competition, though, is something fundamental: the geo-ecological costs of great power rivalry.

The geo-ecological wasn't always hidden. Geopolitics has an older definition, one notorious for justifying German imperial expansionism in Europe during World War II. German geopolitics (*Geopolitik*) held that great powers were living organisms in a competitive struggle for space. Deprived of national territory and colonies by the Treaty of Versailles, intellectuals and revanchist politicians called for greater *lebensraum* (living space) for the German people. This latter word became a rallying cry in Nazi Germany, one used to justify the territorial expansion of the Third Reich and the creation of a "new order" in Europe organized around life and prosperity for Aryan Germans at the expense of all others. This is the dark mirror of the conventional understanding of geopolitics—geopolitics as racial geo-ecological imperialism.

As climate breakdown deepens across the planet, the politics of living space is returning anew with great urgency. The Earth's biosphere has clear material limits and tipping points, most obviously the level of greenhouse gas concentrations in the planet's atmosphere. This so-called carbon budget for keeping heating below 1.5 degrees Celsius has largely been used up by just a few world powers—led by the United States and China—at the expense of everyone else. The resulting effects—climate breakdown, global heating, desertification, unprecedented flooding, and wildfires—are violently remaking living spaces across the Earth. While some continue to live wealthy high-emission lifestyles, others are having the ground pulled from beneath them. Climate change is rapidly creating unlivable spaces, places too hot, too polluted, too vulnerable to flooding, too ecologically stressed to sustain human flourishing.

In short, we have the return of ineluctable questions of *lebensraum*, this time at a planetary scale. Who gets to live well on the Earth, to have luxury living spaces and lifestyles sustained by extractions and emissions that speed the planet toward climate catastrophe? Who gets marginalized and has to suffer the consequences of climate change brought on by the lifestyles of the rich? Who is forced to move in order to survive, to navigate expanding zones of uninhabitability? Understanding geopolitics as a struggle for *lebensraum* is a critical provocation, one I use to highlight what should not be overlooked: the geo-ecological character of geopolitics.

Defining geopolitics, in short, is more complicated than it seems. There are popular and self-serving ideological understandings of it, and more disturbingly dark ones too. China's island-building in the South China Sea in 2015, in the wake of Russia's seizure of Crimea in 2014, catalyzed renewed discussion of territorial control and geopolitics in the power centers of the Western world. An aspect of this discussion was the naturalization of the West's own geopolitical order, territorial power, and geo-ecological imperialism. Geopolitics was presumed to have "returned" because of the actions of those revisionist powers, rather than to have always been present.[54] The West's geopolitics took the rhetorical form of a liberal international order that aspired to universalism, a sphere of influence above all others. China and Russia were revisionists because they sought neighborhood spheres of influence that aggrandized their own state territory and challenged the West.[55]

Great power competition displaced the global war on terrorism as the prime directive for US defense policy in the 2017 US National Security Strategy document.[56] Transnational terrorist networks and rogue states were still recognized as security challenges, but Russia and China were at the top of the threat list.[57] The 2018 US National Defense Strategy consolidated the shift by identifying "the reemergence of long-term, strategic competition" from the "revisionist powers" Russia and China as "the central challenge to U.S. prosperity and security."[58] The Biden administration sought strategic stability with Russia in order to concentrate on "strategic competition" with China.[59] This emphasis fell apart with the Russian military invasion of Ukraine. That war has consolidated the notion that the West is in a new era of great power competition with China and Russia, a "strategic competition to shape the future of the international order."[60]

Locating the central challenge to US prosperity and security in the actions of Russia and China is not an objective claim. Rather, it is evidence of the power of geopolitics as a world-making discourse to shape the recognition of threats and the meaning of security in world affairs. The deepening of tensions with Russia and China over Ukraine and Taiwan underscore the capacity of geopolitics to dominate the agenda of global politics and to reach into the everyday life of states all across the globe.

Geopolitics is the triumph of the competitive territorial thinking of world powers. It locates threats in the territorial behavior of rival states. It defines emergencies based on the behavior of other states, and associated non-state actors, and not modernity itself. Pushed to the side, until they make themselves felt, are the much more urgent common threats faced by all humans and other species from our own institutions and practices.

Contemporary Geopolitics and Climate Catastrophe

This book contends that a critical analysis of geopolitics is necessary to understand not only the climate catastrophe humanity is facing, but also why so little has been done to prevent it. Some will no doubt take issue with the word "catastrophe," so let me explain what I mean by it and why I use it. The best available Earth science states that a planetary environment where global surface temperatures have risen about 2 degrees Celsius since 1800 will have catastrophic consequences for the world as we know it. The direct causes of this coming climate catastrophe are modern civilization's gargantuan emissions into the Earth's atmosphere of greenhouse gases—carbon dioxide, methane, nitrous oxide, fluorinated gases, and water vapor—this, along with the degradation and destruction of the planetary mechanisms that helped regulate solar radiation and greenhouse gas levels over the last geological epoch.

Geopolitics is part of the problem, indeed a major part of the problem. It has helped set modern human civilization on a trajectory toward a hothouse Earth. It also inhibits the collective action required to change this trajectory. That geopolitics hastens future climate catastrophe is already clear from even a superficial look at some features of international affairs today. Three in particular stand out.

The first concerns the potential of geopolitical competition to induce a cataclysmic event that could immediately generate a climate catastrophe alongside civilizational collapse. There is always a danger of great power competition spiraling out of control and nuclear war breaking out across the Earth. Such an event, needless to say, would be disastrous not only for the areas targeted and the states involved, but for the Earth as a whole. A nuclear war involving two or more great powers would likely trigger a nuclear winter as enormous clouds of dust and debris would be driven into the upper layers of the Earth's atmosphere. Nuclear radiation fallout would spread across the Earth's surface, poisoning the biosphere possibly for thousands of years. Both events would radically alter the planet's biosphere and the life support systems for human settlements across the globe. Nuclear war would be an instant climate catastrophe. It would likely prompt an initial global cooling as debris clouds would prevent sunlight from reaching the Earth's surface. Unfortunately, we can no longer assume that this is a very low probability event. Nuclear tensions escalated considerably in the wake of Russia's flailing invasion of Ukraine and the West's considerable military support for Ukraine's aspiration to drive the Russian military out of Ukraine. The world's nuclear weapons control architecture is now in disarray. The possibility of a cataclysmic, system-wide nuclear war is always with us.

The second is how geopolitical competition undermines the ability of the world's leading powers to work together on common security concerns. To have any chance of avoiding the worst outcomes of climate change, the largest state producers of greenhouse gases need to cooperate. China currently produces the largest tonnage of emissions, followed by the United States, which is the largest historical emitter and still the highest per capita by far. But geopolitical competition between the United States and China, especially over the status of Taiwan, blocks significant cooperation. The visit of then–US House Speaker Nancy Pelosi to Taiwan in August 2022 led China to cancel the modest dialogue that did exist.

One analyst, the political scientist Michael Klare, puts the matter starkly: "geopolitics will cost us our planet."[61] Klare argues that both China and the United States need to establish a common front focused on the climate emergency, which he terms the US-China Climate Survival Alliance. All other matters need to be subordinated to the goals of this alliance, which is to stop the continued production of the greenhouse gases that are imperiling not only the future of both states, but the future of all states in the world. The stakes could not be any larger.

Yet this is not happening. While the United States and China have resumed talks about climate change issues, there is no joint action commensurate with the alarming nature of the climate change threat to both of them and everyone else. Both are investing in competition. What makes the situation stranger is that most world leaders agree that climate change is a scientific fact and that it poses a major threat to how humans currently live. Yet, in practice, climate change takes second place to geopolitics. It is a new agenda item, not an item requiring a completely new agenda. Thus, there is no US-China Climate Survival Alliance, but rather competition over future technologies and current spheres of influence. Climate action, the development of decarbonization infrastructures and clean energy technologies, is caught in competitive, not collaborative dynamics. Put bluntly, the geopolitical status of Taiwan and Ukraine appears more important than the future of humanity.

The third is the connection between geopolitical practices and greenhouse gas emissions. Geopolitical competition and war are powerful drivers of fossil fuel use. Over the past two centuries, the competition between large industrial states has run on hydrocarbon energy. All of the so-called great powers—Great Britain, Germany, France, the United States, Russia, and later China—were endowed with considerable reserves of coal and exploited these to industrialize and grow their economies while also strengthening their militaries. That military capacity allowed them to expand their imperial ambition by projecting fire power.[62] Maintaining military capacity itself through securing reserves of hydrocarbon energy well beyond their borders became a mission in itself, with the British Empire leading the way in creating an oceanic chain of coaling stations for its navy, and others, like the United States, playing catch-up. The shift from coal to oil as the fuel driving military machines—from battleships, trucks, and tanks to fighter aircraft and rockets—changed the game considerably, for now control over oil production and supply lines was imperative for military capacity. It became an imperative for economic growth, too, as the many material advantages of oil over coal as a source of energy became apparent.[63]

After World War II, the modality of empire changed and an informal oligopoly of Western oil companies—the "seven sisters"—dominated the world petroleum market until the 1970s.[64] The US military slowly adopted the role of a protection service for the hydrocarbon production and circulation system of the capitalist global economy. This worked in the Middle East through arms sales to Saudi Arabia and Iran (until popular revolution in the latter upended that relationship). As producer state power increased, and hawkish geopolitical scaremongering rose also, the US military was drawn further into the region as an interventionist force. The result was a series of wars with the control of oil reserves a persistent concern.[65]

The massive smoke plumes generated by Iraq's destruction of Kuwaiti oil well towers, and deliberate burning of oil lakes and trenches, in the Gulf War of 1991 visualized how destructive wars can be to the planet's atmosphere and ecology. The United States evicted Iraq from Kuwait that year using military firepower like M1A1 Abrams battle tanks (now operating in Ukraine), a vehicles that consume two gallons of jet fuel per mile.[66] US fighter jets are even more voracious users of petroleum. Dominating its rivals in military expenditure, the US military is the largest single institutional consumer of hydrocarbon fuels in the world.[67] It has long been the largest polluter in the United States and is likely the most polluting institution in the world. Yet, because of its privileged position in the state, US military emissions are untouchable. Indeed, the Kyoto Protocol of 1997 specifically excluded any counting of military emissions due to US lobbying.[68] This state of affairs has shifted somewhat as consciousness has grown that the deep cycle of fossil fuel use in the militarized pursuit of security directly contributes to a similarly fueled militarism by rival states, and the collective destabilization of the world's climate.[69] The carbon footprint (or so-called bootprint) of the military complexes

of world powers is now being questioned.[70] There is a growing realization that carbon combustion–based security undermines itself by
fueling climate insecurity.

There are many other features of contemporary geopolitics that
also contribute to the prospect of climate catastrophe: the financial
power of petrostates and their efforts to greenwash their role in accelerating global heating; the influence of the carbon-combustion complex in capturing states and throttling anti-carbon action across states
and within international organizations.[71] There is also an emergent
toxic culture war over climate action that features attacks by far-right
forces on the transnational climate action movement. Add to this the
long-standing challenges to strategic collective action planning: the
power of immediacy, discounting the future, entrenched interests, ig-
norance, short-termism, and risk uncertainties.

Some accounts of geopolitics and climate change are preoccupied
with what climate change means for a future balance of power, who
wins and who loses. The chessboard shifts—there is a "new map" of
energy and power—but the game is presumed to continue much
as before.[72] I want to suggest that this chessboard conception of the
planet is part of the reason why we have a climate emergency. It
conceptualizes the Earth as the playground of great powers, a material space to be occupied and controlled to advance the victory of
one power over another. The entrenched power of institutions built
around this conceit helps explain the climate crisis. The metaphor dis-
places the material reality of the Earth, a dynamic planet of complex
interdependencies and interlocking processes. In doing so, it hides the
ecological costs of "playing geopolitics."

Geopolitics as Territorial Competition

Geopolitics did not always exist. It is not an inevitable feature of how
humans live on the Earth. As a set of modern human beliefs and practices, it has a history and geography. Geopolitics first emerged as part

of the modernity ushered in by European overseas expansionism and Christian imperialist capitalism. The first world powers, states with the capacity and reach to project power across the surfaces of the Earth, were European empires legitimated by papal decree to occupy and seize land. As these European states deepened their ambitions to exploit faraway territories, they developed competitive strategies to control terrestrial and maritime spaces.

Geopolitics was born amidst imperial rivalry and extractive enterprises, civilizational missions and territorial conquests. Its practices are part of the emergence of an integrated and singular Earth-as-globe whose lands and seas—with the exception of the high seas and regions inhospitable to human settlement—were organized as territories that belonged exclusively to certain empires, states, and state-affiliated organizations. Geopolitics facilitates the claiming of the planet by modern humans.

The British geographer and imperial reformer Halford John Mackinder (1861–1947) termed the period of European overseas imperialism the "Columbian epoch." He described this, in Eurocentric terms, as a period of exploration and discovery of territories new to European eyes. But this epoch of open space, of unclaimed land, was over had ended in the late nineteenth century. A post-Columbian epoch of closed space, of occupied and claimed territories, had arrived. World powers were now in a new struggle—a struggle over the relative efficiency of their use of the earthly spaces they already controlled. Empires needed to modernize how they organized and exploited their territorial holdings.

Mackinder is a helpful figure in thinking about geopolitics. Sometimes described as the "father of geopolitics," he was an aspirational organic intellectual of empire at the outset of the twentieth century, an educator and writer who described the geographical foundations of world power, and prescribed what the British Empire needed to do to strengthen its own foundations. Using Mackinder's work as a point of departure, this book develops a critical framework for the analysis of geopolitics as a set of competitive territorial practices by world powers. Here I consider three distinct practices: (i) the pursuit of territorial security and control by competing world powers; (ii) the competing missionary claims by world powers to organize global space; and (iii) the drive to harness geospatial technologies to enhance the military power of states across the horizontal and vertical territories of the Earth. All of these practices are embedded in broader structures of modernity and global capitalism, so they operate alongside economic forms of occupying and organizing the Earth. *Territory* is a key term in this book. Drawing inspiration from contemporary geographical scholarship, I do not restrict it to a purely statist understanding, namely as the legal property of the state.[73] Rather, we live within multiple territorial regimes, from the geo-ecological to the geo-economic and geopolitical. All these are entwined, though the geo-ecological and geo-economic are often obscured and hidden in daily life. Also, I do not confine it to "terra," to fixed dry land. To fully "Earth" geopolitics requires recognition of the many territories beyond terra—mountains, rivers, marshes, coastlines, deserts, lakes, ice sheets, glaciers, deltas, air spaces, sea floors, underground and underwater spaces—whose interactions are crucial to sustaining the world we find familiar.

The structured way of seeing the planet enabled by geopolitics casts the world as a chessboard of rival great powers competing over hydrocarbon energy, strategic minerals, trade, finance, and people. This obscures the long-standing and now dangerously accumulating environmental costs of modernity. There is a disjuncture between the geopolitical world people live in and the actual material realities of geo-ecological processes. Many, if not most, people do not see themselves living within a fragile and precarious biosphere on a dynamic planet, even though they are, but in a world of geopolitical drama. The terms of this drama dominate the everyday life of states, and arrange world powers against each other in struggles over economic resources, strategic states, civilizational values, world order, and ways of life. This is geopolitics world: compelling and absorbing, but also obscuring the Earth as an ecosphere. Geopolitics locks global politics into antagonistic territorial practices, justifying unsustainable exploit-ation of the planet's resources in the name of security, sovereignty, and freedom. In doing so, it accelerates the climate emergency while preventing collective action to address it. It deserves our full attention.

Book Outline

This book is called *Oceans Rise Empires Fall* because this felicitous phrase, which derives from the chorus of a song from the musical *Hamilton*, summarizes the clash that defines the present. This is the clash between Earth system dynamics and the world power structures that humans have built into and upon the planet, changing it in the process. It is a clash between the materiality of the planet (including its atmosphere) and the world of geopolitics, between vibrant geo-ecological matter and human territorial projects and infrastructures. There is, of course, only one ocean on the planet. But that we think in terms of named oceans—the Atlantic, Pacific, Indian, and so on—is a reminder of the power of human habits of territorialization to shape our experience of the Earth's most basic materiality. Empires appear in the world of geopolitics as plural and rivalrous. Yet from the per-spective of Earth system science, there is just one collective anthropo-genic empire, a globalized civilization of modernizing and competing world powers that have cut deeply into the Earth's surface and spewed prodigiously into its atmosphere, altering the planet's living spaces in doing so. It is the condition where geopolitics is all around, in the air, in the water, and across the Earth. Indeed, geopolitical rivalry gen-erated the strata of plutonium fallout that is the leading indicator of the Anthropocene, a proposed new geological epoch in the history of the Earth.

Because geopolitics is an elastic term, I consider the history of the term and its leading meanings in Chapter 1. I also reconsider my own efforts in the past to develop a critical geopolitics, and some of its weaknesses. I then consider the challenge of developing a critical

conceptual framework to understand the relationship between geopolitical practices and the looming climate crisis.

In Chapter 2, I argue that Mackinder's work is a helpful starting
point for identifying the practices that characterize geopolitics. In
contrast to international relations theories of geopolitics, which marginalize the geo-ecological while reifying the structure of the state
system, Mackinder placed human-environment relations, and technological innovation, at the center of his analysis. He saw international
politics as how world powers went about organizing the exploitation
of the territories they controlled. The ugly aspects of Mackinder's
writings—his racism and chauvinism—instructively reveal how
human inventions of racial hierarchy justified unequal exchange and
imperial rule.

In Chapter 3, I use the notion of *lebensraum* to critically rethink
the concept of geopolitics and tie it to the making of the modern
world. In doing so, I make the case for a critical reworking of three
concepts within Mackinder's work that can be used to understand
geopolitics as territorial struggle. I then devote a set of chapters to
elaborating these concepts and their relevance to explaining why geopolitics inhibits collective action on climate. Chapter 4 argues that
world powers have strong state territorial concerns and anxieties. This
leads them to prioritize their own territorial security dilemmas over
those of the planet as a whole. Chapter 5 argues that world powers
are also characterized by visions of their own exceptionality, greatness, and mission in world affairs. These senses of mission, however,
rest upon the exploitation of hydrocarbon energy regimes, and a politics of perpetual growth, that have polluted the planet's atmosphere
and hastened global heating. The connections between missions and
emissions raises uncomfortable questions about current liberal ideas
of freedom and peace, which tacitly naturalize growth without limit
or end.

Chapter 6 considers the concept of geospatial revolutions to explain
the ethos institutionalized by the emergence of rocket technologies
after World War II and the entrenched commitment to revolutions of

space and speed in the military-industrial complexes of world powers. The desire for unrestrained military power over the Earth's spaces
deepens collective insecurity and undermines collective action against
climate change. Chapter 7 chronicles the contemporary geopolitical
condition, one where the geo-ecological transformation of the planet
is about to overwhelm the geopolitical preoccupations of world powers. Within the next year or so, the average surface temperature of the
Earth will rise to more than 1.5 degrees Celsius above that experienced just two and a half centuries ago. We are entering a new world
of territorial dislocations. I conclude by considering possibilities for
restraining and transcending geopolitics.

I

Geopolitics All Around

In the summer of 2021, the French President Emmanuel Macron traveled over 15,000 kilometers to confront a difficult legacy.[1] Before an audience on the storied island of Tahiti in the South Pacific, Macron acknowledged that France owed the faraway region a debt. Between 1966 and 1996, France detonated a series of atmospheric and underground nuclear explosions on islands and atolls in the area now known as French Polynesia.[2] The French state first seized the area in the mid- to late nineteenth century. The paintings of Paul Gauguin made it famous as an idyllic paradise to a metropolitan Western imagination.[3] But that did not prevent it from becoming a testing ground, in the second half of the twentieth century, for the most destructive weapons devised by French military scientists. The tests left the remnants of atolls and surrounding ecosystems contaminated with radioactivity. Nearly all human residents in the area at the time were exposed to toxic fallout.[4] "I think it's true that we would not have done the same tests in La Creuse or in Brittany," Macron conceded, tacitly acknowledging the hierarchies of place and people that made it possible for France to explode nuclear bombs in paradise.[5] Faraway places, peoples, and ecologies were exposed to toxic weapons of death so homeland places and people could live in security. Or so the thinking went.

Yet what happened in the South Pacific did not stay in the South Pacific. Ever since the first explosion of the nuclear age in Alamogordo, New Mexico, hurled a radioactive fireball more than ten miles into

the atmosphere, the presumption that nuclear fallout would be localized was questionable. That explosion was more powerful than expected while its irradiated mushroom cloud rose much higher than
anticipated. Downwind became an ominous expression for those on
the ground, and subsequently a radiation exposure identity ('down-
winders'). Caught in the jet streams of the upper atmosphere, the
fallout zone became continental, reaching forty six states as well as
parts of Canada and Mexico. The US, in effect, nuked itself and its
neighbors.[6]

The subsequent use of even more destructive thermonuclear
bombs blasted radioactive isotopes into even higher altitudes which
produced regional to global distributions of fallout. Between 1945
and 1998 there were over two thousand nuclear weapon tests, mostly
in the Pacific Ocean, Central Asia, Australia, and the western United
States. Five hundred and forty-three of these were atmospheric tests.[7]
Civilian nuclear power program releases, deliberate and accidental,
also entered the Earth's atmosphere. The result was that anthropogenic
radionuclides—strontium 90, cesium 137, plutonium 239 and 240—
were dispersed across the planet by high altitude wind and oceanic
circulations. A nuclear release anywhere in the world became a nuclear release across the world, even from seemingly remote locations
like the South Pacific.[8] From frozen poles to mountain tops, lakes, and
marshes to country farms and cities, researchers found traces of Cold
War radionuclides. This dispersal is so marked that some have argued
that the geochemical signature of radioactive isotopes are suitable
candidates for defining the Anthropocene, the "golden spike" that an-
nounces humanity as a geological force.[9]

Geopolitics, thus, is all around us. Not only does great power competition shape the trajectory of human affairs; it also shapes the Earth
itself, the air we breathe, the water we drink, the ecologies we depend upon for life. Since the early nineteenth century, it has been
fueled by the burning of hydrocarbon fossil fuels that have dumped
trillions of tons of greenhouse gases into the Earth's atmosphere. The
waste products of geopolitics past are still with us, most especially

from the coal, and later oil, that powered industrial revolutions that made a small country like England into the core of a world power and allowed its navy to master lands and seas thousands of miles from home ports. The gas byproducts of the industrialization of the United States, the Soviet Union, and many other states are still in the air. So also is pollution from two world wars, the Cold War, and many other kinds of conflicts across the planet. Still in the atmosphere are the consequences of interstate highways, drive-through automotive convenience living, cities that know only hydrocarbon combustion to function. Joining their occupation of atmospheric carbon space are the greenhouse gases now produced in enormous quantities by China, India, and other developing states as they industrialize, ur-banize, and globalize. Added to the mix today, of course, are industrial pollutants and novel viruses that concentrate minds on what precisely is in the air. Amidst rising world temperatures and the coronavirus pandemic, we are forced to feel and breathe geopolitics, to take it into our bodies.

Geopolitics is not what an objective Earth makes people do. Rather, it addresses what people upon the Earth have created, what people and Earth make together, not geo→politics but geo↔politics, a hybrid entanglement of different powers rather than a simple causal story. Disentangling these different powers and analyzing how hu-mans have built worlds with the heterogenous materialities of the planet is not so easy.

Great powers have long sought to mold the physical environment to their defense and economic needs. They have built fortresses on high ground, prominent physical landmarks and at the confluence of strategic rivers and roads. They have engineered lands and landscapes to serve their interests. They have relied upon natural breaks and bor-ders as well as climatic conditions ("General Winter") for security and defense.[10] And they have harnessed fertile lands and abundant resources to keep them strong. In this sense, geopolitics seems like an old story of earthly power and human ingenuity, with humans the creative but dependent party. However, the compound term itself is a relatively recent coinage in European languages, just over a hundred years old, a mere instant ago in the timescale of the human presence on the Earth. Furthermore, the story it reveals over the past 125 years is an exceptional one of rising Western imperial power across the Earth as age-old constraints fell away. From the new imperialism in Africa to mechanized slaughter in the First World War, from fascism to total warfare and genocide in World War II, and from nuclear terror to the fossil-fueled great acceleration of the Cold War and beyond, geopolitics is more the story of acquired human superpower, one largely concentrated in the industrial West, than earthly control.

This chapter provides a brief introduction to the history of geopolitics as a traveling concept with multiple meanings and considerable historical baggage. It was born in a period of inter-imperialist rivalry and evolved as the nature of that rivalry changed and transformed. There are now competing understandings of geopolitics, and the concept has drifted considerably beyond its origins, and earthly ground. There is today also a robust tradition of critical geopolitics, developed by scholars over the past quarter century. This chapter reviews these different uses and makes an argument for a renewed engagement with those aspects of geopolitics that placed international politics within the context of earthly processes and dynamics. Conventional conceptions of geopolitics, and some critical ones too, tend to obscure the ecological foundations and biopolitical preoccupations of geopolitics. But these are the structures that must be exposed and their connections to the deterioration of the Earth as a shared living space revealed.

A Short History of an Elastic Catchword

Any study of geopolitics faces an enduring intellectual challenge: specifying precisely what is, and what is not, the subject matter of geopolitics. Is it a set of ideas and doctrines, a minor genre in the history of international thought? Or is geopolitics the competitive behavior of imperial states, and territorializing practices that have been around for centuries? Or is it simply just a synonym for international relations? And what about that standard dictionary definition one often encounters, the study of the influence of geography on politics? No wonder many find the word slippery and difficult to pin down.[11] One author wrote that the most dreaded question for any geopolitician is: "What is a simple definition of geopolitics?"[12] Another summed up the problem: "the primary drawback of geopolitics is that it is conceptually so broad that it can and does mean all things to all people."[13]

The word *geopolitics* has a history that is complex, confusing and, in parts, quite disturbing. Coined by the Swedish political scientist Rudolf Kjellén (1864–1922) at the end of the nineteenth century, the term is often associated with the writings of Friedrich Ratzel (1844–1904) and Halford Mackinder, German and British professors of geography, respectively, though neither man ever used the word.[14] Neither did the American naval strategist Alfred Mahan (1840–1914).[15] For Kjellén, who was also a conservative politician, geopolitics is just one of five aspects of the study of the state, namely the state as a territory.[16]

Geopolitics was quickly adapted for broader themes, for it was an appealing compound word, with generative capacity.[17] The Hungarian-born scholar of world history Emil Reich (1854–1910) was among the first to circulate the term in English, using it to name how the physical characteristics of the Earth shaped human history. The first time the word "geo-politics" appeared in the *New York Times*—it was hyphenated to underscore its compound construction—is July 1903, in an article discussing Reich on the American war of independence.[18]

But it was only when a former German general called Karl Haushofer (1869–1946), a veteran of the Eastern Front in the Great War, drew on the writings of Ratzel, Kjellén, Mackinder, and others to promote the "new science" of *Geopolitik* that the term started to attract both notice and notoriety in the English-speaking world.[19] A professor of political geography at the University of Munich in Weimar Germany, Haushofer was befriended by Rudolph Hess (1894–1987) and through him encountered the imprisoned radical nationalist Adolph Hitler. Tutoring the messianic politician in Landsberg prison between June and November 1924, Haushofer helped Hitler find a vocabulary to justify his belief in the necessity for German territorial expansionism in Europe.[20] The catchword Haushofer conveyed from Ratzel to Hitler was *lebensraum* (living space). Yet this same general had a Jewish wife. He also struggled with the tension between the environmental determinism of his vision of German *Geopolitik* and the biological determinism of Nazi ideology.[21]

Haushofer's association with Hitler brought him initial influence, but later infamy and disaster. One of his sons was imprisoned after the failed attempt to assassinate Hitler in July 1944, and was shot dead by retreating SS remnants as Red Army troops entered Berlin in April 1945. After a brief interrogation for possible trial at Nuremberg—during which Haushofer met Hess who, faking mental illness, pretended not to know his old mentor—Karl Haushofer and his wife committed suicide in March 1946.[22]

The influence of Haushofer and German *Geopolitik* on Hitler spawned a series of conspiracy theories in the United States.[23] Was Haushofer really "Hitler's brain truster," as *Life* magazine declared in November 1939?[24] Establishing that he was not, which was the truth, went against the grain of the sensationalist popular culture of the time. The prominent American geographer Isaiah Bowman (1878–1950), an adviser to US presidents since serving as Woodrow Wilson's geographic expert at the Paris Peace Conference at Versailles, was pulled into the controversy.[25] Bowman condemned German *Geopolitik* as a perversion of the truth and contrasted it to political geography, which in his eyes was scientific and, at the same time, pro-American.[26] Another wartime American geographer pronounced it an "intellectual poison."[27]

Others, however, accepted that geopolitics was a necessary form of geostrategic thinking, something from which Americans could learn. It clarified what the United States needed to do if it were to seize the moment, indeed the future itself. Tyranny may demand living space,

Henry Luce wrote in his influential 1941 essay *The American Century*, but "Freedom requires and will require far greater living space than Tyranny."[28] Luce advocated a civilizational mission for the United States in the world, a campaign to claim as much earthly space as possible for "freedom"—that is, American style capitalist modernity as a way of life. Isaiah Bowman gave this idea of a global "open door" for US business across the Earth a politically incorrect name: "American *lebensraum*."[29]

Strategists like Edward Mead Earle (1894–1954) and Nicholas Spykman (1893–1943), and moralists like Father Edmund Walsh (1885–1956), were intellectual entrepreneurs for an interventionist US foreign policy with global ambition.[30] Geopolitics was presented by them and others as a vital visual mode of thought by which the United States could "see the world" as a singular global geostrategic chessboard and thereby devise a bold global military strategy to pursue against its enemies.[31] Geopolitics was grand strategy on the globe.[32]

Nevertheless, because of its Nazi associations, the word *geopolitics* faded from public discourse even as the Cold War was organized around controlling great spaces, containing enemy spatial expansion, and competing over resources and people in fluid "third world" spaces. Its re-emergence as a popular term of art in the study of international relations came from a surprising source. Henry Kissinger (1923–2023), a Jewish refugee from Nazi Germany who became a professor of government at Harvard University and later US Secretary of State and National Security Adviser, put the term to use for his own purposes.[33] Fashioned as a "hardheaded" style of statesmanship concerned with "balance-of-power" politics by Nixon and Kissinger, the language of geopolitics rationalized many bold and controversial policies during their tenure.[34] One of the more notorious was their clandestine support for a military coup in Chile. The junta that seized power imprisoned more than a hundred thousand people in its first three years, tortured nearly forty thousand, and murdered over three thousand. The dictator at the center of this paroxysm of state violence was General Augusto Pinochet (1915–2006), a former military academy instructor. Largely unknown until then, Pinochet was the author of a small book with a one-word title: Geopolítica.[35]

Surprisingly, despite this blood-stained history of association with fascism and state violence, *geopolitics* became a commonplace term in English-language writing on international affairs. This says something about what was seen and unseen in US Cold War culture. Kissinger's memoirs further popularized the term, though many others also adopted it, not least his long-standing rival as an intellectual of state-craft, Zbigniew Brzezinski (1928–2017), another European émigré.[36] Kissinger's employment of the term endowed it with an appealing Old World cultural gravitas which journalists, diplomats, and commentators emulated, especially from the 1970s onward. In the English language (though not in German), *geopolitics* transcended its Nazi-era associations to become a synonym for a particular mode of Cold War thinking, one that placed hard power interests before human rights in foreign policy calculations. At the same time, a more generic meaning of the word was also taking hold, one where it functioned simply as a familiar descriptor for varied aspects of competitive relations between states.

Analysis of the frequency of use of the term in English-language book titles reveals a dramatic spike during the war years 1940–1945 and then a sharp drop to 1949. Thereafter it rose to a minor high in 1952 before fading somewhat until 1979, when it surpassed the 1952 peak. The term grew in popularity in the last decade of the Cold War and continued to remain popular thereafter, reaching a new peak at the centenary of its coinage, near the end of the twentieth century. A frequency graph of its appearance in the *New York Times* reveals a similar trajectory, and a further steady upward trajectory in the early years of the twenty-first century that reached a peak in 2014, the year Russia annexed Crimea and destabilized eastern Ukraine. In the past years, following Russia's invasion of Ukraine and tensions over Taiwan, use of the word has surged to a new high. The word is stretched in lots of surprising ways. A glance at its use in the *New York Times* in recent years, for example, reveals titles such as "The Geopolitics of Jay-Z,"

"The Geopolitics of Soap Operas," and "The Geopolitics of Name-Dropping."[37] Its use in academia is broader still, with a great variety of subjects acquiring a supposed "geopolitics" in recent decades. In short, *geopolitics* is an elastic word that has been stretched to all manner of contexts and uses.

Four Understandings of Geopolitics

A nominalist account of geopolitics in the English language that is focused just on the word and its use is a poor guide to its intellectual core. Certain foundational intellectuals, like Ratzel and Mackinder, do not use the term. Those that invent and use it find it appropriated by Nazi-supporting intellectuals and later tarnished by association with Nazi expansionism. The term nevertheless still circulates and is re-appropriated by émigré intellectuals of statecraft in the United States as a synonym for what is presented as realist foreign policy practice (in actuality, right-wing militarism). But that meaning does not stick. The term drifts to signify competitive international statecraft, and becomes an appealing synonym for international politics. And it strays and stretches in popular culture and academia as cultural commentators and critical scholars play with it further. How do we make sense of all this?

Geopolitics may be a floating signifier, but it is freighted with historic cargo and has a familiar set of harbors in the English language, a term mostly attached to four different understandings and uses. These are distinct but have a common history as they emerged within the context of inter-imperial state rivalries and the Cold War. The four uses range from the specific and precise to the broad and general, but they are connected by a common thread of concern with the territorial behavior of states, particularly large states that are competing with each other across the Earth. Briefly, these four understandings are as follows.

1. Geopolitics as the Struggle for Space in International Relations

We need to remember that the word *geopolitics* was coined by an academic. Accordingly, it is a theory, an original bold contention, and subsequently a series of variants on this contention and theme. This theory was derived from the most influential intellectual theory in the second half of the nineteenth century, Darwin's theory of natural evolution. Social Darwinism describes the somewhat heterogeneous complex of ideas that drew inspiration from Darwin's ideas on evolution, and those of other thinkers, and sought to apply them to human societies and their development. Ascendant intellectual systems in natural history were extended to also explain human history, with the natural sciences viewed as a model for emerging social sciences. Geopolitics began as a form of social Darwinism applied to states and international politics.[38]

In an irony of intellectual history, it was a Swedish follower of Ratzel, Rudolf Kjellén, who coined the term *geopolitics*, as noted earlier, not the man who was its intellectual inspiration. Ratzel is often credited with inventing the closely associated catchword, *lebensraum* (living space), but others had used it before him.[39] Ratzel did, however, formulate the catchphrase that was the bold theoretical contention behind geopolitics: *the struggle for space.*

Trained in biology and zoology, Friedrich Ratzel's first work was strongly influenced by Darwin and German naturalists like Ernst Haeckel (1834–1919), the zoologist who, among other things, coined the term *ecology*. Ratzel fought in the Franco-German War of 1870–1871 and afterward began international research travel. In 1874–1875 he journeyed to North America. There he was greatly impressed by how historical processes of settler colonialism, industrialization, and urbanization, together with the transcontinental railways, produced the United States as a dynamic territorial state. Upon his return to Germany, he became a prolific author and influential professor of geography, first in Munich and subsequently in Leipzig.

Ratzel is famous for the idea of *lebensraum* because that is the title he gave to a short book he wrote in 1901 that gathered ideas that he worked with throughout his career. Ratzel's claims are large and totalizing: "All earthly being rests on one single law: the greatest and the smallest being depend on the basic properties of the planet."[40] Life is the essential restless dynamic force in Ratzel's writing but it is earthbound, a condition of material spatial limits: "Everything that wants space on our planet Earth must draw on the finite amount of 506 million square kilometers of its surface. This number, therefore, represents the first spatial factor where the history of life is concerned, and it also represents the last. It determines all other factors."[41] This emphasis on finite limits echoed claims made famous more than a century earlier by Thomas Malthus (1766–1834).[42]

Ratzel's essay is remarkable for the ease with which he jumps between examples featuring flora, fauna, and then particular moments in human history such as the European colonization of the New World, where imperialism is ecological as well as political, economic, and racial. The history of America's colonization "began by stripping the indigenous population of their lands and subsisted on it through hunting and agriculture; the result was a battle of annihilation where the prize at stake was space—the soil. It was the Indians who lost this battle, having but a weak grip on the soil."[43] In passages like this, it is clear how Ratzel's idea of *lebensraum* could subsequently rationalize Nazi imperialism during World War II. His general thesis is based on a clash between life and Earth. "There is a tension between the movement of life, which never rests, and the space on Earth, which does not change. It is from this tension that the struggle for space is born." The struggle for life, Ratzel declares:

> primarily means nothing more than a struggle for space. For space is the very first condition for life and space is the yardstick by which other living conditions are measured—especially that of food. In the struggle for life, space has a similar significance as those decisive climaxes in the struggle of nations that we call battles. In both cases what is at stake is the acquisition of space in movements of advance and retreat.[44]

"Life" (*Leben*) is the super-agent in Ratzel's thinking, and his essay offers over two dozen compound words qualifying it, while space (*Raum*) gets over a dozen.[45] *Lebensraum* becomes the catchword for this entire mode of reasoning. It pivots around a life-space-Earth nexus of interaction that is held to be governed by general developmental laws across the natural and human sciences.[46] The discipline of geography serves as a bridge between the natural and the human, and in Ratzel, human geography is but a branch of a broader field of biogeography that encompasses the study of the spatial distribution of all living things across the planet.

In his work, Ratzel famously analogized states to living organisms that are in a struggle for survival and, therefore, are in a contest over space. Ratzel tended to conceptualize living space in his writing on states to the geographical surface area required to support a state population at its current population size and mode of existence. In practice, this meant land or, more precisely, adequate fertile soil capable of producing sufficient food to sustain a growing state population. Unlike Malthus, Ratzel did not believe that population growth could or should be checked. States ineluctably were in a struggle over space because life was unstoppable and earthly space limited. States must expand or die. Those that demonstrated the best mastery of space, the most efficient grip on the soil, would survive.

This reasoning was seriously deficient but no less influential because of it. Ratzel effectively denies the distinguishing feature of humans as a species of animal: that we are capable of reflective thought and behavior. States are not organisms but institutional complexes. The concept of *lebensraum* provided a ready justification for imperial expansionism. Not surprisingly, Ratzel's ideas appealed to the political right in Germany and elsewhere for they legitimated aggression and violence by naturalizing it. The "struggle for space" would become a catchphrase in Nazi Germany, and *lebensraum* a magic word in the Nazi lexicon. Yet, at the same time, the idea that world powers are in a struggle over territory and resources became a widely accepted truth in international affairs. The Nazi vision of *lebensraum* was tied

to territorial aggression and agricultural colonialism. The American
lebensraum envisioned by Isaiah Bowman was different, an economic
global empire detached from territorial control.[47] This 'American
century' vision, the post–World War II Pax Americana that grew into
the self-styled "liberal rules-based international order" organized by
US military primacy, still endures.

2. Geopolitics as Kissinger's Philosophy of Statecraft

It is unclear why Henry Kissinger decided to use the word "geopolitics" to describe the theory of international politics and realist philosophy of statecraft he developed as an academic at Harvard University
and then sought to put into practice when he served in the administrations of US Presidents Richard Nixon and Gerald Ford. Given the
notoriety of the term in his homeland during his youth, it seemed a
risky move on his part. But perhaps not. Since World War II, the term
was favored by a few US foreign policy strategists, including fellow
émigré scholar-practitioners like Vienna-born Robert Strausz-Hupé
(1903–2002).[48] That particular constellation of philosophy and policy,
however, was associated mostly with right-wing Cold War strategists,
those who later became staunch critics of the Nixon-Kissinger policy
of peaceful coexistence with the Soviet Union.

In the first volume of his memoirs *White House Years* (1979),
Kissinger describes geopolitics as "an approach that pays attention to
the requirements of equilibrium" in international politics.[49] The definition is vague and has scant regard for established usage, as Hedley
Bull noted in a review.[50] This notion nevertheless has a place in the
rhetorical structure Kissinger develops to explain his philosophy and
practice of statecraft. In *White House Years*, he used the word "geopolitics" just four times, but "geopolitical" fifty-three times.

The concept has three major features in Kissinger. First, it is the
name of a supposed absent tradition of thought in US foreign policy.
"There is in America," he writes, "an idealistic tradition that sees

foreign policy as a contest between good and evil. There is a pragmatic tradition that seeks to solve 'problems' as they arise. There is a legalistic tradition that treats international issues as juridical cases. There is no geopolitical tradition."[51] Although that was not quite right, Kissinger wanted his framework to be seen as not only distinctive but superior, and misunderstood because of this.

Second, he casts geopolitics as a tradition of thinking strategically about state national interests that emerges from the material geographical realities of world power. States are forced into thinking strategically because of their geographic situation and military strength relative to neighboring states. Protected by two oceans, this supposedly does not happen with the United States. Instead, it adopts idealistic and moral framings of international politics, the opposite of the grounded material calculations that characterize geopolitics. The Cold War and evolution of military technology, however, make geopolitical thinking imperative.

To Kissinger, geopolitics is statecraft beyond ideology, the rational pursuit of state national interests by mature leaders. He describes China's leadership under Mao, for example, as "beyond ideology in their dealings with us. Their peril had established the absolute primacy of geopolitics."[52] Again, this framing has rhetorical effects that should be questioned, serving, among other things, to naturalize the ideological commitments of those pursuing geopolitical strategies in the 1960s and 1970s, such as bombing Vietnam, invading Cambodia, and subverting an elected government in Chile.

Third, geopolitics is a perspective that is distinctively global. It is a view from the mountaintop of international affairs, a vision that is innately superior to other "regional" and "local" perspectives because it can see how things fit together as a whole, how they are interconnected. US State Department bureaus, for example, are routinely criticized by Kissinger for exasperating regional thinking. Contrasting his approach to Nixon's first Secretary of State William Rogers (1913–2001), for example, he characterizes his approach as "strategic and geopolitical; I attempted to relate events to each other, to create incentives or pressures in one part of the world to influence events in another."[53] The policy of "linkage"—tying policy progress in one region or domain to that in another—was one outcome of Kissinger's geopolitical practice.

Kissinger presented geopolitics as a hardheaded rational strategy that steers clear of the moralism of the left and right. Their emotion-alism risked endangering US national security, in pursuing ideological crusades or hastily withdrawing US commitments from allies across the globe. Yet, the concept of geopolitics was also part of his own ideological sophistry to justify the maintenance of US hegemony while adjusting to Soviet nuclear power parity and the re-emergence of China and regional powers across the world. In Kissinger's lexicon, geopolitics is a philosophy of statecraft that presents itself as materi-alist and realist, and in opposition to arguments that it characterizes as ideological and normative. That was its rhetorical claim at least, its dis-cursive self-presentation. Kissinger's realism, however, was an insider philosophy of state. It took for granted the geo-ecological territories that supported US hegemony in the world, that powered the US military and fueled his shuttle diplomacy. It did not see the emerging environmental crisis, even though there were signs of it all around.

3. Geopolitics as the Game of Great Power Competition

From the outset, geopolitics drifted beyond its origins to refer to more general questions and themes in international affairs. It became a name for approaches that explored geographical influences on the conduct of foreign policy and statecraft. While the notoriety of the German school of *Geopolitik* discredited the term among some, es-pecially geographers, it did not among certain US-based strategic thinkers, like Father Edmund Walsh, Robert Strauss-Hupé, and John Kieffer, who recuperated it in different ways.[54] Geopolitics was less a school of thought than a description of the geographical dimensions of great power competition.

Kissinger's elevation of the term facilitated its movement into everyday political discourse in the English language. By virtue of the United States' centrality to world affairs, the word diffused into the major newspapers of the world as an American, not a German, word. By the 1970s the term was shorthand for superpower rivalry as a competitive game. Analogies to chess and card games like poker abounded. Game metaphors were particularly popular in journalistic analysis and commentary.

This conception of geopolitics as a competitive game is the most common understanding of the term today. The game metaphor has multiple interpretive effects. First, there is an emphasis on rules and norms. In the same way that games have rules and norms that structure competition and behavior, geopolitics operates within a set of agreed-upon understandings and rules, though these are liable to be broken and violated on occasion. Second, just as games have participants or players, geopolitics involves actors such as great powers, regional powers, international organizations, and non-state actors who compete for resources and influence. Overt and covert deals are made and broken. Third, similar to a game, geopolitics requires strategic thinking and decision-making, as actors must weigh their options, make calculated moves, and anticipate the actions of others in order to advance their own interests. Fourth, as in a game, actors in geopolitics compete for power and prizes, some tangible and material, others about status and prestige. Fifth, like sports competitions and tournaments, geopolitics is understood to have attentive audiences, some as fervent supporters, others as opponents, and many impressionable nonaligned neutrals. Sixth, geopolitics has a playing board, ostensibly the globe as a whole but extended beyond the Earth by the race to explore outer space. This global chessboard is understood to be interconnected, but there are also distinctive regional theaters of play too. In the geopolitics-as-game metaphor, the geosphere and biosphere are treated as largely inert backdrops to human-centered action.

One of the many negative framing effects of this gamification of global politics is that it marginalizes systemic questions, like poverty and inequality, and common security challenges, such as pollution and planetary degradation. Popular media, from the illustrated news tabloids of the early twentieth century to social media today, reinforce this gamification and pander to it. This leads to a kind of spectator-sport militarism in the societies of major powers that sometimes flares in times of political crisis.[55] How wars are mediated, visualized, and experienced with pleasure and hatred on social media today is a digital version of the jingoistic yellow journalism that emerged in the late nineteenth century.

4. Geopolitics as the Influence of Geography on History

The fourth understanding of geopolitics is the broadest. The *Oxford English Dictionary* defines geopolitics concisely as "politics as influenced by geographical factors."[56] This definition constructs geography and politics as two separate realms structured by a relationship of significant conditioning, if not determinism. Emil Reich was the figure who first popularized the word "geopolitics" in the English language as shorthand for how geographical factors shape human history, including politics. "Geopolitics . . . is one of the most decisive elements in human institutions," he wrote in the introduction to the first of his two volume *Handbook of Geography* (1908).[57] One reason why the term held appeal is that it renamed, in a concise modish manner, long-standing questions in Western intellectual thought about the relationship of the natural world to human societies and cultures.

In his study of this tradition of thought, Clarence Glacken identifies three persistent themes: the idea of a divinely designed Earth, the influence of environments on humans, and humans as modifiers of the habitable Earth.[58] There are other themes too, like the application of organic analogies to the growth and decline of nations, peoples, and the Earth itself. The broadest understanding of geopolitics is one that resonates with such long-standing traditions of inquiry into the naturalistic foundations and relations of human civilizations.[59]

The subject matter of geopolitics can thus be traced back to Plato and Aristotle writing about the role of climate, topography, distance, and land/sea dynamics on political life. Indeed, one of the enduring metaphors in geopolitical thinking comes from classical Greece. This is the notion of a *Theatrum Mundi*, a Great Theatre of the World, which analogizes human history to theatrical drama. In rendering human history as a spectacle observable by a detached viewer, this metaphor also helps specify the relation of geography to politics as that of a stage to the drama that unfolds upon it. Geography is the stage, the natural world, the Earth, the setting for human-centered drama. Politics is the domain of agency and action, of hubris and tragedy. The stage metaphor enables the view-from-nowhere that characterizes geopolitical thought, a master-of-the-globe god-trick.

In sum, the meaning of geopolitics can stretch from a specific German concept to the whole subject of human-environment relations. And it stretches further for it has become an organizing concept of a knowledge industry of think tanks, intelligence units, risk analysis firms, and professional writers selling "geopolitical analysis" and "geopolitical insight." Geopolitics is a business. And it is a subject of considerable debate within academia.

Critical Geopolitics

As an intellectual activity tied to imperial rivalries, geopolitics has always attracted criticism. Ratzel's conservative reactionary politics and forceful advocacy of German naval expansionism and colonialism in Wilhelmine Germany drew opposition in his day.[60] Mackinder's advocacy for the modernization of the British Empire did the same. The English philosopher Bertrand Russell (1872–1970), for example, was a critic of his imperialist advocacy.[61] German *Geopolitik* provoked opposition and criticism from German Social Democrats who rightly saw it as a militaristic creed.[62] Hitler's expansionist foreign policy motivated widespread critique of geopolitics, though some of that was opposition to Hitler and not to geopolitics per se. Similarly, scholars in the Soviet Union scorned geopolitics as Western imperialism while ignoring Soviet foreign policy. Kissinger's geopolitical rationales for US foreign policy activated strong opposition from both the left and right within the United States.

Following political upheavals in the 1960s tied to defeat in colonial wars in Indochina and Algeria, France developed a strong anti-imperialist perspective on geography and geopolitics. In 1972 the French geographer Yves Lacoste gained considerable international media attention by documenting US bombing of the Red River Delta in Vietnam.[63] He argued that the river's dikes were deliberately targeted to destroy the area's fragile cultivated ecology, an act he termed "geographical warfare." In 1976, he published *La Géographie ça sert d'abord à faire la guerre* (Geography serves first to wage war) that exposed how much military concerns dominated the emergence of the discipline of geography.[64] Together with others, he founded the journal *Hérodote* the same year as an outlet for critical contemporary scholarship on geopolitical affairs. Another French geographer, Claude Raffestin, based in Switzerland, was also thinking critically about space, power, and territoriality at this time.[65] In the United States, geographers, radicalized by the Vietnam War protests, developed accounts of how capitalism produced space in racially unequal ways, with some areas privileged and others ghettos.[66] There was, however, little sustained engagement with geopolitical thought or detailed analysis of how geopolitics actually worked.[67]

Rising superpower tensions and existential fears of nuclear war in the early 1980s spurred the development of a new critical geopolitics within Anglo-American geography.[68] Drawing inspiration from post-structural and post-colonial thought, critical geopolitics sought to expose geopolitical reasoning as imperialistic. In *Creating the Second Cold War* (1990), a study of the hawkish US Cold War lobby the Committee on the Present Danger (CPD), Dalby showed how US security discourses were far from objective analyses of international affairs, but rather ideological scripts that organized the world into rigid categories of self and other, friends and enemies.[69] Groups like the CPD used deterministic geopolitical tropes to systematically produce discourses of threat and danger irrespective of empirical facts. Theirs was a deeply conspiratorial worldview that sought to justify hardline policies and greater military spending by the United States and its alliance systems.

My own work *Critical Geopolitics* (1996) sought to make the case for a critical approach to geopolitics. Three lines of critique were particularly salient in the book and in other publications. The first was an argument about the connection between imperial states and geographical knowledge. Drawing upon critical histories of European science in colonial conquest and imperialism, I argued that geography is about power not nature, about the capacity to write and represent the world within European systems of knowledge. To look at geography was not to look at "raw nature" but to look through an archive of representations of nature and landscape.[70] As a new genre of strategic prognostication for imperial states with global ambitions, geopolitics was part of a long tradition of technical knowledge serving as an aid to statecraft and state power. I used the word *geo-power* to describe the symbiotic relationship between geographical knowledge and state power. Geography as a scientific discipline was power because it was an intelligence system, a technical force and technological capacity, an epistemological edge for those states that supported it. The argument placed geopolitics within the broader history of modernity as expressed by European imperialism. Geopolitics was just one of many forms of human endeavor to engage, manage, and master the Earth.[71] Geographical techniques and practices were integral to the expansive imperial power systems creating the modern world: all modern power is always geo-power.[72]

The second argument was a critique of the privileged form of seeing that characterized geopolitics. In conceptualizing international affairs as a *Theatrum Mundi*, modern political geographers positioned themselves as detached viewers of the spectacle of political drama. Theirs was supposedly a view from nowhere but, at the same time, we know they were active political partisans, some like Kjellén and Mackinder serving for years in parliament for conservative political parties. Geopoliticians were implicated within, not removed from the dramas they described. They help constitute that which they claimed they were merely observing by touting cultural frames and political interpretations as self-evident truths. Imperial vision was made innocent by geopolitics, a mere "looking at the map." The task of critical geopolitics was to reveal the cultural assumptions and discursive strategies that produced such geopolitical vision.

These first two arguments were critiques aimed at the classical geopolitical tradition. The third argument was that geopolitics was a broader cultural practice than geo-strategy. All states situated themselves in the world by deploying certain geographical imaginations and visions of civilizational belonging. Geopolitics could be thought of as having not only a formal or elite geo-strategic expression, but also practical and popular expressions. This argument linked up with research studying how "us versus them" or identity-difference dynamics were central to the foreign policy practices of states. It also connected with research on the significance of geographical imaginations in shaping how powerful cultures organized and understood the world beyond their borders.[73] Edward Said's *Orientalism* (1978) documented how Western area experts of various kinds created visions of the East as an exotic Other to the West which reflected not empirical study but the prejudices and conceits of imperial societies.[74] Attentive to the operation of geographical imaginations as vehicles for identity construction, critical geopolitics found these in the routine practice of statecraft by political leaders, as well as in the products of popular culture, in cartoons, magazines, films, novels, sermons, and news media.[75] Prevailing forms of geopolitical reasoning require study of the broader social and cultural networks of power within and across states.

The critical study of geopolitics became a lively research field within Anglophone geography over the past three decades.[76] The perspective attracted criticism both from defenders of classical geopolitics and from those who found fault with some aspect of its initial articulation.[77] It also produced more conceptual stretching of the word.

The Weaknesses of Critical Geopolitics 1.0

In retrospect, there were two major weaknesses of the original articulations of critical geopolitics. The first is that critical geopolitics did not develop an alternative geographical theory of international politics. Shaped by a deconstructive open source ethos, critical geopolitics prioritized critique of the classical geopolitical tradition and the development of themes and ideas from theorists in literary theory, cultural studies, and critical political theory. While critical geopolitics did begin to formulate a set of new theoretical tools to understand and analyze geopolitics—most especially the formal, practical, and popular geopolitics distinctions—it failed to build upon these to develop a broader framework of engagement with fundamental questions in the study of global politics.

The reasons for this are many, but one of them was a desire to avoid state capture. Dominant approaches in the study of international relations—variants of realism and liberalism—tended to be caught up in problem-solving for the state, rather than questioning power structures.[78] Alternative perspectives like world-systems theory and international political economy were more appealing, though it was apparent how limited both were in explaining the danger of nuclear war.[79] Practices of statecraft and the contingencies of geopolitical struggles are not easily explainable by the logic of a capitalist world system.

Other scholars, particularly feminist political geographers, did develop critical geopolitics in creative ways, but these tended to drift
away from the study of statecraft and great power competition in
international politics toward the study of everyday intersections of
geopolitics and gender identity.[80] It can be argued that the open and
necessarily interdisciplinary features of this research were a strength,
not a weakness: critical geopolitics as "build-it-yourself" critique.
Whether this is the case or not, it became a heterogeneous field of
critical research on all aspects of global politics, rather than a distinct
theory of international relations with a developed and shared conceptual infrastructure.[81]

The second weakness of critical geopolitics was its tendency to be
drawn to the discursive rather than the material and earthly context
of geopolitical practices. Like many social theory–inspired approaches,
it was preoccupied with the human world, particularly its discursive
formations and power structures. More than most approaches, though,
critical geopolitics was critiquing a classical inheritance where the
natural world was a central force and actor. This could have produced
more engagement with the lively materiality of the Earth system than
it did, but here critical geopolitics, like postwar US political geography more broadly, was anxious to disassociate itself from any sugges-
tion of environmental determinism.

Thus, critical geopolitics tended to settle for critique of the ways
in which classical geopolitics naturalized the ideological worldview
of imperialist intellectuals through appeals to the environment, geography, and the natural world. This was and remains a valid and important exercise. But the broader intellectual questions associated with
the influence and force of the materiality of the Earth—everything
from the configuration of landforms, the fertility of soils, the variability of temperatures, and distance to rivers and seas—were considered old-fashioned problems.[82] These questions, though, are hardly
that, and have pressing relevance to contemporary debates on how societies will adapt to climate breakdown and ecosphere crises. None of
this is to affirm the muddled and cliché-ridden 'revenge of geography'

narratives in circulation which remain stuck in unexamined imperial conceits.[83] A better formulation of critical geopolitics is required.

The Climate Crisis and Geopolitics

The initial impetus behind critical geopolitics was born of anxiety about the terrifying prospect of nuclear war, and potential nuclear winter thereafter, between the West and the Soviet Union. The original wave of critical geopolitical scholarship was driven by the experience of this anxiety and a desire to respond intellectually to enduring imperial practices in international affairs.

The contemporary climate emergency presents an existential condition that is more complex and entwined with additional matters of serious concern to human flourishing.[84] The nature of the crisis, and the concepts that are being developed to understand it, have heightened attention to past traditions of thought on human-Earth relations, and on the ecological assumptions of political thought more generally.[85] It has also provoked new forms of critical geopolitical thinking while stimulating renewed interest among prominent intellectuals in the history and meaning of geopolitics.[86] Scholarly works in the subfields of international relations, critical security studies, environmental politics, gender studies, political ecology, science and technology studies, and political theory have extended critical approaches to geopolitics and climate in creative ways, creating what might be termed a "critical geopolitics 2.0" that addresses the climate emergency.[87]

Within this large literature, it is frequently remarked that climate change is transforming the very terrain of global politics and great power competition. Simon Dalby, a key figure in deepening the connections between critical geopolitics and political ecology, sees this as a defining feature of what he terms "Anthropocene geopolitics."[88] "Rising sea levels, potential agricultural disruptions, the dangers of

wildfires, droughts, and extreme weather," he writes, are the new context of geopolitics.[89] This changing terrain is the result of decisions
made by major powers themselves and the modernity they express,
project, and protect. Political decisions about modes of economic production, especially decisions about energy sources, are "remaking substantial parts of the 'geo' and directly shaping the future spatial context
of humanity."[90] What is clear is "that the geographical fixity assumption on which territorial jurisdiction operates is literally being eroded
as sea levels rise."[91] The continuation of great power competition as
usual only perpetuates this.

Latour, whose final works partly engaged with classical geopolitics
concepts, argued that climate change shifted agency within geopolitics.[92] What was taken as a passive background is no longer so, but active and lively. "People generally talk about geopolitics as if the prefix
'geo' merely designated the framework in which political action occurs. Yet what is changing is that, henceforth, 'geo' designates an agent
that participates fully in public life."[93]

Claims such as these are helpful in the abstract but are insufficiently
cognizant of the actual intellectual history of geopolitics. Geographical
features and factors were never passive for thinkers like Ratzel and
Mackinder. In contrast to later theories of international relations
where geography fades into the background, they took the agency of
geo-ecological factors seriously and thought about the dependencies
and vulnerabilities, as well as possibilities and imperatives, faced by
states because of these. In the following chapter I turn to the life and
work of Halford Mackinder to show how his initial formulation of
geopolitics was tied to an imperialism that was geo-ecologically anxious. To remain in the first rank of world powers, Mackinder argued
that Britain had to modernize its empire to more efficiently exploit its
vast territories and resources. In Mackinder, an entire superstructure
of state strength, missionary ideals, and technological innovation rests
on geo-ecological foundations.

2

Grounding Geopolitics

On March 8, 1947, the *New York Times* published an obituary of a British professor, a figure not well known in the United States. Sir Halford John Mackinder, the newspaper explained, was a noted geographer. He made a name for himself as an explorer and educator and, through advocacy and political service, became "a leader in applying science to British imperial problems." Two of his publications, a 1904 address to the Royal Geographical Society (RGS) and a book addressed to diplomats gathered at Versailles after the Great War, the obituary explained, subsequently acquired great significance for US strategists "because of their world connotations."[1]

Underscoring Mackinder's perceived significance at that moment, the next day the same paper published an editorial entitled: "The Father of Geopolitics."[2] This explained that the recently deceased British geographer was "a nobler cast" than those in Germany, like Professor Karl Haushofer, who "furnished the intellectual underpinnings for the doctrine of 'lebensraum,'" the Nazi ideology justifying territorial expansionism. In contrast, Mackinder was a British patriot who "strove for freedom, democracy and peace." This sympathetic view of a British imperialist reflected tacit beliefs at the time. The Anglo-American "special relationship" forged by the Atlantic Charter and subsequent war were informed by conceits of Anglo-Saxon racial virtue and superiority. Central to this was the specification of rising threats. Here Mackinder's writings from decades earlier proved useful. Mackinder, the editorial explained, "invented the name 'Heartland' for the strategic core of the European-Asiatic landmass." He clearly saw "how this immense area, with adequate manpower, would have space in which to outmaneuver and defeat an enemy advancing through 'a broad isthmus' between the Baltic and Black Seas." But what neither he nor Haushofer foresaw were "the effects of a westward thrust carrying Russian power to the Stettin-Trieste line," a demarcation that echoed Churchill's famous "Iron Curtain" speech in Missouri a year earlier. Russia's "westward thrust," the editorial concluded, was the threat at the gates facing the Western powers today.

The circumstances by which Halford Mackinder came to be known as the "father of geopolitics" are accidental. Mackinder never used the buzzword in his writings and reportedly disliked it.[3] Furthermore, his subsequently influential publications were largely forgotten after their initial appearance. They had little discernible influence on British foreign policy thinking and imperial strategy at the time. Instead, what made Mackinder famous in the United States at the outset of World War II was a conspiracy theory about Germany. Journalists were attracted to the idea that Karl Haushofer was "the brain trust" behind Hitler.[4] They noted Haushofer's reverence for Mackinder and Haushofer's connection to Rudolph Hess and Hitler during the writing of *Mein Kampf*. From this they imputed that German *Geopolitik* was the key to a supposed Nazi "grand strategy." Mackinder, in other words, became the patriarch of geopolitics because the leading figure in German *Geopolitik* held him to be so.

Yet, just as importantly, the US state was actively debating its global strategic position, and Mackinder's 1919 book, *Democratic Ideals and Reality* (published in the US in 1942), was cited as a prophetic text in this discussion. Edward Mead Earle, a leading advocate of grand strategy and US interventionism in Europe, praised its "rare quality of timelessness," declaring that "there is no better statement anywhere of the facts of geography which condition the destiny of the world."[5] In a separate foreword, the popular military analyst Major George Fielding Eliot declared his astonishment at Mackinder's strategic insights decades earlier.[6]

As a result, geopolitics emerged in the United States amidst fear over Nazi Germany's territorial expansionism. This easily morphed into fear over the territorial gains by the Soviet Union by 1945 and the worldwide spread of communism. An emergent concern in the United States' ambitious postwar global geopolitics was preventing a single major power from dominating the Eurasian landmass. It was Mackinder who helped justify this geo-strategic disposition by naming a north central region within Russia the "heartland of world power." This reinforced the new US geopolitical fixation on Russia and burdened it with an imperial mission justified by paranoid cartographic vision.[7]

The material realities of climate breakdown today are forcing new thinking on the "facts of geography which condition the destiny of the world." Mackinder helped usher in a new global geo-strategic vision of the Earth's geography. But there is a lot more to Halford Mackinder than the two enduring catchphrases—the "geographical pivot of history" and "the heartland"—with which he is associated.[8] A founding figure in the establishment of the discipline of Geography in British education, a prolific geography textbook author, a parliamentarian and public intellectual, Mackinder was among a series of intellectuals in imperial states in the late nineteenth and early twentieth centuries who transposed central metaphors from Malthus and Darwin to the emerging study of international politics. Mackinder's arguments have been described as a "pre-theory" of international relations.[9] He approached international politics, though, as a geographer, and sought to create a political geography that was both scientific and practical. This makes his work interesting because, in contrast to much of what subsequently became International Relations in the Anglo-American realm, his thinking is grounded in the geological and ecological realities of the Earth (as he saw them). Geographical good fortune and climate, coal and empire, technology, education, and race: these are the factors central to Mackinder's narratives. The geopolitical gaze on the Earth that Mackinder helped establish was geo-ecological, but an imperial one.[10]

Most discussion of Mackinder tends to focus on his strategic ideas, instead of the conceptual foundations that get him to these claims. But these foundations are crucial and a productive starting point to consider the deep structure of the relations between geopolitics and climate change. In this chapter, drawing upon Mackinder's writings and parliamentary speeches, I discuss six dimensions of the conceptual system he develops. These help us understand how geopolitical thought was grounded from the outset in attitudes toward the Earth, interpretations about geo-ecological factors in world history, and in imperial anxieties about land, food, resources, and racial order. At the end of the chapter, I briefly address some limitations of how Mackinder grounds geopolitics before considering how some of his ideas can be repurposed to critical geopolitical ends in the next chapter.

Dynamic Interaction: The Earth's Influence on Human History

Mackinder's work is grounded in recognition of the Earth as a dynamic geophysical system that decisively shapes international politics. Classical geopolitics is frequently dismissed as geographically determinist, but the arguments of its key thinkers are more complex than this. Mackinder argues that physical geography is the foundation of political geography.[11] He conceptualizes this foundation as the interaction of three different geophysical spheres. The Earth's surface and landforms are its lithosphere, the Earth's climate its atmosphere, and the Earth's seas its hydrosphere. Their dynamic interaction is physical or pure geography, as opposed to applied geography. Pure geography, he wrote, is "essentially a branch of physics: it aims at showing as a dynamic system the reciprocal influence over the world whole earth of landforms and air and water circulations. In other words, its chief-subject matter is the control of climates by landscapes and of landscapes by climates, and the control by both of the environment of living beings."[12]

Mackinder grasped the unique nature of Earth in the solar system as a planet that sustains life. Indeed, he even approaches an early version of Lovelock's Gaia hypothesis when he writes: "Is it not the fluid envelopes, the water and the air, which by their circulations, their physical and chemical reactions, and their relation to life, impart to the earth's surface an activity almost akin to life itself?"[13] He appreciated how, within the vast realm of space, planet Earth presented "the infinitesimally rare conditions under which life becomes active," a condition attributed above all to the hydrosphere.[14]

Physical geographic conditions on planet Earth create propitious conditions for the development of multiple forms of life. Reflecting prevalent thinking at the time, Mackinder discusses the relationship between the physical environment and biology in Darwinian terms. Certain physical environments create opportunities for particular species and through processes of natural selection—Mackinder renders this as "the survival of the fittest"[15]—a hierarchical order of local varieties of species come to inhabit a region.

Mackinder's discussion of plants and animals conceptualizes them as constraints and opportunities. They can be potential hindrances to human habitation—for example, the prevalence of diseases in certain locations—but also resources for human exploitation. Concepts like the fertility of the land and the abundance or scarcity of resources in a region are conceptualized as natural phenomena even though they are clearly anthropocentric notions. Accompanying this is a normalized settler colonial mentality toward land (similar to Ratzel): it is natural that more advanced societies would want to seize land and resources that are not being used effectively. All organisms are in a struggle for survival, and stronger groups naturally look to secure their survival and future growth through expansion.

While human beings are the dominant species in the biosphere, they are far from being alike. Race and racial difference are fundamental realities for Mackinder, the product of environmental difference but also genetic inheritance, a domain of scientific debate emergent at the time. Mackinder thought that the white Anglo-Saxon race was at the top of a natural racial hierarchy in the world. Yet this had to be enforced and races kept separate, lest there be racial degeneration.

Writing in 1908 while traveling in Canada, he supported the right of Canada's Anglophone establishment to exclude immigrants from British India. His justification for this is revealing: "If there is one object of policy on which thinking Canadians are firmly united it is that of a white Canada. Mixture of the races must result either in intermarriage, with physical and moral consequences which, to say the least, are deeply uncertain, or in a caste system fatal to democratic ideals." Violence was justified in keeping white and non-white races separate. "Brute force is no doubt a terrible arbiter . . . but if force be ever justifiable it must surely be for the preservation of the very texture of social order, painfully woven during long history."[16] Mackinder had sanctioned force personally on the expedition to climb Mount Kenya in 1899, with some of his porters murdered for ill-discipline.[17] Force was necessary to protect that which was supposedly natural.

The New Geography that Mackinder advocated for in the late nineteenth century was a discipline that promised to bridge the physical and human sciences. Geography, he proposed in 1885, is "the science whose main function is to trace the interaction of man in society and so much of his environment as varies locally."[18] The prestigious model of science at the time was positivist, so describing variations in human-environmental interactions was a way of framing the New Geography as a law-seeking science. Instead of filling out the map with discoveries and descriptions, it would provide causal explanations for the geographical distributions across the Earth's surface. But this set a geographical determinism trap for New Geography because the scientific inclination was to trace causal arrows from the physical environment to human institutions. Mackinder's emphasis on "interaction" was an effort to avoid this trap. So also are his considerable qualifications around the notion of geographical causation in his 1904 address to the RGS on the geographical pivot of history.[19]

But Mackinder never escaped the shadow of geographical determinism. One reason was that he remained trapped, as many of his contemporaries were, in oppositional abstractions like Nature and

Man, Geography and History, even as he complicated and questioned them. In his advocacy lectures for New Geography, Mackinder borrows a schema enunciated before the Royal Geographical Society by James Bryce (1838–1922) in 1886. Bryce, an Irish-born academic, historian, explorer, liberal politician, and later British ambassador to the United States (1907–1913), presented a lecture entitled "Geography in Its Relation to History" a year prior to Mackinder's first major address on the subject.[20] Bryce argued that Geography "had to look on man as a part of nature who is conditioned in his development and progress by the forces which nature brings to bear upon him; in other words, he is in history the creature of his environment—not altogether its creature, but working out also those inner forces which he possesses as a rational and moral being." History is shaped, in other words, by environmental forces interacting with human potentialities, though Bryce tilts toward geographic determinism in suggesting that it is "largely determined and influenced by the environment of nature."

Bryce conceptualized the relationship of geography to history as the operation of three distinct environmental influences. The first is the configuration of the Earth's surface, that is the distribution of land and sea, mountains and valleys, rivers and basins. The second is the influence of climate on the conditions of life in distinctively configured locations. The third is the resource endowment of a particular earthly territory, what it offers in terms of minerals, vegetables, and animals to "human industry." Mackinder endorsed this schema and used it in writing his descriptive geography textbooks. These texts are full of elaborated descriptions of physical geographic forms, climate and resource endowments, and the opportunities these provided for human shelter, settlement, growth, and expansion.

It is commonplace to translate the relationship of geography to history as a relationship of Nature to Man, or of a constraining environment to human agency in geopolitical writing. Mackinder's 1904 address on the geographical pivot of history, after all, supports this reading. There he proposed to describe "those physical features of the world which I believe to have been most coercive of human action." To this he adds a famous summary statement: "Man and not nature initiates, but nature in large measure controls."[21]

Influential as this passage is in the history of geopolitical thinking, Mackinder's thinking on geographical causation is more complex than this sentence suggests. The relationship between humans and the environment is dynamic: initiative and control can shift. Constraints and opportunities are never fixed. Organizational, technological, and scientific changes make it possible for advanced human societies to overcome barriers and exploit resources not previously mastered. The trend line was greater human power relative to earthly power. "In no small measure," Mackinder wrote in 1919, "man now controls the forces of nature."[22] That control, though, is conditional and not absolute.

Human geography examines how human societies adapt and respond to their geographical setting, and how different communities build their distinctive habitats. Mackinder's conceptualization of how humans make space utilizes two concepts that are uncommon today: going concern and momentum. Both are terms he uses to describe the dynamic qualities of human organizations. A "going concern" is a complex organization that is well ordered and growing in its environment. The term refers to the political economy of a state, to its industrial, financial, and human capital systems. The metaphor is mostly mechanical—a going concern is a vast and delicate machine—but there are also implicit analogies to living organisms.[23]

"Momentum" is another name for the pace of growth. Here Mackinder's argument is more elaborate. Through initiative and dynamic work ("energy"), certain societies acquire first-mover advantages and structure the material environment that faces other societies as they begin to self-organize. Though a small island state, Great Britain was able to establish a worldwide empire and political economy that structured commodity trade and finance flows across the globe. This privileged the city of London, and it grew to an extent that was well beyond what was sustainable by its local environment.[24] This created dependence on overseas lands for Great Britain, most especially for food. Momentum may be launched by initial geographical advantages, but it becomes social as superior organization and habits of efficiency. While circumstances change, and new states rise, the pathways established at the outset exercise an enduring influence.

Mackinder's broad conception of geography, and geographical causation, is an important background for understanding how he theorizes international politics or what he termed "political geography." Geography is not simply the influence of the physical environment, but also the influence of a biosphere structured by the law of the survival of the fittest. Here he normalizes Anglo-Saxon supremacy and, more generally, racial hierarchy as simply part of nature. Yet this same "natural order" requires force to keep it in place. The important point is that geography is not fate: it can be molded by human organizations and technological systems, and the path dependencies they create.

The Cartographic Expression of the Eternal Struggle for Existence

While Mackinder did criticize Darwinian thinking for fatalism, he nevertheless thought largely in Malthusian and Darwinism terms about international relations. "Nature is ruthless," Mackinder remarked in one publication, "and we must build a Power able to contend on equal terms with other Powers, or step into the rank of the States which exist on sufferance."[25]

The phrase "struggle for existence" was first popularized by Thomas Malthus. He used it to describe what population growth amidst limited land and food resources portended for human societies. Absent the possibility of emigration, Malthus foresaw a "struggle for existence" that would take the form of a "perpetual struggle for room and food."[26] This phrase "struggle for existence" was later used by Charles Darwin to explain his theory of evolution by natural selection. As we have noted, German Darwinians like Ratzel rendered this as a struggle for *lebensraum* and applied it, like social Darwinians in many countries, to interpret international politics. Mackinder did not outright declare that international politics was a "struggle for space" in the manner that Ratzel did. As the British Empire covered nearly a quarter of the Earth's land surface in the early twentieth century, stories of space scarcity had little public salience in British public life, relative to Germany. And yet his thinking is along the same lines. In 1902 Mackinder identified what he called five "great world-states": Britain, France, Germany, Russia, and the United States. In a book meant for schoolchildren, he was direct. The "most important facts of contemporary political geography are the extent of the red patches of British dominion upon the map of the world, and the position of hostile customs frontiers. They are the cartographical expression of the eternal struggle for existence as it stands at the opening of the twentieth century."[27]

Mackinder's argument was that as a small island state with a limited territory, Great Britain was vulnerable without the lands it had acquired overseas. Other great powers had vast territories at their immediate disposal. Britain did not: it depended on its dominance of the sea to secure its lines of flow with its overseas territories. Concluding the last of his secondary school geography textbooks (first edition published in January 1911), Mackinder emphasized the importance of four steam routes converging on Britain over the Atlantic ocean: eastward from Canada and the United States, northeastward from the West Indies and the soon-to-be-completed Panama Canal, northward from South America and South Africa, and westward through the Mediterranean from the East:

> That these ways should be kept open is now vital to Britain, for her supply of food and raw material is dependent on the ships which traverse them. Therefore Bermuda and Malta and Gibraltar, and the fleets on the Mediterranean and North American stations, should be regarded as for essential purposes a part of the Home Land. The strength drawn from over the ocean enables our nation, pent within these small islands, to hold its own with the great states of the adjoining continent. But a

fresh and serious risk is being run. Never before have we depended on our ships for fully half our supply of food. That is a new fact in the present generation. The freedom of the ocean ways, the command of the sea—these are expressions which have an urgency of meaning for us they had not for our ancestors even in the days of Trafalgar.[28]

Mackinder's political career was built upon the contention that Great Britain needed to think about the future and reform its imperial relations if it were to survive as a great power. Anxiety that global power trends were tilting against Britain and its empire pervades his work and parliamentary speeches. In his first year in Parliament, he remarked that competition and the scale of production are "no longer in our favor." Britain needed to add to the productive basis of its power by looking to the large spaces of its empire. "The broad acres necessary are to be found in our great Colonies."[29] But if Canada is drawn into the orbit of the United States, the dismemberment of the empire is possible, with Australia potentially drifting away also. Britain would then be left alone trying to maintain its position with India and facing the prospect of its empire collapsing.[30] Commenting on the prospective opening of the Panama Canal (it eventually opened in 1914), he argued that the very center of world politics was shifting and that the Dominions of Canada, Australia, New Zealand, and even South Africa were "passing into the frontline of the battle."[31]

Mackinder viewed international relations, like racial relations, as shaped by force. This was something he stressed in his maiden address in the House of Commons in 1910.[32] The British acquired its empire by force, and it held its markets by force. It used its navy to intervene across the world to secure positive outcomes for itself.[33] In an appendix to *Democratic Ideals and Reality* he stated bluntly that world order ("the rule of the world") "still rests upon force notwithstanding juridical assumptions of equality between sovereign states, large and small."[34] This was one of the many realities he considered important to recognize if peace was to be created by the League of Nations.

Mackinder interpreted the origins of the Great War as a master–slave struggle. The war began as a German effort to subdue "Slav

Serbia" after the assassination in Sarajevo. "But it cannot be too often
repeated that these events were the result of a fundamental antagonism
between the Germans, who wished to be Masters in East Europe, and
the Slavs, who refused to submit to them."[35] He found an even more
primordial reason behind this, namely access to food. Germany "was
out against the Slavs for markets, for raw materials, and for wider
fields to till; a million people were being added annually to her stay-
at-home, kept-at-home family."[36]

The Great War returned the question of food security to everyday
life across Europe. As Mackinder anticipated, the material reality
of Great Britain's reliance on faraway grain harvests, world trading
markets, and the unimpeded movement of shipping for its food-
stuffs became an acute vulnerability during the war. German submarine warfare, first from August 1914 to September 1915, and again
from January 1917, sought to starve Britain into submission. Britain
was forced to introduce selective rationing at the end of 1917, and
Mackinder wrote *Democratic Ideals and Reality* amidst this scarcity and
the "Spanish influenza" pandemic. Improving the efficiency of imperial shipping and trade was one locus of Mackinder's work after
losing his parliamentary seat in 1922, but there was no solution to
Britain's dependence on overseas lands for its food. Britain reintro-
duced rationing in 1940 and retained select rationing for years after
World War II.

The Geographical Foundations of Great Power

Mackinder thought of the international arena not as an interstate
system of equally sovereign states, but as a system dominated by great
imperial powers. The fate of any empire in the international arena was
dependent upon their material geographical environment and how
they responded to it. All great powers were situated within geophysical and bioecological regions which came with a great diversity of
constraints and opportunities. The configurations of the Earth's surface left states with varying physical formations and locations relative

to each other. Climate shaped how these formations, lands, and locations might be developed. It conditioned what soils were productive and which crops were grown where. It made certain human habitats possible. Resource endowments and soil fertility created opportunities and possibilities, while the lack of these imposed hard constraints.

Writing in the geography textbook *Our Own Islands* (first edition, 1906), Mackinder answered the question of how "so small a country can be the home of so great a people" by citing four factors. The first was a moderate climate that enabled year-round work, the second Britain's wealth in coal and iron resources. The last two had to do with Britain and the sea. This provided strategic protection from hostile invasion but also the ability for Britons to "go out into all the world to trade and to found colonies."[37]

Climate, geology, and location shaped the fate of nations. Mackinder described the use of fossil fuels for energy as "the great source of change in the modern world." Mechanical power "has wrought so great a change on the face of the earth that in the last three or four generations there has been a greater addition to the resources at our command than in all the scores of generations which preceded."[38] This great transformation came with the use of coal. It was a key foundation of Britain's national wealth and prosperity. Writing in the early 1920s, he wrote that "[t]he modern wealth of Britain lies, of course, not only in her soil but also in her coalfields." Noting that nearly a tenth of the population depend directly on coal mining, he added: "On the foundation of coal, an industrial, commercial and financial superstructure of many storeys has been raised."[39] Mackinder says nothing about petroleum reserves, even though Great Britain had switched its naval fleet from coal- to oil-powered engines at the instigation of the then First Lord of the Admiralty Winston Churchill in 1911. This initiated a concerted effort by the British state to secure access to new oil deposits in Persia.

Germany also enjoyed fortunate geology in having extensive coal reserves in the Ruhr Valley. Like many, Mackinder connected German coal and steel to militarism. It used Ruhr coal and iron ore from the annexed Lorraine "to prepare war against the world."[40] He adds: "One of the most inconvenient facts in Geography is that History has thus left us a debatable zone of territory precisely where the ground is underlaid by some of the greatest riches in the world."[41] Commenting presciently, he notes that "if humanity is to know any rest in the future, there must here be a practical recognition of the necessity of peace for history has produced enmity just where the civilization of the twentieth century demands a friendly co-operation." French insistence at Versailles on the occupation of the Saarland in compensation for its destroyed coal mines, however, ensured that control of coal remained a divisive political issue on the European continent after the Great War. It was not until 1951 that the European Coal and Steel Community began to give structural form to the sentiment expressed by Mackinder in 1924.

The major distinction that Mackinder and others used in thinking through the geographical foundations of state power is between land and sea powers. Sea power rested on both internal geographical advantages—fertile lands and resource endowments—and external geographical advantages, the defensive benefits and seafaring traditions created by water. It grew as states acquired the capacity to navigate to new lands, as they seized strategic harbors and built coastal defense systems. This allowed them to dominate certain maritime spaces and deny these to rival powers. Sea power enabled small islands like Great Britain to acquire the overseas colonies that it needed to compete with large-space states like Russia and the United States. But wealth, like that of the British Empire, built upon sea power was vulnerable because colonies were distant and naval supremacy difficult to sustain.

Land power rested on fertile heartlands, demographic power, and the capacity to move without impediment along rivers and later railways. Land empires were expansionist for a variety of reasons. More territory meant more agricultural land for food, and more resources for exploitation. Germany in the Great War sought industrial plants in France and Belgium to improve its productive capacity. In the east it sought land, but also, according to Mackinder, people to incorporate as "half-slaves" into their wartime productive system.[42] Harnessing the "human energy" of those made racially subordinate was another geographical foundation of state power, one Mackinder identified with respect to Germany but not the British Empire or the United States. The challenge of developing "manpower" to boost national strength is a dilemma Mackinder first articulates in 1905 in the wake of Britain's poor performance in the Boer War.[43]

Land and sea, in classical geopolitical thought, are elemental forces fundamentally at odds. Drawing upon a long tradition of liberal political thought and assertion, Mackinder linked sea power with the British Empire and democratic ideals. Land power, by contrast, is associated with authoritarianism and tyranny. Land invasions from the east were the "pestle" that pounded Europe into its modern shape.[44] Mackinder saw the future of British democracy as resting upon the exploitation of its non-white-majority tropical colonial holdings. Citing Athenian democracy, he argued in Parliament in 1919 that these British colonies were its "mines of Laurium. We have vast tropical areas in which hundreds of thousands of square miles of fertile soil are to be found." The development of this storehouse of resources could bring forth a Britain its forefathers never imagined.[45] The implication that British democracy was an exclusive white racial project, resting upon the subordination of non-white populations and places, was not acknowledged, but clear nevertheless.

Mackinder is well known for the fear he expressed in 1904 that the balance between land and sea power was tilting to land power because of the ability of railways to move troops quickly to distant frontiers and thus project power effectively across vast distances. This was a simplistic interpretation and rather directly contradicted by the Russo-Japanese war of 1904–1905 that began a few weeks after his address. Nevertheless, it served an alarmist narrative about the need for the British state to strengthen its army as well as its naval forces. Mackinder argued that Britain depended too much on its fleet to defend its islands instead of training its population sufficiently to render any invasion impossible.[46] He was also concerned about the capacity of the German state to ally itself with Russia and thus acquire access to the heartland and a supposed unrivaled storehouse of resources.[47] This fear, ironically, persuaded some German factions that it represented sound strategy.

Whether states seize the opportunities that their geographical situation creates or not depends upon their social organization and Mackinder's notion of momentum. States, he argues, are products of human division of labor and the accumulated productive habits of their populations. "Society reposes on the fact that man is a creature of habit. By interlocking the various habits of many men, society obtains a structure which may be compared with that of a running machine."[48] Set upon certain pathways of routine functioning, they become "going concerns" with a directional "momentum" that is hard to change. Only in times of revolution and war is it possible to reset the structures and habits of the state.

Those states that are well organized and develop efficient forms of bureaucratic organization will compete effectively and seize the opportunities that are available to them. Some states will enjoy first-mover advantages and accumulate power resources that are beyond what they might ordinarily expect. Here social momentum consolidates accumulated advantage and particular path-dependency in the international system. The British Empire runs on a particular social momentum which has free trade and naval supremacy at its center. British maritime colonialism propelled Great Britain to the first rank of world powers and London to the apex of world cities despite the relatively small size of Great Britain and its capital city. The challenge for the British Empire is to hold together its geographically diverse and distant dominions.

States can lose their social momentum. This is where Mackinder's commitment to imperial reform comes in. Mackinder argued strongly for economic reforms to improve the position of the British Empire in this struggle with other states. Large states are in a competition with each other for resources and markets. According to imperial modernizers, Great Britain needed to abandon its laissez-faire liberalism and impose tariffs to protect its industry at home and secure its economic relationships with other parts of the British Empire. There is also a struggle for relative efficiency in industrial production and in the recruitment of "man-power."[49] "You cannot in the long run hold the position of a great power in the world unless you are reasonably equal in resources to the great Powers with which you are competing."[50] Looking to the future required, to Mackinder, "regarding human life as capital for fighting, for work, and for creating wealth."[51]

Mackinder relates social momentum to questions of state leadership. He constructs a figure he terms the "organizer," who is an ambivalent agent of change. Unsurprisingly outlined in patriarchal terms, he is a man of action and leadership, a figure who thinks clearly about what the state requires to survive and prosper. A materialist thinker, he can break the power of inertia and change the direction of a state. Some organizers, like Napoleon, lead their states to ruin after initial brilliance. Bismarck was a successful organizer, according to Mackinder, because he showed a capacity to also reckon with what he terms "spiritual forces."[52]

Geographical Imaginations and Geopolitical Culture

Halford Mackinder is not known as a social constructivist, nor as a figure who wrote about geographical imaginations. Yet in *Democratic Ideals and Reality* he contends that the influence of geographical conditions upon human activities depended "not merely on the realities as we now know them to be and to have been, but in even greater degree on what men imagined in regard to them."[53] The statement is a surprising one, given Mackinder's well-known association with natural and materialist arguments. Yet, from the outset, the prevailing societal perception of space is an important theme in geopolitical thinking.

Classical geopoliticians like Ratzel and Kjellen discuss the importance of space perception and advocate for new ways of seeing space, most especially for thinking in terms of great spaces (*Grossraum*).[54] Geographical realities may be objective and ineluctable, but they are not imminently meaningful. They must be studied, grasped, and acted upon. Culture and history shape the interpretive process. "Our view of the geographical realities," Mackinder writes, "is coloured for practical purposes by our preconceptions from the past. In other words, human society is still related to the facts of geography not as they are, but in no small measure as they have been approached in the course of history."[55]

This is where geographical education could make a difference. Inspired by the example of German geographical education, Mackinder viewed the institutionalization of geographical modes of thought as necessary for Great Britain to be a successful imperial power. It mattered greatly how states thought about their place in the world, how location was both a material fact and a geographical viewpoint. Nascent within Mackinder's work is the concept of geopolitical culture, what states make of their material geographic location. But this idea sits alongside other passages where he naturalizes the operation of geographical imaginations, attributing them to fixed national mentalities or elemental determinism (e.g., "the seaman's point of view" or the "landman's point of view").[56]

Yet Mackinder is clear that geographical imagination is something that is taught, and that all states have geopolitical cultures, some highly developed whereas others are lagging. Denouncing Prussian militarism, for example, in *Democratic Ideals and Reality*, he nevertheless admires aspects of the culture it helped foster. "Maps are the essential apparatus of *Kultur*, and every educated German is a geographer in a sense that is true of very few Englishmen or Americans. He has been taught to see in maps not merely the conventional boundaries established by scraps of paper, but permanent physical opportunities— 'ways and means' in the literal sense of the words."[57] The widespread circulation of maps in a state promoted the capacity of people to visualize international affairs on a "mental relief map." Decades of instruction in German classrooms on geography and politics provided

Germans with a powerful "map habit of thought." Because of this, Halford Mackinder feared even a defeated Germany because it was better positioned than the allies to win the peace. At Versailles, "our statesmen will, no doubt, have the advice of excellent geographical experts, but the German representatives will have behind them not merely a few experts but a great geographically instructed public, long familiar with every important aspect of the questions which will arise, and quick to give a farsighted support to their leaders. This may easily become a decisive advantage, especially should our people pass into a magnanimous frame of mind."[58] To "most Anglo-Saxons," thinking geographically was "a new mode of thought." Underscoring how this is a popular culture of visualizing space, he suggests this capacity has been "lately and imperfectly introduced among us by the rough maps of the newspapers."[59]

Mackinder, in other words, recognizes the importance of popular geopolitics—the everyday geographical imaginations that circulate among the masses within large states—in how states act in international affairs. His goal is to incite imperial consciousness within the British public through geographical education. Though he never developed the notion that each state has its own geopolitical culture, it was part of his thought. Mackinder was, in his own time, a geopolitical culture advocate for empire.

Spatial Revolutions

Mackinder is rarely discussed as a theorist of technology and power. Indeed, the word "technology" does not appear in his written work. Nor does the phrase "spatial revolution."[60] Yet the question of how technological change transforms spatial relations is a fundamental one in Mackinder's New Geography. "While the mountains change their form almost imperceptibly in long ages," Mackinder wrote in an 1890 essay, "a daring leader, a mechanical discovery, a great engineering monument, may revolutionise man's relations to geography in the third of a generation."[61] Leadership, technological innovation, and

infrastructural projects are all important sources of systemic transformational change in international affairs.

Mackinder's 1904 RGS address presents a condensed story of international politics as a spatial history of invasions shaped by the interaction between geophysical endowments and what he calls "mobilities
of power." Today these might be termed "infrastructures" or "logistics
of power projection." These are the means of movement by which
particular people project their power onto other people's lands. His
earliest example is the Roman Empire and its system of roads, though
it is only cited in passing. Featured more prominently are the series of
horse-riding peoples from Asia that advance through the open spaces
of southern Russia into Hungary and "the very heart of the European
peninsula."[62] The Vikings and their boats were a rival mobility of
power. Muslim Arab empires (named Saracens by Mackinder) combined mobilities, using camels and horses on land and ships on the sea.

The ships that made the Spanish and Portuguese seaborne empires
possible inaugurated a spatial revolution in Europe and its relationship
to the rest of the world. "The revolution commenced by the great
mariners of the Columbian generation endowed Christendom with
the widest possible mobility of power, short of a winged mobility."[63]
The broad political effect of this was to reverse the relations of Europe
with Asia. Whereas before Europe was "constantly threatened by the
superior mobility of the horsemen and camelmen, she now emerged
upon the world, multiplying more than thirty-fold the sea surface
and coastal lands to which she had access, and wrapping her influence
round the Euro-Asiatic land-power which had hitherto threatened
her very existence."

A fresh spatial revolution, however, was afoot in Euro-Asia, driven
by the spreading networks of a new mobility of power: the railway.
"[T]rans-continental railways are now transmuting the conditions of
land-power," Mackinder declared, "and nowhere can they have such
effect as in the closed heart-land of Euro-Asia, in vast areas of which
neither timber nor accessible stone was available for road-making.
Railways work the greater wonders in the steppe, because they

directly replace horse and camel mobility, the road stage of development having here been omitted."[64] Presented a year after the Wright Brothers first flew an aircraft, Mackinder's emphasis in 1904 on transcontinental railways as a transformative technology may seem antiquated. But, with North America as the exemplar, the development of railway networks signaled development and modernization, the state becoming more connected and coherent. Railways also enabled land powers to more rapidly project power over large distances. "It was an unprecedented thing in the year 1900," he argued, "that Britain should maintain a quarter of a million men in her war with the Boers at a distance of 6000 miles over the ocean; but it was as remarkable a feat for Russia to place an army of more than a quarter of a million men against the Japanese in Manchuria in 1904 at a distance of 4000 miles by rail."[65] Almost twenty years and a worldwide war later, these events were still impressive cases of power projection to him.

By 1919, Mackinder included airplanes, submarines, and motor cars in his discussion, which he grouped together as the internal combustion engine, but without any in-depth consideration.[66] Just as the Spanish and Portuguese explorers had demonstrated the unity of the oceans, modern methods of communication by land and air were supposedly realizing the unity of continental areas. Nowhere was this more consequential, he argued, than in north-central Eurasia: "The opening of it by railways—for it was practically roadless beforehand—and by aeroplane routes in the near future, constitutes a revolution in the relations of men to the larger geographical realities of the world. Let us call this great region the 'Heartland of the Continent.'"[67] Railways, motor cars, and airplanes, he contended, shift the balance of power in favor of land power. "In the days of air navigation which are coming," he suggests, "sea-power will use the water-way of the Mediterranean and Red Seas only by the sufferance of land-power, for air-power is chiefly an arm of land-power, a new amphibious cavalry, when the contest with sea-power is in question."[68] The word "amphibious" is one he would return to late in his life.

Mackinder appears today as a limited theorist of technological change and strategy. His remembered emphasis on railways appears old-fashioned while, in his published work at least, he had little to say on the most revolutionary technological developments of his time. These were technologies like aircraft flying high in the air and submarines stealthy lurking in the ocean depths, military technologies that traversed vertical spaces as much as horizontal spaces.

Mackinder's parliamentary speeches, however, reveal a figure keenly interested in changes in transportation and military technology. For example, he was one of the few British members of Parliament to travel in an early model airship. The R.36 was a modified Zeppelin design British airship built near Glasgow and the first to obtain a civil registration. On June 21, 1921, Mackinder was part of a group that took a two-and-a-half-hour trip over Norfolk and the North Sea organized by the Air Ministry.[69] Soon thereafter, Mackinder advocated in *The Times* for the British government to continue state support for airship development. Airships offered "potentialities of speedy air transport over long distances."[70] They held considerable potential in binding the distant lands of the empire closer to the British homeland.[71] His intervention garnered support, with one advocate summarizing the case: "It is as necessary for us to rule the air as to command the seas."[72] The following month, though, a somewhat larger R.38 airship crashed spectacularly off the coast of Hull with the loss of forty-four lives.[73] It was among the first of many accidents that doomed airships as a mode of transportation and military power.

Mackinder, however, remained enthusiastic and included a picture of the R.36 he traveled upon in his short 1924 textbook *The World War and After*.[74] In it he declared that "the time has come when men will truly think in terms of continents and oceans." This was because "[b]efore very long the airship will take you from London to Australia in ten or twelve days and 'Egypt,' 'India,' 'Burmah' [*sic*] and 'Singapore' will be the names of stations on the way."[75]

Mackinder represented a major shipbuilding constituency in Glasgow and was always attuned to changes in shipbuilding technology and the needs of shipbuilding firms. He later served as the chair of the Imperial Shipping Committee, an organization created in 1920 to address problems arising between shipowners and shippers over port facilities, trade freight rates, maritime insurance, and optimal travel routes between the different dominions of the British Empire.[76] Here he advocated, among other things, for subsidies to increase the speed and optimal efficiency of vessels moving between Australia and the United Kingdom.[77] He believed greater trade and better connections would strengthen the imperial ideal.

The Geopolitical Condition

Mackinder's 1904 address to the RGS provides a compelling origin story for modern geopolitics, a series of striking claims about a new universal order of space and time at the outset of the twentieth century.[78] The era of geographic exploration is over; there are no more "blank spaces" on the globe. The "outline of the map of the world has been completed with approximate accuracy."[79] A new spatial condition beckons, an interconnected system of closed space that is of "world-wide scope." Everything is now supposedly interconnected and dangerous. "Every explosion of social forces, instead of being dissipated in a surrounding circuit of unknown space and barbaric chaos, will be sharply re-echoed from the far side of the globe, and weak elements in the political and economic organism of the world will be shattered in consequence." Tacit consciousness of this condition of global spatial interconnectivity, he claimed, was "at last diverting much of the attention of statesmen in all parts of the world from territorial expansion to the struggle for relative efficiency."[80] These claims were astonishingly glib and hyperbolic for a geographer. The latter proved particularly wrongheaded.

Nevertheless, Mackinder's claims in this address provided subsequent geopolitics with a grand "master-of-all-I-see" style to emulate. His discussion in this 1904 address of three epochs of human history— pre-Columbian, Columbian, and post-Columbian—posits that there is a systemic geopolitical condition that analysts can aspire to describe and characterize. This is more than a portrait of who are the rising and declining powers of the age. Rather, this is a certain order of time and space shaped by geo-ecological endowments, economic divisions of labor, great power territorial competition, and the ascendancy of certain technologies of communication, transportation, and warfare. Mackinder, in other words, aspired to describe meta-structural factors shaping the conduct of international politics. An underappreciated aspect of his work is its ambition to describe how shifting time-space relations in any geopolitical condition restructures competition between major powers.

After the republication of *Democratic Ideas and Reality* in 1942, Mackinder was invited to write an essay for the US establishment journal *Foreign Affairs*. While the article largely revisits earlier claims, Mackinder uses the description "amphibious powers" to describe the United States, Britain, and France, a phrase that recognizes the hybrid nature of military power projection at the time and the limits of the sea/land power dichotomy. The observation was, no doubt, shaped by Britain's experience during World War II and the massive logistical effort involved in staging the D-Day invasion of France in 1944. This leads him to a striking image of the assemblage of power needed to contain German power: "a bridgehead in France, a moated aerodrome in Britain, and a reserve of trained manpower, agriculture and industries in the eastern United States and Canada."[81] Where once Mackinder celebrated Britain and the British Seas, his final published essay describes it as a "moated aerodrome." Air power had reduced an imperial country to a bit part in a trans-Atlantic military assemblage run by the United States.

Conclusion

Halford Mackinder's minor international fame as a writer came very late in his life. He was eighty-one when *Democratic Ideals and Reality* was republished in the United States, and he was prominently remembered, upon his death, as "the father of geopolitics." Yet this minor fame has endured rather well. At the height of the Cold War, the fiftieth anniversary of his 1904 address was celebrated by the US Council on Foreign Relation's periodical *Foreign Affairs*.[82] The centenary was also marked by various publications, and the establishment of a Mackinder Forum to promote geopolitics. Journalistic writers on geopolitics invariably cite Mackinder at some point. Their references are usually celebratory, viewing him as a prophetic and gifted strategist. His racism is rarely noted.[83] Mackinder's fame has endured beyond the Anglosphere as well. Intellectuals and policymakers in other world powers still cite Mackinder as a prophetic strategist.[84]

Mackinder has relevance in the age of climate breakdown because his work reveals geopolitics as geo-ecological. Like many intellectuals of empire, Mackinder used Malthusian-Darwinian metaphors to cast international affairs as a struggle for existence. In an oval-shaped Mercator projection map accompanying his 1904 RGS address, Mackinder presented the Earth's surface as a singular space of competition over "natural seats of power" between rival empires. As the Oxford historian Henry Spencer Wilkinson (1853–1937) put it, commenting that evening, Mackinder's lecture revealed that "the world is an enclosed chess-board and every movement of the statesman must take account of all the squares in it."[85] Here we confront a paradox. Though inspired by a geo-ecological map (there are no states on Mackinder's map), this chessboard metaphor took on a power of its own which, in practice, occluded Earth system processes. Its visualization of the planet as a competitive global chessboard provided a deep structure of intelligibility for twentieth-century geopolitics. But it also rendered the geo-ecological costs of geopolitics unintelligible and invisible.

Mackinder's works reveal that the stakes of world politics are geo-ecological and racial. The lands and resources of colonial territories were to be organized to preserve not only great power status but also racial hierarchy. Foreign lands and foreign peoples were meant to be efficiently organized to support the power, prestige, and affluent lifestyle of Britons as a white imperial race. This connection of geopolitics to the preservation of hierarchy and privilege is an insistent question today.

Mackinder's grounding of geopolitics in geo-ecological foundations and struggles has serious limits. Reasoning from within the imperial elite, and its self-aggrandized sense of itself as the bearer of "civilization," Mackinder ignored the human and ecological costs of the imperialism he advocated. In recognizing the centrality of coal mining to British prosperity, for example, he overlooked the respiratory diseases that scarred those working in the country's pits. He did not register the pollution of British cities. Similarly, he chose not to see the widespread impoverishment and inequality held in place by British imperial rule on the Indian subcontinent, in Africa, and much closer to home in Ireland. It is understandable that he did not grasp that the coal power that drove the British Industrial Revolution and British imperial power would so pollute the Earth's atmosphere as to radically alter the climate. Yet his inability to see the pollution and environmental degradation, already apparent in his time, is symptomatic of the narrowness of vision that characterizes the geopolitical gaze he helped create.

Grounding is not earthing. The latter aspires to a comprehensive appreciation of Earth system processes and interconnectivities, including the crucial role that humans have made in altering these processes. Mackinder's grounding of geopolitics is not the comprehensive earthing of geopolitics our present requires. But, as I argue in the next chapter, we can repurpose some of his concepts to help us develop this.

3

Making Geopolitics Critical

The most famous claim in classical geopolitics is a rhyming slogan. It owes its remarkable stickiness to a literary device called anaphora, the deliberate repetition of the first part of a sentence for artistic effect, alongside a cognitive bias associating rhyme with wisdom. Summarizing his fear of a potential alliance between Germany and Russia, Halford Mackinder suggested that British statesmen at Versailles ought to have some airy cherub whisper in their ear:

> Who rules East Europe commands the Heartland:
> Who rules the Heartland commands the World-Island:
> Who rules the World-Island commands the World.[1]

East Europe did not really exist at the time Mackinder wrote this. It was his name for varied territories from Germany to Russia, identified not in their own terms but as the in-between lands where a racial contest between Teutons and Slavs was playing out.[2] The terms "World-Island" and "Heartland" were Mackinder inventions, not real places but giant labels conjured by his imagination of global space. "World-Island" is Mackinder's term for the continents of Europe, Asia, and Africa as a single landmass, a hyperbolic reframing of vast spaces into a familiar British geographic category.

Mackinder's 1904 address uses the terms "Euro-Asia" and "Pivot Area" interchangeably, only incidentally describing it as a "heart-land." By 1919 these terms are replaced by a capitalized and de-hyphenated "Heartland" as the preferred name for the geographic plain east of the Urals that runs from the Arctic to Iran, incorporating the West

Siberian plain, the Kazakh steppe, and lowlands toward the Zagros mountains. The defining characteristic of this region is its vastness, the continental or Arctic drainage of its rivers, its supposed inaccessibility to oceangoing commerce, and its reputed store of material resources. Mackinder is not consistent in his geographic description of the Heartland, but he is consistent in describing it as a strategic prize, a pivot around which all else revolves.[3]

Mackinder's claims reveal more about anxieties in British imperial culture at the time than about geographical realities. The thesis that any state "ruling" the in-between lands therefore "commanded" the center of Eurasia is a hyperbolic claim, as is the idea that this state then controlled all of Eurasia. The final corollary—that the dominant power in Eurasia, therefore, would command the world—borders on a paranoid fantasy. Yet anxieties and fears such as these often drive policy. Preventing a single world power from dominating the Eurasian landmass became the single most important geo-strategic principle of the West's Cold War strategy. Indeed, it is an axiom whose power endures to this day.

Mackinder wrote in rhyme for deliberate effect. He once stated in Parliament that if you want to "establish an idea in the mind of the nation it must be by some dramatic stroke of policy, or by some great and oft-repeated phrase, as well as by striking illustration."[4] His anaphora echoes, most likely deliberately, that from Sir Walter Raleigh (1554–1618) at the outset of European overseas expansionism: "For whosoever commands the sea commands the trade; whosoever commands the trade of the world commands the riches of the world, and consequently the world itself."[5] Numerous variants of this rhetorical device have been articulated since—involving everything from spice to semiconductors. All strive to express a central strategy required in order to triumph in the competitive game of world power: control this territory, this element, this resource.

In this chapter I want to build upon Mackinder's discussion of the earthly dimension of politics and international relations in two ways. First, I discuss the general issues involved in thinking about human territoriality and the imperial making of the modern world. Second, I take three ideas within Mackinder and reformulate them as critical tools to analyze geopolitics as territorial politics. This discussion helps move us toward the following three chapters, where I put these concepts to work and trace how they are entwined with the climate crisis.

Territorializing the Earth

What makes Ratzel and Mackinder worth rereading in the era of climate change is how they connect international politics to broader Earth processes. The Earth solidified into a planet about 4.5 billion years ago. The first bacterial life form on it likely arose more than 3.8 billion years ago. The emergence of *Homo sapiens* as a distinct species is a very recent development within this long geological history, about 300,000 years ago, alongside other tool-making and fire-controlling hominin species. In the cosmic time calendar year analogy, humans only appear in the final minutes of the last day of the year. European overseas expansionism only begins at 23:59:59 on December 31.[6]

The climatic regime of the Holocene, the geological epoch that began after the last glacial retreat some eleven thousand years ago, created the relatively benign living space for the emergence of human civilizations and the acquisition by *Homo sapiens* of greater capacities and powers over its immediate conditions of life. Surface Earth temperatures never strayed beyond one or two degrees Celsius over this period. What humans take as the norm is, in geological terms, an unusual regime of climatic stability. Instability, wild swings in surface temperatures, and rapidly shifting sea levels are part of the empirical history of Earth as a planet. All human civilizations were built during a benign stretch of congenial climate.

In seeking shelter and survival, prehistoric human communities manipulated the raw materials of the Earth to create habitats they judged favorable to sustain life within their own time horizons. In evolutionary biology, this is termed *niche construction*: leveraging location,

repositioning resources, constructing physically secure homes.[7] Early
humans survived by collective cooperative action, using fire and
other tools to sculpt their surroundings and shape the ecologies they
needed to acquire food and successfully reproduce. How they did so
varied tremendously, with climate, ecology, seasonality, and culture all
shaping behavior. The earliest known evidence of human social life
"resembles a carnival parade of political forms" rather than any clear
sequence of forms or ideal types.[8] In his writing on these matters,
Ratzel used the term *lebensraum* in a species-wide manner to collect-
ively describe the parts of the Earth settled by humans, what the ancient Greeks termed the *ecumune*. He also used it in a group-specific
manner to refer to the particular Earth habitation systems created by
distinct societies.[9]

Terraformation is the process by which communities of humans
occupy a particular territory and organize it to support them with
food, shelter, and resources. The symbolic designation of places as belonging to particular human communities is a complex question. At
its heart is the question of territoriality, the act of claiming controlling power over a delimited geographic space. In more formalistic
specification, territoriality involves three Ds: the act of *demarcating* a
particular space; the public *declaration* of a desire to control access to
it; and the practice of asserting *defensive dominance* over that space. In
animals, all these behaviors are often combined in public displays to
competitors. Territoriality, though, is frequently contingent—only for
a certain time at a certain place in certain seasonal conditions—and
varies greatly by species. Its contextual, tacit, and unmarked aspects
are important.

Human territoriality emerges as part of human cultural development in certain geophysical contexts. It is not a universal human behavior but a contingent one that depends on resource abundance and
perceived survival needs.[10] How this works is still a matter of considerable debate among social biologists and anthropologists. Some
argue that territoriality is an effective strategy for survival and maxi-
mizing reproduction.[11] Not doing so may imperil the survival of the

community. Controlling access to certain natural resources, granting it to kin while denying it to outsiders, may be an adaptive survival mechanism for human groups, especially in conditions of competition and scarcity.

Human territoriality is most likely a combination of human physiological and psychological dispositions that are activated by the challenge of survival in certain environmental conditions.[12] A series of observable human "cognitive biases"—the endowment effect, loss aversion, and "first owner" bias—provide a psychological foundation for territorial thinking.[13] Part of this activation involves seeing certain spaces claimed by the group as indivisible and sacred.[14] Territorial indivisibility is the belief that a claimed space cannot be divided; it must be defended as a whole, and not partitioned or sectioned and given to competitive claimants. A sacred space is a territory with transcendent symbolic meaning to a community.

Not all biomes are amenable to human territorial behavior: deserts and tundra, high-altitude mountains, and extensive seas are difficult spaces to demarcate and control. But some, like grasslands and steppe, forests, and river valleys, have allowed human communities to flourish and have stimulated territoriality. Cutting forests and clearing fields to cultivate plants, to till the soil and to harvest crops, require delineation and fencing. Herding animals requires access to certain pastures and grazing lands. From the very acts of human settlement upon fertile spaces of the Earth comes an imperative in some cultural groups, seasonal at first but later more enduring, to organize space, to divide, delineate, and distinguish.

One of the signatures of early state formation, according to James C. Scott, is territoriality.[15] The building of a city wall is the delimitation of a polity, an imagined community of people living in one place. Some of the largest early cities were in Mesoamerica. Other organized settlements developed in the Black Sea region.[16] One of the more famous ancient cities with walls is Uruk, built between 3300 and 3000 BCE.[17] The rise of early modern states initiated the slow process of the political partitioning of the Earth's land surface, a process that sped up considerably with Western imperialism and came to encompass the entire land surface of the planet.

Carl Schmitt identified the origin of human law in the standards and rules of human cultivation of the Earth.[18] What he described as the nomos of the Earth is the spatial order created by powerful European empires and given legal form in international laws, treaties, conventions, and rules. Its foundations are human niche construction, terraformation, environmental engineering—acts that seek to occupy, cultivate, and modify the Earth for human needs. But what is distinctive about the rise of modern humans is their conception of the Earth as a storehouse of resources for exploitation by the most industrious and enterprising. Early modern states created distinctive entwinements of power, land, and people, a trilogy that would become the basis for legal codes on sovereignty, dominion, and population.

There are many histories of the relationship between sovereignty and what became known as "territory" in early modern Europe.[19] These trace the emergence of rules organizing the political demarcation of land, and later the sea, and eventually the air. This long process leads to the emergence of legal systems to measure and codify the Earth, coastal sea waters, and vertical airspace as territory that is demarcated and governed by certain shared rules of sovereignty.[20] The line, wall, and border become the indexes of emergent spatial orders organized around territorial fixity and sedentarism. But coexistent with these spatial orders were other indexes of spatial orders organized around connections, networks, flows, and linkages. Jane Jacobs suggests that the power structure of early modern states featured struggles between guardians and traders.[21] To guardians, the territory of the state was something that had to be secured and fortified. To traders, the territory of the state was something to be managed to facilitate exchange with the world beyond the city wall. This was the spatial order of trade routes, commodity flows, and migrations.

The French geographer Jean Gottman—born Ivan Gottman to a Jewish family in Kharkiv/Kharkov, Ukraine, in the Russian Empire in 1915—described this as a clash between two different logics of territorial production. "The search for security will often clash with the yearning for broader opportunity. The former calls for relative isolation, the latter for some degree of interdependence with the outside."[22] He posited two opposing and enduring tendencies in Western thought about territory: the Platonic, territory as a self-sufficient container; and the Alexandrian, territory as a network of flows and circulation.[23] Many treat networks as separate from territory, and imagine routes and roots as mutually exclusive spatial organization principles. But others, correctly in my view, point to their interdependencies and argue for understandings of territory that are relational, topographical, and ecological, not just statist and legal.[24] Territory, in other words, needs to be thought of as multifaceted: it has a formal legalized political aspect, but it also has extended economic, strategic, and ecological dimensions. Conventional territorial maps obscure this, but some of the language we use—terms like "backyard" and "footprint" and "sphere of influence"—disclose this broader sense of territory.[25]

A critical juncture in the emergence of modern humans as territorializers of the planet is the expansion of European civilization overseas into the so-called New World. John Agnew suggests this moment marks the emergence of a modern geopolitical imagination.[26] Four fundamental practices underpin this: the cartographic visualization of the world as a singular global space, an accompanying Eurocentric arrangement of global space into modern and backward places, the framing of space as exclusively about territorial state sovereignty, and the narrativization of global politics as a competitive game between great powers pursuing primacy. Agnew argues that the modern geopolitical imagination was born in the sixteenth century when cartography rendered the world as a tableau of lands and seas, with ownership claims and a singular global unity. But it is only in the nineteenth century that the European global view begins to approximate reality, as places are integrated by imperialist structures and capitalist production and trading networks.

European overseas expansionism from the fifteenth century created a worldwide geopolitical field that grew in thickness and density
of flows as time passed and forms of capitalist production intensified. Recent scholarship makes a persuasive case that European empires were weak relative to non-European forces until the eighteenth
century.[27] The capitalist world-economy was far from being global
when it was established. But its often violent extension to encompass more and more space as relational territories created a geopolitical force field that eventually reached the ends of the Earth.[28] New
forms of imperialist control and capitalist extraction thickened the
range of geopolitical fields, globalizing a once Eurocentric world-
economy. In state territorial terms, however, it was only in the late
nineteenth century that most spaces across the globe were locked into
a sovereignty system based around territorial demarcation and ownership. Even then, however, vast swaths, particularly in polar regions,
remained uncharted and unresolved in status, though not without
claims of ownership.[29] Other regions, like the vast stretches of ocean,
were designated as high seas and a shared commons. Not captured
by the map was the ecological footprint of great powers which was
slowly altering the chemistry of the atmosphere.

Chakrabarty helpfully reveals the disjuncture between the
European-led processes of globalization and territorialization, on the
one hand, and Earth as a planet, on the other hand.[30] To him and others, the triumph of the modern geopolitical imagination is the process by which the materialities of the planet are rendered as a globe.
The global is the human-centric creation of five hundred years of
European expansionism and imperialism, the rendering of the Earth
as a measured and mapped product of a world attentive to capitalist
and geopolitical logics. The planetary is the Earth as a dynamic and
interconnected system of diverse geophysical processes, an order of
knowledge much more recent than that of the globe but recording
processes which are much older and broader. The globe is a human-
centered vision of the Earth, whereas the planetary is an Earth-life
vision where humans are far from the center of things. It is the Earth

as a planet with an atmosphere made unique by the interaction of biophysical processes and geophysical processes which have rendered it habitable to oxygen-breathing life forms.

The timescales between the two concepts are vast: millions of years, in contrast to the past five hundred years of thinking of the planet as a globe. The latter world is a vision of Earth that is parochial and narcissistic, the Earth as the human planet. By contrast, the research of atmospheric scientists and interplanetary scientists have re-situated the Earth within the solar system as a planet where humans are an incidental feature. The planetary model of thinking that emerged with the development of Earth systems science in the late twentieth century and the early twenty-first century foregrounds the issue of what makes the Earth habitable to abundant forms of life and to human flourishing. Its answer is a set of conditions that are much more precarious than previously thought.

This distinction between the globe and the planet has important implications for critical thinking about geopolitics. It helps frame the current climate crisis as a clash between a hegemonic view of the Earth as global geopolitical space—territorially demarcated homelands of recognized nation-state communities—and the ever materially present and inexorable planetary dynamics of the Earth. The current conjuncture is one where that geopolitical order—a product of five hundred years of imperialism and capitalist globalization—is facing the shifting dynamics of the planetary.[31]

This manifests itself as a struggle over living space in at least two ways. There is first a global struggle between humans and all other species for the right to live and prosper on the Earth. Here we have an undeclared struggle for space to live well between the claims of an advanced modern faction of humanity and the claims of millions of nonhuman living species to nourishing ecosystems and a healthy biosphere. But this is no simple zero-sum war of humans against nonhuman species for survival. Rather, it is a struggle that threatens to rebound on humans in very negative ways. The accumulating evidence for a possible sixth extinction of animal and plant species across the planet, driven by the toxicity of our modernity for the planet's eco-sphere, is evidence of this, a dangerous degradation of the life-support systems that all human societies require.[32]

The second is a civil war struggle within humanity between those marginalized by the current world order—Indigenous communities and impoverished millions across the world—and those who are at the top of the economic and racial pyramid, those who get to im-agine themselves as "sovereign consumers" and "liberal subjects" with an expanding spectrum of rights. This struggle finds expression in the efforts of Indigenous communities to block development projects that they view as toxic to their way of life. In many instances, be-cause Indigenous communities are already marginalized, these strug-gles are lost, and extractive projects proceed. Other instances include the struggles of small island states on the so-called frontline of climate change (its more a drowning line), like Pacific Island states, to hold those historically and presently responsible for the greenhouse emis-sions that drive the rising sea levels submerging their territories. In late March 2023, Vanuatu, population 300,000, scored a symbolic vic-tory in the UN General Assembly with the passage of a motion asking the International Court of Justice to issue an opinion on whether governments have "legal obligations" to protect people from climate hazards and whether failure to meet those obligations could bring "legal consequences."[33]

The larger point is that there is an increasingly visible struggle in our modern world over territories and living spaces. Latour casts this as a disjuncture between the territories we live in and the territories we live from.[34] Pierre Charbonnier deepens the point in arguing that because modern peoples are everywhere on the planet, we have set-tled simultaneously in two territorial regimes, not just one. The first is our place of cultural belonging and identity, our official homeland. This is the state that appears as a bloc of homogenous color on a world political map. But there are also the geo-ecological territories that make possible the economic networks and flows that underpin modern life: "this is the amount of space needed to produce the goods that are consumed and to absorb the waste and pollution that are generated—a space much larger, on our case, than the territory that is officially conceived of as "ours."[35] Our territories are shared, multiple, and entangled, but our prevailing perceptions are trapped in state territorial visions. We think of land, sea, and air as discrete elements in abstract space: our soil, our waters, our airspace. But contemporary modernity is global, our living space planetary. And the extraordinary territorial demands made on the planet by modernity have compromised its ability to continue to support life like it has throughout human history.

Concepts for Thinking Critically about Geopolitics

We can think of the territorialization of the planet by capitalism and geopolitical rivalries as a five-hundred-year-plus process. Within this, we can identify more specific periods where this territorialization process took distinctive forms and found characteristic expression. Mackinder's conceptualization of the planet as a closed space of global competition between rival world powers in 1904 was a parochial imperial view. Yet it did raise the issue of how spatial relations were changing in international politics. The afterlife of Mackinder's strategic ideas suggests that these resonated with an emergent condition where the world's continents and oceans were indeed a connected global space. His post-Columbian epoch is characterized by imperial consolidation not expansion, by frontiers imaged as closed not open. Ratzel's struggle for living space is reimagined in Mackinder as a struggle among world powers over the efficiency of their organization of territorial possessions. Mackinder's work suggests three ways in which this finds expression.

The first is Mackinder's identification and conceptualization of international politics as a global geopolitical field featuring certain pivotal spaces, strategic prizes, and zones of inter-imperial competition.

Rival empires are in a struggle for resources and position across an un-even playing field. The second is the struggle over competing geopol-itical ideas and visions. The grand strategies of imperial states matter, as do what habits of thought prevail within their educational insti-tutions and ruling circles. The third is the struggle over technologies and infrastructures of time-space compression. Mackinder's particular concern is the binding power of transport and communications, and the relative mobility and speed of military power.

Mackinder's life and work suggest that the struggle for living space needs to be understood more broadly. The Nazi version, namely the territorial conquest of the agricultural land of neighboring states to grow food for a privileged racial community, was the application of ra-cial imperialism within Europe. Imperialism more broadly is a forced organization of living spaces, a geo-ecological structure of power that appears as comparative advantage in trade or a "natural" international division of labor. As Mackinder's works reveal, it is about the establish-ment of a dominant position across the world's continents and oceans. It is also about the securing of a particular world order and way of life (with implicit ideas about racial hierarchy and resource allocation). And it is about the development of effective technological infrastruc-tures and ever faster means of projecting military power across the horizontal and vertical spaces of the planet.

To better elucidate this, I want to reformulate Mackinder's ideas into three critical geopolitics concepts: geopolitical fields, geopolit-ical cultures, and geospatial revolutions. These concepts are connected but can be separated out for the purposes of analysis. I argue that together they provide a conceptual framework for the critical ana-lysis of geopolitics within broader structures of modernity and global capitalism. The analysis that follows chronicles a security contradic-tion that is now fully present today. In seeking to secure their own living spaces, the competitive territorial practices of great powers have undermined the broader living spaces that sustain human flour-ishing on Earth.

Geopolitical Fields

Classical geopolitics, for all its faults, was a sustained effort to examine the conditioning influences of the Earth's features and characteristics on the behavior of great powers. But its foundational conceptualizations were corrupted by racist preconceptions. Mackinder's sweeping notion of "geographical realities" needs to be disaggregated into what could be characterized as first- and second-order material geographical realities. The first concerns those of the Earth system and the geophysical and bio-geophysical dynamics that characterize it. These are the materialistic affordance structures of the planet. The second are those created by human niche construction, the material environment produced by human labor. Both are now thoroughly entwined, of course. The term "field" is helpful in conceptualizing this second order because it signifies both something that is earthbound yet also a product of human cultivation.

Mackinder's argument about the strategic significance of Eastern Europe is an argument about geopolitical fields. His claim, after all, is not only about raw geophysical realities, but about the relative location of great powers on the Earth across geo-strategic space. The significance of relative location is a given in classical geopolitics, though it gets limited theoretical treatment. But the relative location of great powers to axial regions and strategic prizes is crucial to the stories that are told by classical geopolitics.[36]

This is recognized and foregrounded by modern defenders of classical geopolitics. Kelly, for example, reframes classical geopolitics as an international relations theory that holds that a state's immediate environment conditions its international behavior.[37] For him, spatial position is to geopolitics what power is to realism. In this account, one that sidesteps its imperial origins, classical geopolitics is a relational theory of international politics where a state's behavior is shaped by its relative location within a structure.[38] This is a somewhat whitewashed view of classical geopolitics, but it has the virtue of identifying the basis for productive dialogue between classical and critical geopolitics.[39]

The concept of *fields* is an important tool for theory building in contemporary social science, associated most prominently with the influential work of the French sociologist Pierre Bourdieu.[40] Bourdieu used the term to describe a structured arena of conflict in which a series of differently positioned actors compete over a variety of prized resources.[41] The concept has three associations that are helpful in thinking about competitive struggles: a spatial setting, a configuration of forces, and a positional game.

The first association is the idea of a field as an arena or a theater of struggle. Sociologists do not always emphasize the spatial qualities of fields, not to mention their earthly foundations, but these are worth underscoring. Fields are materialist formations made by human labor through cultivation and terraformation of the Earth. They are structured by and dependent upon dynamic Earth systems, geophysical processes of energy circulation and biophysical processes of growth and decay. They are material terrains and settings produced by the work of generations of human settlement. Field in this sense combines both the materiality of Earth systems and the accumulated work of human occupation, cultivation, and dwelling. It is a terraformation, the geosphere and biosphere exploited and arranged by human modes of production. Geopolitical fields are the material landscapes made by histories of human settlement upon the Earth.

The second association is the idea of a field as a configuration of actors and positions, a field of forces that struggle on multiple fronts for valued resources. Here we can speak of four major fields—strategic, economic, sociocultural, and diplomatic—each of which is characterized by distinctive concerns and all of which sit within geo-ecological structures. The strategic field is shaped by the desire of different actors for territorial security and protection. The major players in this field are military institutions and networks, which can take the form of cross-state alliance systems. Other actors that try to utilize violence as a means of advancing their interests—terrorists, gangs, and militias, for example—are part of the struggles that characterize this field. The economic field is characterized by patterns of production, labor, investment, trade, and consumption. Actors are involved in struggles over the rules governing "the economy" and over the various practices of capital accumulation. Here are where practices of Earth extraction and environmental pollution are most visible, and generate the material foundations for ways of life. The sociocultural field is characterized by heterogeneous imagined communities and bonds of affection and antagonism. Actors within this field are entrepreneurs for particular forms of identity and belonging. This field features competitions over standing, status, and prestige, with educational qualifications and cultural achievements part of the struggle. The diplomatic field is characterized by a hierarchy of perceived power and influence. It is ostensibly the most powerful coordinating level among all the fields, with power concentrated in the hands of state leaders, federal groupings, military alliances, and international organizations, like the United Nations.

The third association the word "field" has is with the playing of a competitive game. Here agency requires consciousness of the rules of the game and the prizes at stake. Players generally hold to a broadly agreed set of rules. But there are often struggles over how the rules are applied and how they are to be understood. Some players that are disadvantaged by the socially prevailing rules may try to change both to advantage themselves, redefining the game and its rules in the process. An added complication is that many agents are nonhuman forces— like viruses and greenhouse gases—that do not act with conscious intentionality. As noted earlier, viewing geopolitics as a competitive game between states is perhaps the most widespread understanding of the notion.

Geopolitical fields are "thick" in three distinct ways. First, they feature scalar relations between very different arenas of action and interaction. The planetary scale is the most determinative materialist context that is ever present and characterized by Earth system processes that encompass the interconnected atmosphere, biosphere,

hydrosphere, and lithosphere. The global scale is made by human organization and technosphere construction. It creates an environment
that is exploitable not only by the powerful, but also by minor players
who wish to hide themselves within its niches. The regional scale
provides its own set of relationships and conditioning forces. The state
society scale represents another crucial arena that shapes possibilities,
but this depends upon the capacity of the state to bring resources to
bear and to implement policy. Finally, the local scale is an arena that
has the potential to be decisive in shaping actions and outcomes. How
actors across different scales interact, whether they converge or di-
verge, congeal or dissolve, shapes the power geometries of geopolitical
fields. Actors have capacities to rescale their activities, to downscale or
upscale as they pursue their goals and interests.

Geopolitical fields are thick in a second sense because they are influenced by prior configurations and spatial histories. Previous competitions over rules of the game, and subsequent outcomes, shape
current understandings. This is also the case for past territorial configurations of the field. Old infrastructural patterns endure and shape
emergent forms. The geographic inertia that Mackinder described —
the continued dominance of imperial metropoles, for example—is a
function of first mover advantages creating durable network effects.
Memories of past rules and past geographies are always in the background of current competition within geopolitical fields. Historical
and economic geographers conceptualized human landscapes as the
product of different rounds of historical accumulation and divisions
of labor. Each regime of accumulation carved itself upon the Earth as
a socio-spatial division of labor, an assemblage of human and nonhuman elements that created contingent power formations. Successive
regimes of accumulation and power formations produced a layered
human landscape that has sedimented elements and legacies from different regimes and power formations, past and present. The thickness
here is the spatiotemporal record of the human terraformation in a
particular region and place.[42]

Geopolitical fields are thick in a third sense in that they weave other fields together. The geopolitical is in theory an aggregate meta-field, one that arranges a series of other fields and has ultimate authority over them. It can be argued that the most important subfield for states is the geo-strategic field, the field that shapes the prevailing rules of survival and defense for territorial entities in the arena. Yet security is broader than the hard security provided by defensive fortifications, alliance structures, and weapons systems. Here the other fields—the economic, the sociocultural, and the diplomatic—condition and shape the broader arena. These various fields are enmeshed with each other and the infrastructural space that binds them. Separating them out as different subfields can be analytically useful, as they are not necessarily in sync with each other and have their own defining logics and rhythms.

Geopolitical Cultures

As I suggested in the previous chapter, Mackinder's writings operate with a nascent concept of geopolitical culture but rely, at the same time, on some dubious claims about essential national mentalities, collective psychologies, and environmentally shaped outlooks. His idea that states have a landman's or seaman's point of view, for example, caricatures and homogenizes entire societies.[43] Such concepts reduce analysis to stereotypical categories.[44] Alternative concepts like geopolitical codes and strategic culture are better, but also have limitations.[45] The former inclines analysis toward limited content analysis, whereas the latter inclines toward how state security elites interpret and process military-technical questions.[46] The concept of a geopolitical culture is better because it allows complexity and recognizes that states have internal power structures that shape their outward facing narratives.

Geopolitical cultures are what states make of its geographic and power position in world affairs.[47] They are built around the spatial narratives that states use to specify their territory as a place, homeland, community and location in a world of other states and communities.[48] They situate states within the world through use of geopolitical imaginaries, representations of transnational communities of identity, belonging, and fate in international affairs.[49] These may be imaginaries that are organized around collective identities like language, culture, religion, and political values. But the foundations of geopolitical cultures are the national territorial identity regimes within states. Both the power structures of states and their political system shape how geopolitical cultures are made and remade through debates within factions and between different foreign policy traditions in a state's culture. The geo-ecological condition of the state—its endowments and dependencies—is a material restraint on geopolitical culture that finds different forms of expression. So also is the prevailing balance of power in its immediate and larger geopolitical field.

Considerable critical geopolitics research has already appeared on geopolitical cultures.[50] The initial threefold distinction between formal, practical, and popular geopolitics has been extended by feminist researchers to consider everyday geopolitics and an intimate geopolitics of birth, marriage, and death, all part of demographic anxieties within and among states.[51] There is now abundant research on media and geopolitics, and how state actors use communications technologies and media ecologies to spread propaganda and disinformation. My colleagues and I conducted research on the geopolitical orientations of ordinary people in the in-between states between Russia and the European Union in 2019.[52] We asked, for example, the people we surveyed to locate their country on a ten-point spectrum between the West and Russia. We then asked them to place where they think their country should be located. From this research we were able to learn about the aspiration of many Belarussians, especially young Belarussians, to move their country closer to the West and away from Russia.[53]

A geopolitical culture is never just an expression of domestic power structures. Rather, geopolitics is always an "intermestic" matter, an entanglement of the international and the domestic in each other.[54] How a state culture articulates this depends upon its prevailing practices of framing international events within domestic politics. In a manner comparable to studies of securitization as a speech act in domestic politics, there is room for the analysis of geopolitics as a speech act in the domestic politics of states. This refers to the decision by certain political actors and institutions to name and frame a particular issue as a matter of geopolitics, to adopt, in other words, a conscious policy of *geopoliticization*.[55] This act is a rhetorical gambit to remove a question from the realm of domestic politics and reframe it as a matter involving great power politics and the location of the state within geopolitical fields.

Deploying such a move can scale up domestic political struggles into matters of great power competition, potentially advantaging one side over the other by broadening the stakes and rallying allies beyond the state to one's cause. One salient example of this was the competing framing used by Western leaders to the election protests in Belarus in August 2020. Both US presidential candidate Joseph Biden and EU Council President Charles Michel argued that the protests were not about geopolitics.[56] The Lukashenka regime, by contrast, decried the protests as a geopolitical plot by the West against Belarus. Russia's leadership agreed—it was "all about geopolitics," according to the Russian Foreign Minister Lavrov—and provided Lukashenka the necessary technical and financial support to suppress the protests.[57]

The case of Belarus in 2020 opens up a broader set of questions about the relationship between the geopolitical culture of individual states and hegemonic (and counter-hegemonic) narratives of world order. Here we confront the issue of how world powers imagine their collective identity and forge exceptionalist myths and heroic roles— special missions, crusades, and quests—for themselves in world affairs. The geopolitical imaginations that states use to situate themselves in the world are constructed from shared cultural narratives, histories, and language communities.

"Anglo-Saxonism," the late nineteenth- and early twentieth-century creed that held that English-speaking peoples were a distinctive civilizational group in international affairs, is a good example from Mackinder's time.[58] Some of its proponents dreamed of a joint Anglo-American federation.[59] The creed was also a vehicle for visions of racial separation and the superiority of 'English-speaking races' over others in world affairs.[60]

The idea of a *Russkii Mir*, a distinctive Russian world in international affairs, is a Russian-language equivalent that was sponsored by various institutional entities within the Russian state before being adopted and adapted by the Putin regime as an ideological justification for its invasions of Ukraine.[61] Meta-geographical signifiers like "the West" and "Europe" also serve as powerful geopolitical imaginaries tied to civilizational identities and missions in world affairs.[62]

Imagined collective identities can become the basis for historic mission discourses that bind together world powers and states that become allies. This tends to happen when imagined transnational identities become activated by violent eventful processes and congeal into distinct affective communities. An affective community is an imagined community of shared sacred values, experiences, and emotions.[63] It is a community with common structures of feeling, affective dispositions that are often the product of shared histories of experience, including and, indeed especially, suffering, violence, and pain. Structured around experiences such as war and terrorism, it is a community that requires stylized memory rituals and affective performances to cultivate and maintain. These are usually state sponsored and can, over time, become appropriated by political factions to legitimize themselves and their policies. The Russian Federation's use of May 9 (Victory Day) and memory of the Great Patriotic War—the Soviet regime's construction of World War II—to legitimate its invasion of Ukraine is a clear contemporary example. Affective communities can be contingent and fleeting, but sometimes they are the basis for deepening military ties and a formal military alliance.

The United States created a powerful affective community during World War II that became central to its missionary self-image thereafter. The US was officially neutral at the outset of the war, much to the frustration of the British government. The British embassy in Washington, DC, organized an influence campaign, including disinformation operations, to get the United States into the war. Public sentiment began to change as Great Britain came under sustained attack during the Blitz. The US public experienced this as a radio war, with Edward R. Murrow's live broadcasts from a London rooftop attracting large audiences. "You burned the city of London in our homes and we felt the flames," the poet Archibald MacLeish later wrote in tribute.[64] Murrow's broadcasts, and those of other correspondents, were greatly facilitated by the British Ministry of Information. It also worked to produce and distribute, without claiming attribution, a documentary film about the Blitz, *London Can Take It*, aimed at the US movie-going audiences. By the spring of 1941 an estimated sixty million Americans had seen the propaganda film.[65]

US media framing of the Blitz as plucky British resilience under fire helped foster sympathy for the very real suffering of the British people. The image of Britain as a country of class hierarchy and empire was displaced by the image of "common people" suffering under the bombs of a violently expansionist Nazi empire. The Atlantic Charter of August 1941 represented the culmination of Anglo-Saxon sentiment in elite circles. Churchill and Franklin Roosevelt sang songs like "Onward Christian Soldiers" on the deck of the British battleship *The Prince of Wales*. Both men later recalled the moment as a particularly emotional one.[66] The emotion was only increased by the fact that a few months later *The Prince of Wales* was sunk in the Pacific by a Japanese submarine with the loss of hundreds of lives.

The Atlantic Charter was a declaration that expressed respect for "the right of all peoples to choose the form of government under which they will live." [67] As leader of the British Empire, Churchill was not credible as an advocate for the self-determination of all peoples. But the aspirational language proved powerful. So also did the linkage of the liberation of peoples to the liberation of the Earth's resources.[68] The Charter promised to "further the enjoyment by all states" of access "to the trade and to the raw materials of the world which are needed for their economic prosperity."[69]

This was the US answer to Nazi *lebensraum*, an American *lebensraum* that served all humanity. This presumed confluence between American and universal interests became a foundational conceit in US geopolitical culture as it assumed world leadership after the war. A spaceless language of liberal universalism served to obscure massive asymmetries of power and messy geographies of production and extraction. Everything was in an aspirational condition of freedom: free peoples, free markets, free trade and free access to the Earth as a storehouse of resources.

American *lebensraum* took cultural expression as the idea of a Free World. Working from US Vice President Henry Wallace's characterization of World War II as a "flight between a free world and a slave world," *Prelude to War* (1942), the first of the US War Department's propaganda film series *Why We Fight*, gave it the visual form of a brightly illuminated planet where "men of vision" believed that "all men, in the sight of God, were created equal." The slave world was visualized as a darkly shadowed planet. This literal black-and-white contrast reduced international politics to a struggle between good and evil, a moralizing tendency that was bad for geographical knowledge of the world but good for belief in the righteousness of America's cause. Subsequently, the idea of the Free World gave meaning to the struggle against the Soviet Union and the formation of US military alliances. It was evoked during the US's Global War on Terror and it remains powerful today as an organizing geopolitical imaginary Obscured by the emotive power of this imaginary is the global political economy it helped consolidate and expand, with geo-ecological costs that are now all around us.

Geospatial Revolutions

The notion of spatial revolution is not particular to the study of geopolitics. Rather it encompasses the history of capitalism, the development of a modern world-system, and the technological society that characterizes modernity. The spatial revolution par excellence for Mackinder and Schmitt is European overseas expansionism and the birth of the modern world-system in the fifteenth century. The whole of the Earth is made visible as a globe for the first time. Vast new spaces are "discovered" and seized by European powers. The foundations of a trans-oceanic capitalist world order are established, initially on the basis of raw material extraction and accumulation through dispossession, but soon thereafter on a triangular trade in commodities and human beings anchored around brutal plantation capitalist enterprises.

In Schmitt's account, the most important actor in advancing this spatial revolution is not Spain or Portugal, nor the Dutch, but England. England heralds a new global spatial revolution because it is the first European state to choose maritime power over land power. It "was the English who finally overtook everyone, vanquished all rivals, and attained a world domination erected upon the domination of the oceans."[70]

The study of spatial revolutions, thus, needs to be embedded within the study of the development of a capitalist world-economy in the sixteenth century and a particular regime of elemental domination by its leading state, Great Britain, in the seventeenth century. The triangular trade in slaves and commodities across the Atlantic of mercantile capitalism would provide the stimulus for industrial capitalism in the eighteenth century. Marx and Engel's famous description of capitalism in the *Communist Manifesto* (1848) links how the bourgeoisie revolutionized the instruments of production, and thereby the relations of production, and the entire relations of society to restless globalizing imperatives.

> All that is solid melts into air, all that is holy is profaned, and man is at last compelled to face with sober senses his real conditions of life, and

his relations with his kind. The need of a constantly expanding market for its products chases the bourgeoisie over the entire surface of the globe. It must nestle everywhere, settle everywhere, establish connections everywhere. The bourgeoisie has, through its exploitation of the world market, given a cosmopolitan character to production and consumption in every country.[71]

This famous description of capitalism doubles as a description of modernity, a condition of space-time compression.[72] Capitalism, modernity, and great power competition, of course, are deeply entwined in each other. The revolutionizing of the instruments and relations of production are only possible because a hegemonic state is willing to spend money on public goods provision to secure the world-economy it creates and re-creates. Modernity, however, is not the possession of any one state, no matter how powerful, but a systematic way of life that envelopes states within worldwide processes of capitalist production, circulation, and accumulation. Modernity, of course, took many different forms within the world's leading states in the nineteenth and twentieth centuries, including a nominally anti-capitalist but no less brutalizing industrial form in the Soviet Union.

Spatial revolutions are, thus, aspects of an extractive capitalist world-economy as a whole. They are enabled by transformative change in modes of production, transportation, communication, and destruction. Indeed, separating innovations in military technologies from these other processes is nearly impossible: mutual entanglement and co-production is the condition of things. Further, spatial revolutions are, strictly speaking, revolutions in space and time relations. Part of the revolution in question is in the relationship of dimensions of space (spatialities) to the dimensions of time (temporalities).[73] In reality, spatial revolution is a catchphrase for a very broad set of questions about human-environment relations and the dimensions of modernity.

Given the centrality of railways, aircraft, and naval power to their thought, it is surprising that Ratzel and Mackinder had little to say about these as technical systems. The same is also true for energy regimes, which get some attention as we noted in the previous chapter, but not nearly enough in geopolitical thought. The significance of new modes of transportation and communication is acknowledged, but the concepts developed to describe this are limited and undeveloped.

This does not mean they are without value. In spotlighting the mobility of power, for example, Mackinder addresses an enduring problem for empires: how to effectively project power over long distances in a timely manner. The cases that impressed him prior to the Great War—Britain fighting the Boer War and Russia fighting Japan in Asia—are horizontal projections of military power. But he sees them within a larger geopolitical shift from seapower to landpower and also within a struggle for relative efficiency among empires. After the war, he updated this to recognize the importance of movement in the air: "Aircraft will now complete the freedom of human movement."[74] While mentioning submarines, aircraft, airships, and wireless telegraph, his work lacks any elaboration of these as technologies enabling the mastery of vertical space by one power or another. Further, while his work hints at an emergent struggle for pace, it never elaborates this.

The argument I have developed in the book so far is that geopolitics is actively involved in shaping the territories of the modern world, in terraforming the Earth to serve the needs of dominant states and their ways of life. It is not one thing, but a series of practices. We now turn to examine one of these practices, the ways in which world powers seek to control territory.

4

Territorial Anxieties

World powers are anxious about territory. They worry persistently about their borders and territorial integrity, and about threats in their neighborhood, most especially those they can connect to rival powers. They are also persistently concerned about their access to vital resources and about the security of flows considered necessary for their prosperity. This territorial behavior is not because great powers are like organisms, as Ratzel claimed, but because they are power structures run by modernizing elites with a keen interest in securing and strengthening their position. Further, in world powers, territorial anxiety tends to stoke territorial ambition.

Vladimir Putin ordered the Russian army to invade Ukraine on February 24, 2022. He had several motivations for doing so, but persistent features of his public rhetoric for fifteen years were complaints about NATO encroachment into areas deemed vital to Russia's national security interests. Specifically, Putin condemned the Cold War military alliance's drive to extend membership to two core members of the original Soviet Union, Ukraine and Georgia. This, according to Putin, was a "red line" for Russia. NATO deliberated about extending a membership action plan to both states in April 2008 but chose in the end not to do so formally. Yet, in symbolic compensation, and in a direct challenge to Putin's stated position, it announced "that these countries will become members of NATO."[1] Four months later, Georgia and Russia were at war. In March 2014, Russia invaded Ukraine for the first time and annexed Crimea. It invaded again in response to what Putin saw as an intolerable gathering geopolitical threat on Russia's borders.

Russia's invasion of Ukraine is not a response to the actual proximity of NATO to Russia's borders. NATO was already at Russia's borders, and now much more so, since Finland, in response to Putin's war, joined the alliance. During the Cold War, NATO and the Soviet Union bordered each other in both the north and south of the European continent, with NATO members Norway and Turkey sharing a border with the Soviet Union. The United States and Russia have long been neighbors, separated by the Bering Strait. After the Baltic States joined NATO in 2004, the military alliance and the Russian Federation had a new contact border. This was unsettling to Moscow because, as hard-liners saw it, former Russian and Soviet lands were now aligned with a historic enemy alliance system. Encroachment is an interpretive matter within the geopolitical culture of world powers. It is also, as Putin repeatedly stressed in speeches on NATO missiles and infrastructure next to Russia's border, a matter of geospatial revolutions in military affairs.

It might be suggested that this state of affairs is an accident of Russia having a leader with antiquated ways of thinking about security and defense. While international affairs are indeed full of contingencies, great powers have an enduring tendency to prioritize their own territorial security over that of anyone or anything else. State territory comes before the Earth system and the planet. State interests come before corporate interests and the environment.

In this chapter I sketch out a series of territorial security dilemmas produced by great power competition within a global geopolitical field. They are somewhat simplified and abstracted from the actual physical geography of states and their relationship to each other and the Earth. I am going against the grain of one feature of the geopolitical tradition—ideographic description of the physical geographical situatedness of states—in order to spotlight another—relative location and the structural pattern of territorial security dilemmas. One can see the ideal types as an inventory of the territorial anxieties (and

ambitions) of the ruling elites within great powers, particularly the
political and military power networks ("guardians") within the bureaucratic institutions of great powers. How threats are defined obviously depends on the particular social makeup of the ruling elites at
the center of the state. Yet, irrespective of their particular ideological
beliefs, whoever sits at the center of the state faces recurrent territorial
dilemmas and will have a familiar repertoire of responses to them.

The territorial security dilemmas of world powers matter because
they involve questions of the identity, welfare, and survival of the state.
To live, the state must defend its territory. In world powers that territory is perceived to extend well beyond the official borders of the
state. Great powers thus build military-industrial complexes to secure
themselves and project power. The classic security dilemma is the insecurity produced elsewhere by a state's pursuit of its security. But there
is a climate security dilemma also, the planetary insecurity produced
through pursuing security by burning hydrocarbons. Defending territory through hydrocarbon combustion induces conditions which
threaten that territory. The military-industrial institutions of world
powers are not only carbon-combustion complexes but defenders of
the infrastructures of this complex because hydrocarbons power military strength and economic growth.

But the pursuit of security by this means undermines itself.
Defending state territories, allied state territories, and hydrocarbon
flow networks, is de facto aggression-by-pollution against the planet's
geo-ecological territories and lifeforms. Protecting state boundaries
with greenhouse gas emissions furthers the transgression of planetary
boundaries.

Inner Abroads

Great powers are haunted by fears over their own internal territorial coherence. This is because most great powers become such by
the territorial expansion of an original metropolitan core across a

surrounding range of territories. These are then assimilated into the institutional structures and culture of the metropolitan core. This process of "internal colonialism" is often fraught with difficulties.[2] Certain territories may be difficult to conquer and assimilate because of their physical geographic characteristics. These same territories and others may be difficult to integrate because they are the homelands of non-core national groups. Consolidating territory under the power of a metropolitan core and settler class is often a bloody process.[3]

The term "inner abroad" refers to regions within the state that the metropolitan center fears are places of possible territorial weakness and disintegration. This can be a function of demography, location, or both. A demographic inner abroad is a region that is a historic homeland of a non-core nation. Core nationals are not fully at home in these regions. Non-core nationals may be the demographic majority or retain substantial presence in such places. A geographic inner abroad is territorially remote from the metropolitan center and geographically marginal to everyday life in the state. It may also be a non-core nation region. The key concern for the state is to strengthen its territorial grip over such regions, especially if the remote location is a potential weak point in border defenses.

In Mackinder's day, Ireland was the United Kingdom's unsettled inner abroad. Mackinder was a staunch Unionist all his life and opposed Home Rule for Ireland. However, responding to the revolt of Irish nationalists to British rule from 1916 onward and the Anglo-Irish Treaty of December 1921 (which would leave Ireland partitioned), he adopted a pragmatic line, albeit infused with imperial hubris. Britain could not afford to continue fighting in Ireland, he explained in a speech just days after the handover of power to the provisional Irish government at Dublin Castle on January 16, 1922. The British Army "was not sufficiently strong to carry on the kind of anti-guerilla warfare that was necessary in Ireland." Continued war would further jeopardize Britain's financial position and upon the security of the state's finances "stood the order of the world. If their finances broke there would be Bolshevism through Europe." Mackinder re-scaled the issue: the Irish question was a small one in international affairs. Three million people in the south of Ireland, Mackinder reasoned, "must not be allowed to hold up the destinies of humanity."[4]

All great powers have troubled territorial legacies. As a relentless capitalist colonial settler system, the United States disrupted and destroyed Indigenous ways of life. Native Americans bore the brunt of this manifest destiny, dispossessed of their land and subject to relentless racialized violence.[5] Those who survived were corralled into land reservations. The other settler capitalist system, slavery, rendered African Americans long-standing objects of anxiety about internal revolt. So too were areas of the "greater United States," acquired as colonial possessions after wars but never fully integrated into the territorial representative structures of the US state.[6] At work in the US case, and others, was a racial hierarchy of civilization and belonging, with all non-white and non-Christian groups excluded from full membership in the nation and the rights of citizenship. Such racialized structures of exclusion endure in the contemporary political life of the United States in the form of electoral malapportionment and gerrymandering.

The struggles of the Russian Federation with rebellious regions are well known. Russia has fought two wars to assert its formal sovereign territorial control of the north Caucasus republic of Chechnya.[7] It has also struggled to contain violent religious extremism in other republics. Its "solution" to the Chechnya problem was to concede significant local control to a former warlord, who rules coercively while receiving lavish subventions from the center.[8] Russia too has its racialized hierarchy, and this informs multiple perceived inner abroads in its cities by the ethnic Russian-majority population.[9]

China also has its inner abroads: Xinjiang, Tibet, and Hong Kong. All were incorporated into the expansionist Qing Empire (1644–1912) before its territorial writ contracted. The largest territory is the northwest province of Xinjiang, a historically Muslim-majority region with close ties to Central Asia. Making up a sixth of China's land area, Xinjiang was incorporated into China by Mao's army in 1949.

Writing at that time, the geographer Owen Lattimore dubbed this area, which borders on eight neighboring states, the "Pivot of Asia."[10] Since the late 1970s it has been the site of sustained resource exploitation and modernization projects by the Chinese state. Han Chinese migration to the area has brought economic, religious, and ethnic tensions. Uyghur separatism and an infamous violent riot in 2009 provoked a concerted campaign by the Chinese Communist Party to tackle "terrorism" and "extremism."[11] After four small terrorist attacks in 2013–2014, a new party secretary began a program of intense population surveillance and grid police monitoring.[12] From 2017, under Xi Jinping, this policy intensified in the form of intrusive biometric state surveillance of the non-Han population and the imprisonment of over one million Uyghurs and others in special "re-education" centers.[13] Uyghur have also been subject to coercive population-control policies.[14] Some have charged China with "genocide" in the region.[15]

The highly mountainous and overwhelmingly Buddhist region of Tibet was occupied and incorporated into China in 1951. After a failed revolt against China's rule, the area was territorially rearranged and further subordinated to Han Chinese domination. Transnational Buddhist activists and Tibetan exiles have kept the cause of Tibetan autonomy and independence alive. There have also been internal protests and revolts, the last in 2008. The anti-separatist security efforts of the Chinese government under Xi Jinping have attracted less attention than those in Xinjiang, but state authorities have been no less relentless in attacking Tibetan activism both within the region and abroad.[16]

Hong Kong has proved troublesome for the Chinese state. A British colony held under a 99-year lease, it reverted to formal Chinese sovereignty in 1997 under the principle of "one country, two systems," though Hong Kong was never part of a centralized Chinese nation-state. Communist Party efforts to strengthen its power in the wake of sustained democracy protests in 2019 led to imposition of new national security laws on the territory in May 2020. The move was widely condemned, with the United States revoking Hong Kong's special trade status and Britain promising a pathway to citizenship for those in Hong Kong holding special British national overseas passports.[17] Independent media in Hong Kong were crushed by national security laws, with the anti-government tabloid *Apple Daily* forced to close in June 2021.

Many inner abroads are geographically remote from the center of the state and were acquired initially for strategic reasons. Geopolitical competition was a significant factor in the expansion of the United States beyond North America. Competition with Spain resulted in US acquisition of a series of territories in the Caribbean and Pacific. Geopolitical ambition often clashed with racial anxiety as the US political class decided what to do with its newly acquired territories.[18] World War II added an archipelago of islands and territories that created a greater United States that was invisible on most maps. It also saw an internal militarization of peripheral US territories. The desert Southwest became the central military test site for the US nuclear weapons complex.[19] Hawaii became a lynchpin for the US naval effort to win the war in the Pacific and to project power in Asia thereafter. Alaska's militarization also began during World War II and deepened during the Cold War. Together, these and other territories were conceptualized as "natural environmental settings"—desert, Arctic, and tropic—for military experimentation and fortification.[20] In 1959, the territories of Alaska and the islands of Hawaii were incorporated as states into US governing structures. By contrast, Puerto Rico has been systematically shut out of full participation in US political life, and legacies of colonialism hinder its efforts to manage hurricane disasters.[21]

Similar processes of state militarization of peripheral and remote inner abroads, and deliberate sacrifice of territory to state military imperatives, are evident elsewhere. Between 1949 and 1989 the Soviet Union exploded 456 atomic and thermonuclear bombs, both above and below ground, at its Semipalatinsk test site in Kazakhstan. It also conducted a total of 130 nuclear tests on the mountainous and sparsely populated near Arctic archipelago of Novaya Zemlya between 1954 and 1990. Fifteen explosions were in the atmosphere, the rest below ground and in the surrounding seas.[22] Testing on Novaya Zemlya produced the greatest single source of artificial radioactive contamination in the Arctic region. Yet other tests were conducted in the Urals.[23] The Soviet Union's militarization of the Russian Arctic region has been revived by the Russian Federation in recent years.[24] China has sought to strengthen its border infrastructures across its extensive land borders with Russia and Central Asia. Similarly, India has made a concerted effort to strengthen its territorial presence and control in high glaciers in the Himalayas. The grip of the state upon its own territory, however, is conditional not only on people, but on the Earth's cooperation.

Near Abroads

Who commands the lands beyond the border is never a matter of indifference to great powers. Some have borders that are so-called natural defenses, rivers and sea moats that may not necessarily keep enemies at bay but render invasion dangerous and difficult.[25] Those with land borders that have few or no geophysical barriers to movement are prone to greater nervousness about the orientations of land neighbors.[26] The stopping power of water and the sensitivity of great powers to neighboring land threats is Geopolitics 101, according to US political scientist John Mearsheimer.[27] German jurist Carl Schmitt is blunter in his assessment: "Every true empire around the world has claimed . . . a sphere of spatial sovereignty beyond its borders."[28] Great powers have the desire to shape and control the security environment in their immediate neighborhood. This finds expression along a spectrum of influence-seeking behaviors—from military alliances and bases to economic unions and special trade regimes—that create special territorial ties between great powers and their neighbors.

In all cases, regions beyond the sovereign territory of the great power have storied relationships to it. In some instances, the territory may previously have been controlled by an earlier iteration of the great power. This is the case for territories that are currently sovereign states beyond the borders of the Russian Federation. These regions are often referred to as Russia's "near abroad," a measure of specialness that many argue reveals an enduring imperial attitude on Moscow's part. But this near abroad condition of special entanglement with one's surrounding neighborhood is a more general one. Britain's relationship with Ireland, the United States' relationship with Mexico, the Caribbean, and Central America, China's relationship with Mongolia, Tibet, and other the lands surrounding it, India's relationship with Pakistan and Bangladesh, Turkey's relationship with Syria: all are examples of near abroad spaces, where memories of geopolitics past condition the operation of geopolitics present and future.

In considering near abroads as particular types of geopolitical fields, we encounter two common spatial concerns of great powers which generate struggles over the rules of the game in these locations. The first is the desire of a great power to exercise special rights in its near abroad. While this desire is a long-standing one in international affairs, its public articulation can be controversial and invite challenge. One version of it was famously expressed by the US President James Monroe on December 2, 1823. In a report to the US Congress, Monroe ostensibly wrote in supportive terms about the newly independent states in North and South America. However, his message was also the declaration of the American continent and the American hemisphere as a separate sphere from Europe. Any efforts by various European states to take control of any independent state in North or South America, he wrote, would be viewed as "the manifestation of an unfriendly disposition toward the United States."[29] The United States had little capacity at the time to enforce Monroe's declaration and it continued to recognize and not interfere with existing European colonies in the Americas. It was only decades later that this written report to Congress was upgraded to the status of a doctrine.[30] By then, the United States was a growing force in the hemisphere and world affairs. An anti-interventionist doctrine was repurposed as a justification for US interventionism. The Monroe Doctrine became the normative basis for a series of public extensions and elaborations that expanded the territorial claims made by the United States in the Pacific and Atlantic oceans.

Other great powers, interested in enunciating their own unilateral spheres of influence in their neighborhood, used the Monroe Doctrine as a foundational referent. Carl Schmitt described it as "the first and until now [1938], the most successful example of the *Grossraum* principle in the modern history of international law."[31] *Grossraum* was a concept Schmitt sought to develop as a conceptual alternative to 'Anglo-Saxon' liberal internationalism. All world powers should be able to acquire their own hinterland spaces, large pan-regions that could provide food, raw material, and labor for the center. All great powers should have their own sanctioned sphere of influence: happiness was multiple Monroe Doctrines.[32] This was the normative vision of global space held by leading geopoliticians among the Axis powers (Nazi Germany, Italy, and Japan). It found an imperial expression in fascist Italy's vision of an Italian empire in Africa, Nazi Germany's vision of a German empire in Eastern Europe, and Japan's vision of a Great East Asia Co-Prosperity Sphere.[33] The quest for special territorial arrangements and agreements became a general feature of the diplomacy of the period leading up to and following World War II.[34]

Explicit declarations of great power spheres of influence were discouraged after World War II. Yet, for the most part, the postwar world order was one based on tacit geographic spheres of influence with the many areas in-between within a zone of competition and proxy wars. The Soviet Union created an empire of client states surrounding it on the European continent, whereas the Western powers created a military alliance of anti-communist states. Near abroad control imperatives remained powerful in the West, as French interventionism in Algeria and West Africa, and persistent US interventionism in Central America and the Caribbean, made clear.

Common terms like "backyard" or "front yard" tacitly acknowledged spatial hierarchies.[35] Respect for the equal sovereignty and territorial integrity of states was the formal norm, the organizing principle of a closed space globe, and one that great powers chose to honor, while allowing themselves the right to declare exceptions. The Soviet Union justified interventionism in Hungary in 1956 and Czechoslovakia in 1968 in the name of protecting 'socialist' internationalism. The US justified covert actions across the Americas, Asia, and Africa in the name of preventing the spread of Communism. An important consequence of this litany of interventionism was geo-economic and geo-ecological: the superpowers and their allies had privileged access to the material resources of the states they pulled, often through violence, into their sphere of influence.[36]

The collapse of the Soviet Union created a ring of newly independent states on the borders of the previous core state, which declared its independence as the Russian Federation. With violence characterizing the Soviet dissolution in some regions, Russia's security intellectuals sought to declare their own Monroe Doctrine for the region.[37] In practice, Russia played this role in conflicts in Moldova and Georgia. Responding to renewed fighting in 2008, Russian Federation President Dmitry Medvedev declared the Caucasus a "sphere of privileged interest" for his state.[38] The immediate cause of his declaration was the Georgian government's efforts to reclaim the breakaway territory of South Ossetia, an area controlled by a local regime which the Russian government supported.

Spheres of influence can be theorized as spatial expressions of hierarchical power relations in different ways—military exclusion zones, places of contingent sovereignty, peripheries of an economic core, cultural hearth, or network center—but the concept can also signify a zone where great powers have negotiated explicit rules governing their respective influence.[39] The secret protocol to the Nazi-Soviet Nonaggression pact of August 1939 and Churchill's percentages agreement with Stalin in their Moscow conference of October 1944 are two infamous examples of great powers making deals over the heads of the countries and peoples involved.[40] But they can also potentially be the basis for a stable multipolar world order if great powers agree to restrain their universalist aspirations, and agree not to poach territories in rival spheres.

This raises the second territorial security dilemma, the fear great powers have that hostile states seek a "beachhead" or "foothold" in their immediate neighborhood. These terms suggest a military invasion of a nearby state. That usage reveals an overriding geo-strategic mentality at work. But the terms are often used in a more metaphorical sense to constitute the emergence of friendly relations between the named states and the great power's rival or enemy. The general territorial security dilemma is the perception of encroachment by one great power or military alliance upon the self-constituted security sphere of another.

Some of the most dangerous moments in the Cold War were a product of perception that enemy states were establishing footholds in the neighborhood of a rival great power. Taiwan and Cuba became emblematic of this geopolitical field security dilemma, offshore island states allied to rival great powers. In both cases, crises there nearly escalated to nuclear war. After the outbreak of the Korean war, the United States placed Taiwan under its military protection. The small island of Matsu and island chain of Quemoy were subsequently at the center of two separate military crises between China and Taiwan that involved the United States.[41] In September 1954 the US Joint Chiefs recommended the use of nuclear weapons against China in response to its shelling of the islands. Eisenhower and his secretary of state subsequently threatened to use nuclear weapons against China. A second crisis in August 1958 saw renewed threats of nuclear strikes.

The Cuban missile crisis was so dangerous because of the United States' outrage that the Soviet Union was moving to position nuclear missiles close to its cities on the East Coast. Encroachment fear induced a crisis that nearly triggered a nuclear war. The final settlement recognized that the Soviet Union faced a similar territorial security dilemma from US missiles in Turkey. It would continue to face this problem of proximity with new rounds of US nuclear missile deployments in Germany and elsewhere, just minutes' flying time from

Moscow. The United States, by contrast, enjoyed the perception of relative "free security" provided by surrounding oceans, though this was illusory, as enemy submarines sometimes lurked in their depths not far from the US coastline. Cognitive bias toward visible threats from locatable terrain, as opposed to invisible threats from mobile weapon systems in the ocean depths, play into the symbolic politics involved in great powers wishing to demonstratively roll back rival great power influence in their territorial neighborhoods.

Flowmations

The dominant spatial imagination in geopolitics is that of formations in territorial space, discrete entities with clearly defined boundaries. More often than not, these entities are states, containers of territory, people, and social systems. But geopolitics has always been about much more than blocs of territorial space. Its English origins are in a crisis of connection and control, namely the British Empire's effort to subdue Boer settlers in South Africa.[42] No state is an island unto itself without connections to the rest of the world. The world produced by human settlement across the planet is a function of movement, mobility, and circulation, flows of people, commodities, diseases, technologies, symbols, ideas, and beliefs. Like many geographers of his time, Mackinder termed this "circulation" and gave a series of lectures on the "great trade routes" across Great Britain which emphasized the centrality of shipping to the functioning and prosperity of the British Empire.[43] Rather than formations, these are *flowmations*, spaces of regularized flows of resources, capital, and people.[44] They have long been crucial to the practice of geopolitics, and conceptualized as such, as seen in the previous chapter. Because maps tend to focus on the visualization of fixed spaces, however, the visualization of flowmations has not been as prominent as those of territorial formations. Yet, such visualizations do exist, with maps depicting shipping routes and movements of armies. Propaganda maps adorned with threatening arrows are another way in which potentially hostile flowmations are cartographically presented to a state's public.

As Mackinder and rival German geopoliticians well understood, flowmations are vital to the regularized operation and security of the state. The Napoleonic blockage of Great Britain underscored the vital significance of the British Navy to the security and prosperity of the Empire. During the First World War, the British Navy imposed a blockade on Germany that led to near starvation conditions within the country. At the time, Germany's fledgling submarine fleet began to threaten British supply lines. Their switch to unrestricted submarine warfare in February 1917, targeting neutral shipping vessels around Britain, France, and Italy without warning, created the circumstances which led to the United States' entry into the war.[45] World War II brought a reprise of submarine warfare in the Atlantic and a concerted German campaign to disrupt and sever logistical supply lifelines to Great Britain.

We can identify three different ideal-typical flowmations as geopolitical fields, each specified by its elemental core, either land, sea, or air. Flowmations associated with land comprise transportation routes— roads, railway lines, telegraphic lines, land border infrastructures—but also oil and gas pipelines. Flowmations associated with the sea encompass shipping routes, port facilities, navigation rules, and the material systems put in place to facilitate maritime traffic. Flowmations associated with the air involve airport infrastructures, the codes and procedures that regulate air travel, and infrastructures associated with wireless communication, from broadcasting hubs to relay stations to the hardware that makes this possible. From the 1950s this also included satellite communications in near Earth orbit. This infrastructure grew enormously and today encompasses a global set of networks that facilitate the circulation of data through wireless communication systems.

All of these flowmations involve the construction of infrastructural spaces, usually built by corporations and entities associated with

particular states, or consortiums of states. In practice, flowmation infrastructures assemble two or all three of the elemental forms. Data
transmission infrastructures require land stations and extensive underwater cable systems. The first transatlantic cable networks were laid in
the mid-nineteenth century, initially for telegraphic communications.
Today, there is an enormous infrastructure of underwater cable networks. Trade linkages and supply chain networks involve complex
assemblages of motion across land, sea, and air.

The anxieties of states over infrastructural flowmations are persistent in history. States are concerned about their ability to trade,
to receive and sell commodities vital to their economies. Fears of
blockades and violent disruptions of flows have generated a plethora
of well-known corporal metaphors concerning spaces of circulation: "life lines," "arteries," and "choke points." Recognition of the
strategic significance of choke points led the British Navy to seize
and garrison ports overlooking narrow straits and shipping passages
in the eighteenth and nineteenth centuries. Physical geography was
also spectacularly reshaped to create new choke points, first in Egypt
with the construction of the Suez Canal (opened November 1869)
and later in Central America with US sponsorship of a secessionist
region as a new country and then the construction of the Panama
Canal. As the world economy built thicker and denser networks of
connection and flow, newer types of choke points emerged: critical
supply-chain nodes, energy system grids, pivotal transportation hubs,
and, more recently, data-switching stations, and advanced semicon-
ductor foundries.

Since the widespread adoption of hydrocarbons as a source of energy in the twentieth century, states have had to figure out how they
can ensure reliable access to coal, oil, and gas, if their own domestic
supplies are insufficient. There is no need to rehearse the geopolitics
of energy during this century, one that saw the United States rise to
hegemony on the back of its own considerable store of hydrocarbons
and its creation of a network of client states across the Middle East
to supply it and its allies with oil. Revolution in Iran and the Soviet

invasion of Afghanistan prompted US President Jimmy Carter in January 1980 to declare that "an attempt by any outside force to gain control of the Persian Gulf region will be regarded as an assault on the vital interests of the United States of America, and such an assault will be repelled by any means necessary, including military force."[46] The declaration echoed a similar one by the British Foreign Secretary in 1903.[47] Carter's so-called doctrine led the United States to establish CENTCOM in January 1983, the first of a series of US military world regional commands that sought to cover the planet.[48] Primacy for the United States in the late twentieth century involved a commanding power to shape world hydrocarbon markets.

Anxieties about flowmation infrastructures are everywhere today. Even well before the COVID-19 pandemic, states were moving to decouple their communication infrastructures and production supply chains in response to concerns about potential vulnerabilities and opportunities for spying.[49] The Snowden revelations led to widespread concern about US intelligence-gathering ambitions and instrumentalization of US technology company information flows. Governments and consumers became more wary of the surveillance capitalist model of the so-called FANGs (Facebook, Apple, Netflix, and Google). Concern about the emergence of Chinese companies in telecommunications generated a US government campaign to exclude Huawei from new 5G infrastructure, an effort that has been largely successful.

Recent years have seen considerable research on infrastructural geopolitics, the ways in which flowmation infrastructures not only shape geopolitical struggles, but actively constitute and express geopolitical power and resistance.[50] Contemporary financial infrastructures like the SWIFT money transfer system, for example, have become weaponized by the United States and its allies in concerted campaigns against hostile states like Iran and, more recently, Russia. This in turn has provoked attempts to create financial and digital infrastructures that are outside the control of dominant powers, particularly the United States.

The United States is now actively seeking to decouple itself from dependence on hardware and software technologies from companies with ties to China and Russia and to cut both off from access to advanced computer chips and fabrication facilities.[51] But US national security infrastructures are highly dependent upon ostensibly US technology companies with extensive transnational networks and interests (including within China). 'National security' infrastructures today in actuality tend to be blurred combinations of state and corporate systems. "De-risking," "re-shoring," and "friend-shoring" are the slogans of a decoupling in flowmational geopolitics. Less visible in public policy are the relentless earthly extractions and greenhouse gas emissions involved in keeping all the technological megastructures running. Geopolitical de-risking is merely parochial geo-fencing if decarbonization, the most important de-risking strategy of all, is not prioritized.

In-Between Spaces

The best-known geopolitical fields are those involving territories in-between great powers. Three distinct types can be identified. First, there is the situation where great powers share a common border, a border that may or may not be clearly demarcated and agreed between the two powers. Historically, France and Germany were antagonistic great powers that shared a common border and transferred borderland territories (most famously Alsace Lorraine) after wars.[52] The United States and Russia share a border zone but are happily separated by a narrow passage of sea, the Bering Strait.

Russia and China share a land border that is over four thousand kilometers long. In 1969, there was fighting between the Soviet Union and China near Zhenbao (Damansky) Island in disputed border territory. The Soviet Union and subsequently Russia reached negotiated border agreements with China in 1991 and then in 2004, which resulted in China acquiring territory on Amur River islands which was previously occupied by Russia.

India and China also share a common border, approximately 3,380 kilometers long, and a dispute over the location of their joint border in the Karakoram mountains of the Himalayas.[53] Both states clashed in 1962 and 1967 over territorial claims in the region, creating a contentious line of actual control and no agreed border. In June 2020 soldiers from both sides clashed again, this time in the Galwan river valley in Ladakh, causing the first fatalities in over four decades in this dispute.[54]

Second, there is the situation where two or more great land powers are separated by a zone of smaller states that are nominally independent of both powers. The territories in-between Germany and Russia on the European continent are probably the most debated subject in geopolitics. They were the subject of Mackinder's rhyming message to the peacemakers gathered in Versailles. He labeled the region between Germany and Russia as the "middle tier" and crudely mapped it as a row of nine states from Estonia to Greece with borders still undetermined.[55] Mackinder's contemporary and one-time student, the Scottish educator James Fairgrieve (1870–1953), memorably described the lands between heartland power and sea powers as a "crush zone of small states," an evocative phrase that Mackinder eschewed.[56] This space between Germany and the Soviet Union was a central preoccupation of German *Geopolitik*, with Haushofer advocating for an alliance between the two great powers. Historian Timothy Snyder dubbed the space where the Nazi and Soviet regimes clashed the "bloodlands," a region he specified as central Poland to western Russia encompassing Belarus, Ukraine, and the Baltic States.[57] Fourteen million people were murdered in the twelve years between 1933 and 1945 in this area as Hitler and Stalin's regimes first cooperated and then fought each other while victimizing the residents of this region and beyond.

Certain regions have the distinction of being located within the neighborhood region of multiple imperial systems, a condition often rendered as being at the "crossroads" or "edge" of empires.[58] Historically, the Balkans were an arena of competition between advancing and retreating imperial powers while local factions sought relative advantage in their own struggles. So also the Caucasus, where the Persian, Ottoman, and Russian empires clashed until the Soviet Union established its dominion over the region. Central Asia is another example, indeed the classic illustration of the "great game" of imperial competition. With the collapse of Yugoslavia and the Soviet Union, all these regions have reverted to their former status as locations of variable levels of great power competition in the post–Cold War era.[59] Some political geographers label these regions as "shatterbelts," which they define as spaces that feature both deep internal divisions and interventionist rivalry between great powers.[60]

Third, there is a whole class of maritime states that can get caught between great powers. Nicholas Spykman dubbed these "rimland states." In his scheme, land power empires were at war with maritime empires. Land powers sought to dominate the "World Island." To prevent this, maritime empire powers needed to enlist those states on the edge of the World Island to their cause, with a view to creating an encircling zone of rimland states that thwarts the ambitions of the land power empires.[61]

Great powers fear encirclement and footholds by rival powers in their near abroad. Thus, the alignment and orientation of in-between states is a deeply contentious matter in geopolitics. Schemas to manage the sensitive spatial position of in-between states are equally disputed. Visions of such states as "buffer states" run counter to twentieth-century legal understandings of all states as sovereign and independent entities.[62] In practice, however, state sovereignty is relational and never absolute: all states have to adjust to material realities. It makes pragmatic sense that in-between states acknowledge the power realities of their geopolitical location and accommodate the security concerns of neighboring great powers. Many states do this.[63] After a bloody winter war with the Soviet Union in 1940, for example, the country of Finland adapted itself to its larger neighbor during the Cold War by pursuing a policy of strict neutrality, while retaining its economic ties to the capitalist West. The strategy had cross-party support within Finland. Outsiders, however, condemned the strategy and coined the term *Finlandization* to negatively characterize this practical adjustment by a small state to the realities of its location in a dangerous geopolitical field of power.[64] Finland itself grew critical of its past neutrality. Russia's 2022 invasion of Ukraine pushed Finland's government, in alliance with Sweden, to seek membership in NATO as the best means to guarantee its territorial security and 830-mile border with Russia.

Far Abroads

Great power should theoretically have interests that diminish with distance, and power projection capacities that are subject to distance decay. Power is easier to exercise locally than in far-flung locations. Some empires are predominantly land powers and seek to gather in surrounding territories, whereas other empires, like the British, were largely sea powers that sought to dominate the world's oceans and bind together territories that were geographically scattered and distant. Some empires have geographically limited civilizational missions, whereas others hold that their state represents the interests of all of humanity. Further, the evolving capacities of military technologies and scope of economic interdependencies counter any simple notion that there is an observable declining-with-distance power gradient.

Distance, nevertheless, is an important feature of certain geopolitical fields, what I am terming far abroad fields. Three types are identifiable. The first is the field of proxy conflicts that are roughly equally distant from the competing great powers. The best example of this is the competition between the European powers for colonies in the eighteenth and nineteenth centuries, culminating in the "scramble for Africa" in the late nineteenth century. The second type of far abroad field is where one world power is seeking a foothold in the near abroad of another or pursuing a policy of encircling a rival power.

Considerable infrastructure and capacity are required to project power across long distances, with imperial overstretch and overcommitment constant dangers. The third type of far abroad field is that constituted by one or more great powers designating a particular place as materially or symbolically significant to its interests. Who controls the oil fields of the Middle East is a case already cited in the discussion of flowmations. But this is also an instance of a far abroad geopolitical field for the United States, one that combines the material and the symbolic. Another example is the history of British intervention in Afghanistan, and then a century later, US-led military interventionism in the region. A yet further example is how the Falkland Islands, thousands of miles from mainland Britain, became a symbolic interest for the United Kingdom after their invasion by the Argentinian military junta in 1980. After retaking the islands by force, the Falklands became an expensive symbol of Great Britain as a world power.

If geopolitics were purely a matter of instrumental geo-strategic calculation, states would stay close to home and avoid locations of marginal material strategic value. However, reputation, credibility, and status anxieties can lead world powers to expend inordinate resources to project power over long distances to shore up threatened symbols. That the United States threatened nuclear war over a set of islands in the Taiwan Strait in the 1950s confirms how geopolitical fields are never objective features of global politics, but are always entwined with the geopolitical cultures of great powers.

The Planetary Commons

The final geopolitical field is the planetary commons, spaces that are ostensibly open to use by all and not considered the exclusive property of any one state. The desire of states, and increasingly non-state actors like billionaire entrepreneurs, to explore, exploit, and control these spaces is tempered by international treaties and the great difficulties involved in doing so. Excluding the Earth's core, there are four distinct planetary spaces: the polar regions, the world's oceans, the Earth's atmosphere, and outer space.

Historically, the world's polar regions were geopolitical fields for symbolic competition between great powers for scientific discovery and prestige. British explorers vied with Norwegian, American, and Russian expeditions to be the first to the Arctic pole. Mackinder's initial rendition of the "Pivot Area" in 1904 encompassed a large swath of the Russian tundra and Arctic region. There was some fighting in the Arctic during World War II, and it became a zone of geo-strategic competition during the Cold War. Climate change has reinvigorated competition between the great powers for control of potentially newly emergent Arctic resources, like more accessible oil and gas reserves, and a northern sea route from Europe to Asia.

Unlike the Arctic, Antarctica has never been subject to the same level of geopoliticization. The Antarctic Treaty of 1959, signed by twelve different countries in Washington, D.C., including the United States and the Soviet Union, declared the continent a demilitarized zone available for scientific research only. No state would be permitted to establish a base, conduct military experiments, or dump waste on the continent. A subsequent 1991 protocol banned oil and mineral exploration for fifty years. Both the Arctic and Antarctic play vital roles in regulating the Earth's temperature and sea levels. Ice instability in these regions, and other cryosphere areas like Greenland, has planetary-wide implications.

The world's oceans have long been contested objects, with states like the Netherlands and then Great Britain seeking to promulgate "open seas" regimes, in which they played the role of naval enforcer. Closed seas doctrines endure, and contestation between great powers, and their smaller state allies, over exclusive rights to certain stretches of the world's oceans are routine, as we see in the South China Sea. Oceans are fundamental to the Earth remaining a habitable home for humanity. They have borne the brunt of unsustainable economic growth, pollution, and climate change over the past century. Oceans absorb enormous quantities of carbon dioxide and have become more acidic as their temperatures have risen. Large areas in the world's oceans are now plagued by plastic trash and waste, while the extent of maritime dead zones has increased. In March 2023, UN member states finally agreed, after decades of negotiations, a High Seas Treaty to regulate the almost two-thirds of the world's ocean that lies beyond national boundaries. The treaty, which shall require robust enforcement, will create a legal framework for establishing vast marine protected areas to safeguard biodiversity on the high seas. It establishes a Conference of the Parties forum (CoP) that will meet periodically and enable member states to be held accountable on issues such as governance and biodiversity.[65]

Counter to this significant achievement of diplomacy, though, is an intensified push for deep sea mining to extract minerals in demand for green energy infrastructures. Norway has already moved to open areas of its territorial waters in the Greenland Sea, the Norwegian Sea and the Barents Sea to deep sea mining. The International Seabed Authority is considering the same for the seabed in international waters, with mining companies from Canada, China, Russia, South Korea and elsewhere lobbying for this unique ecological space, designated the "common heritage of mankind," to be open for exploitation. A new frontier of extraction is rationalized by the urgency of the need for rapid decarbonization.

Since the advent of the air age, states have sought to secure the airspace above their territories and develop the capacity to project power in the Earth's atmosphere and beyond. It took some time before the world's states developed common rules and standards governing military and commercial aircraft transportation. These apply to the lower two of the five atmospheric levels conventionally held to be above the Earth, the troposphere (0 to 18 kilometers) and stratosphere (11 to 50 kilometers). The three layers beyond that—the mesosphere (40–50 to 80–90 kilometers), thermosphere (80–90 to 800 kilometers) and exosphere (800 to 3,000 kilometers)—are realms where rules are less standardized. The Kármán line, for example, the imagined boundary between the Earth's atmosphere and outer space, is not universally accepted (at 100 kilometers above mean Earth sea level, it is within the lower thermosphere).

The Outer Space Treaty, signed in 1967 under the auspices of the United Nations, governs the use of outer space. The treaty declared outer space a "province of all mankind" and that its exploration and use should be carried out for the benefit of all countries. Outer space, including the moon and other celestial bodies, is "not subject to national appropriation by claim of sovereignty, by means of use or occupation, or by any other means." Signatories to the treaty undertook "not to place in orbit around the Earth any objects carrying nuclear weapons or any other kinds of weapons of mass destruction, install such weapons on celestial bodies, or station such weapons in outer space in any other manner."[66]

With both Cold War superpowers claiming to act in the interest of a universalized humanity, outer space emerged as a zone of cooperation between world powers. The International Space Station, one of the most expensive objects ever built, became a locus of cooperation after the Cold War. But, cooperation between Russia and Western space agencies is set to end in 2024. In the meantime, these agencies still work collaboratively, despite sharp divisions over Russia's war in Ukraine. China, for its part, launched the central modular unit of its new planned permanent space station in 2021. The European Space agency is keen to become a major actor in space and has drawn up plans to build its own spaceship to take European astronauts to the moon.[67]

There are now thousands of satellites in low Earth orbit around the Earth, many of them with military purposes or deployable for military use. Starlink is a private space company that has deployed more than four and a half thousand small satellites in low Earth orbit to deliver broadband internet to paying users across the globe. Its satellites account for more than half of all active satellites. To aid Ukraine in its fight against the Russian invasion, Starlink made its service available to organizations there, including the Ukrainian military. It quickly became the backbone of its communication systems. Starlink's CEO, Elon Musk, though has restricted its use in offensive military actions. For better or worse, Starlink's empire of satellites has enabled it to acquire a new geo-spatial form of power over territorial states.[68]

Technological capacities such as this, and much more specialized targeting and spying capacities, have predictably generated countermeasures. In recent years the United States, China, India, and Russia have developed and tested anti-satellite weapons.[69] Space is, as a consequence, becoming a nascent battlefield.

Planetary space travel is a field for status displays. The year 2020, for example, saw the launch of three separate space missions to Mars. The United States' *Perseverance* rover touched down on the Martian surface in February 2021, sending back spectacular pictures of its progress, including controlled flight across Mars's surface.[70] It was followed by China's *Zhurong* rover, which landed in May 2021.[71] The Chinese space agency released pictures and videos from the vehicle in June, the mission showcasing Chinese scientific achievement to the world. It was also timed with celebrations marking the hundredth anniversary of the founding of the Chinese Communist Party. The United Arab Emirates financed "the first Arab interplanetary mission" which deployed a satellite into orbit around Mars, to celebrate the country's fiftieth anniversary.[72] Finally, India became the fourth state to land a spacecraft on the moon in August 2023. Its Prime Minister Narendra Modi hailed the event as an achievement for its "human-centric approach" whose success "belongs to all of humanity."[73]

Space exploration has long been justified by appeals to a universal humanity, but has been conducted in the interests of specific territorial states and power structures. In this sense it echoes the original voyages of "discovery" of the Portuguese and Spanish empires to the New World where conquest was presented as altruism.

Geopolitical Territories First

In March 2023 the Intergovernmental Panel on Climate Change (IPCC) released its synthesis report from its sixth assessment. It offered a dramatically updated version of "the geographical pivot of history", a greenhouse gas emission pivot of history, by declaring that the "choices and actions implemented in this decade will have impacts now and for thousands of years."[74] Mackinder's "history" was that of recorded human history. The IPCC's "history" is thousands of years longer, that of the Earth as a favorable living space for humanity and millions of other species.

Presently, those choices and actions are shaped by prevailing state imperatives across geopolitical fields. Territorial competition between Western organized military alliances in Eurasia against Russia and in the Pacific against China set hard constraints on global cooperation. Geopolitics, it appears, always comes first. The immediate contest for territorial security and power between world powers has greater priority than the current and future health of the planet. Geopolitical visions of territory prevail over the geo-ecological materialities of territory. Contemporary struggles over the geopolitical status of Ukraine and Taiwan are accorded greater significance than the future health of the planet. The most consequential decade in human history is dominated by short-term geopolitical anxieties and ambitions.

In this decade of decision, fundamental choices have already been taken. Vladmir Putin made a deeply consequential decision when he alone decided to invade the territory of Ukraine, in March 2014 and again in February 2022. Justifying his stance in December 2021, Putin declared that "we have made it clear that any further movement of NATO to the East is unacceptable." His perception of territorial encroachment by a rival world power was at the forefront of his thinking:

> Are we deploying missiles near the US border? No, we are not. It is the United States that has come to our home with its missiles and is already standing at our doorstep. Is it going too far to demand that no

strike systems be placed near our home? ... What would the Americans
say if we stationed our missiles on the border between Canada and the
United States, or between Mexico and the United States?[75]

Putin's reasoning was conspiratorial and inaccurate, but the territorial
anxiety he articulated had an emotional power of its own, and it led
him, along with other motivations, to authorize a hideously bloody
large-scale war two months later.

Putin, as discussed further in the following chapter, made his decision to invade after meeting President Xi Jinping of China in Beijing
in early February 2022. Like Putin, Xi Jinping also has given voice
to territorial anxiety in discussions of geopolitics. Before meeting
with Putin in Moscow a year into the war in 2023, he told political
delegates that "Western countries led by the United States have implemented all-around containment, encirclement and suppression of
China, which has brought unprecedented severe challenges to our
country's development."[76] Both leaders began their summit the same
day that the IPCC released its "final warning" report.

The ruling elites at the pinnacle of world powers claim to act in
the name of protecting the territory, prosperity, and livelihoods of
their citizens. In all instances, however, these very materialistic and
grounded goals are under threat from climate breakdown. Territory is
much more than what a state holds it to be. It is made from materials
drawn from the geosphere and biosphere, from life-sustaining Earth
system processes that are now disrupted and likely to become even
more severely ruptured. We live, as already mentioned, within multiple territorial regimes at the same time, within ecologies shaped by
Earth system processes and economic markets, within infrastructure
constructed from Earth materials, accumulation logics, and geopolitical calculations, and within jurisdictions of regulation, law, and sovereignty overseen by corporate, state, and international institutions.
To reduce our location to one territory—the map of a state's legal
territory—is to misrecognize our place in the world.

Territories have always been more complicated than how they appear on map. This divergence is only set to widen as the consequences of climate breakdown deepen. State territories will not look the same as shorelines retreat, as mountain glaciers shrink, hydrological cycles break down, lands are parched and flooded, and soils become stressed and degrade. The contradiction of modernity is that its material conditions of existence, its geo-ecological extractions and emissions, threaten everyone's future. Further, prioritizing the lives and livelihoods of residents of affluent world powers through an "our territories first" stance deepens inequities and locks in ever intensifying increments of climate catastrophe for future generations. But that is not the story that world powers tell themselves and the world. It is to this storytelling that I now turn.

5

Missions and Emissions

The creed of liberal modernity presents two compelling promises to human societies. The first is the promise of creating a dynamic and prosperous society by embracing economic, technological, and scientific change. Nature is vanquished and forced to give up its riches. Abundance is achieved. Ever more advanced systems of production and technology make possible new levels of comfort, wealth, and opportunity.

The second is the promise of greater human freedom, an escape from the historic constraints of nature and the oppressions of despotic authority. "Man" (a seemingly abstract universal subject) can achieve greater levels of self-expression and self-realization in social, cultural, and political life. Human self-determination and autonomy are enhanced. The first promise is economic development, the second that of liberation. These promises have different tracks, but they are often interconnected and tied together in expressions of liberalism.

A salient feature of the contemporary climate crisis is the now widespread recognition that the economic promise of modernity is built upon the degradation of the life support systems of the Earth (to say nothing about human-made hierarchies). Attaining greater abundance and prosperity are made possible through expanded and intensified exploitation of earthly resources, the most important of which has proven to be the burning of hydrocarbon fuels. Modernity has long been in denial about its earthly costs, viewing its extractions and emissions as mere "side effects" and "externalities" to the virtuous main show. Though this denial is still powerful, it is asserted in the face of scientific evidence of its falsity. Economic modernity in its current forms, with its prevailing extraction and emission practices, is a compulsion that is destroying the stability of the future.

The connection between the second promise of modernity and climate catastrophe is less obvious but no less significant. This is because the means to realize the promise of liberation for human groups is most often sought through greater growth and development. Growth and freedom are the magic formula of liberal civilization and modernity. With economic modernization comes civilizational improvement.[1] The creed is not only domestic but international. Greater levels of commerce and economic interdependence create the conditions for international peace between states. This, at least, is the theory of liberal peace.[2]

Whatever the merits of these claims, the creed of liberalism that developed in the eighteenth and nineteenth centuries alongside imperialism rendered the expansion of capitalist relations of production worldwide as virtuous and civilizing. Both the British Empire and the United States gave its presumptions and claims great prominence in their geopolitical cultures, presenting different aspects of it as a revealed logic of history that they were sharing with the world. "Free trade" was the British Empire's missionary creed in the nineteenth century, while the "Free World"—the geopolitical imaginary of American *lebensraum*—became the crusading cause of the United States in the second half of the twentieth century. The accent in the later US versions is on the connections between capitalism and democracy, with "market democracy" presented as the winning formula for the creation of a stable international system.[3]

Mackinder remarked that Great Britain raised a superstructure of many stories upon a foundation of coal.[4] That foundation proved to be a crucial support for British imperial power in the world. But British carbon power, like all carbon power, came at the expense of the shared living space of humanity. The planetary atmosphere became a dumping space into which emissions tied to British industrial, commercial,

financial, and military power were released without apparent consequence. When the rival great powers of the world switched to petroleum and strove for greater levels of modernization, this greenhouse
gas emission process only accelerated, and the chemical composition
of the atmosphere began to appreciably change. The subsequent geopolitical rivalries during World War II and the Cold War were built
upon energy regime practices that ineluctably drove climate change.
Though powers differed greatly in ideology, they differed little in pollution practices. This material history raises an uncomfortable question for liberal internationalists today: Is the liberal international order
they champion built upon modernizing practices that are destroying
the planet?

This chapter considers the entanglement of the geopolitical cultures of world powers and geo-ecological materialities. I argue that
great powers tend to create heroic missionary narratives for themselves in world affairs. These narratives justify the claiming of space by
these world powers for their community and cause. Furthermore, all
these narratives, whether supportive or opposed to liberal hegemony,
are currently captive to and dependent upon geo-ecological practices
that hasten climate disaster. Geopolitics is in an undeclared human
war against the Earth.

To make this argument I have divided the chapter into five different
sections. First, I briefly explain the concept of geopolitical culture further and consider the place of missionary stories in the spatial self-
representation and ambitions of great powers. Second, I examine how
the United States adopted an anti-communist missionary role after
World War II at the same time as it was the vanguard of a modernity
that led the world in carbon pollution. Third, I note how the European
security order after the Cold War involved both a missionary expansion of Euro-Atlantic institutions to the East and an interdependent
energy trade regime designed to keep Europe's relations with Russia
peaceful. Fourth, I discuss Vladimir Putin's missionary visions which
led to his invasion of Ukraine, and then examine the missionary attitude of Euro-Atlantic powers. Finally, I discuss the environmental
costs of the Ukraine war and end with some challenging questions

about the relationship between world power missions and emissions in global politics.

Missionary Narratives in Geopolitical Cultures

All states present themselves in positive terms to the international community. Their process of self-identification involves rendering themselves as both unique and part of something broader, a cultural community living in a certain region of the world, or a worldwide community of shared values and identifications (as the liberal international order sees itself). States see themselves as distinctive and define themselves against an Other, perhaps a neighboring state or historic oppressor and enemy. A constructed otherness is the foundation of identity formation, and the mutually constitutive work of the self-other binary means that states are always in a process of becoming.[5] Most states see themselves as exceptional, namely as being not only unique in international affairs, but also morally superior to others (though this is often unstated). Some states go further and imagine a heroic role for themselves in the international arena. Moral superiority is combined with a commitment to take action for the universal good of all. A few states go further still and view their heroic role as messianic. This view imagines a state as a chosen nation with a duty to promote and realize a transcendent cause in the world.

Explaining messianism, Curanović identifies its three basic components: (1) a view of history as linear; (2) a presumption that the realization of a certain historical purpose, ideal, or logic will be good for all humanity; and (3) a commitment to act to help forward the realization of this purpose.[6] The last component is the sense of mission-as-action that one finds in the foreign policy of certain states. Messianic traditions in the geopolitical cultures of states convince their political class, and a certain segment of the population, that their state has an exceptional role in history, that it has the task of carrying forward certain ideals for the universal good.

Great powers tend to think of themselves as having great identities, and one attribute of this is a proclivity toward national exceptionalism and messianic thinking. Empires are formed around certain universalistic conceits and tend to run on ideals of uplift and civilizational beneficence, all the more to justify the unequal exchange mechanisms and racialized hierarchies of power they impose in practice. Imperial centers are conceived as more advanced, as further ahead in time than peripheral backward areas. In modernity's linear view of historical development, space is arranged by time.[7]

Post-imperial great powers usually have competing traditions and power factions representing different orientations in foreign policy, some reworking inherited imperial mythologies while others are formed in response to past conceits and policies. Small and medium states can have geopolitical cultures with strong messianic elements (for example, Israel, Iran, Poland, and North Korea). Today it is the case that great powers tend to be sponsors of certain universalist missionary narratives and to create communities of identity and belief among states around these narratives. The rule-bound liberal international order as imagined by the United States and its allies is a good example, a collective commitment to a vision of modernization through the hegemony of liberal institutions and power structures.[8] The global cities of the collective West are its advanced centers, the future that others have to catch up with. To its critics, like Russia, China, and India, this order is merely the latest iteration of a long-standing Western imperialist attitude toward the rest of the world. Others see racialized rescue narratives—a "white savior complex"—at work in its expression.[9]

Messianic claims express a particular worldview but do not dictate the foreign policy practices of states. National exceptionalism and missionary identity may produce exemplarism, the conceit that one's state is a beacon to the world by the power of its example. By contrast, the same combination may generate a crusader identity and a desire to convert parts of the world to the true path and faith of the missionary state. Here the foreign policy orientation is much more forward-leaning and aggressive in its promotional actions. There is an active claiming of space and a public commitment to expansion to realize the ideal ordering of space across the world.

Missionary narratives tend to come with a rhetorical sacralization of ideals, values, symbols and territory. Thinking of messianism as mostly religious is misleading because missionary narratives are often eclectic in character, mixing and matching elements. Ideas of providential destiny and chosenness can be informed by religious inheritances but secular in expression. The identity, ideals, and symbols of the state can constitute a civil religion that justifies enduring patterns of action in the world.[10] I have already noted the importance of the sacred, not as the marker of religion but as a rhetorical expression of that which is held to be beyond transactional thinking and strategic calculation. The sacred is that which is held to be definitional of the community, a transhistorical value that cannot be compromised or conceded without significant damage to the civil religious sense of self.[11]

Contemporary geopolitical narratives are captive to ideas of mission and sacred values which are understood differently by rival world powers. In these narratives, the geo-ecological condition of the world rarely features (though this is changing). Rather, it is the struggle for terrestrial space between the hegemonic order of power and the emergent counter-hegemonic alliance between the Russian Federation and China that dominates. More significantly, all the narratives of these competing world powers are captured by a deeply embedded commitment to modernization and economic growth. All are built upon economic practices that have a toxic relationship with the Earth and its atmosphere as geo-ecological space.

The Cold War and the Great Acceleration

From the perspective of the current climate crisis, Cold War history looks quite different from how it is conventionally told by diplomatic historians. The geological history of the Earth and the geopolitics of international affairs are supposed to work on separate timelines and timescales, the first incremental and slow, the second full of dramatic events and critical junctures. But it is Earth scientists who are the ones reaching for superlatives when it comes to the geohistory of the Earth after World War II. Environmental historians and Earth scientists term the period in planetary history after 1945, and most especially 1950, the Great Acceleration.[12] It featured a sharp increase in the amount of greenhouse gases that human activity released into the planet's atmosphere. In 1945 the global greenhouse gas emission estimate was 13.44 billion tons of carbon dioxide equivalent. By 1991, the year the Soviet Union dissolved, that figure was at 38.19 billion tons per year.[13] The number of people in the world tripled between 1950 and 2015, while the number of city dwellers rose from about 700 million to 3.7 billion.[14] These changes occurred within the span of two human generations. McNeill and Engelke describe this period as "the most anomalous and unrepresentative period in the 200,000 year-long history of relations between our species and the biosphere."[15]

These emissions are deeply entangled with Cold War geopolitics and the competing modernities sponsored by the two superpowers. The Cold War was clearly conceptualized and lived as a struggle for space—territorial containment and expansion were its obsessive themes—and also as a struggle between two different ways of life. Materially, though, the struggle ran on regimes of hydrocarbon extraction and energy use that were not dissimilar, and these made possible a massive expansion in industrialization, urbanization, and infrastructural systems and ways of life that were self-confidently modern. Soviet modernity ran on the exploitation of the enormous mineral wealth that lay across its fifteen different constituent republics, and in its satellite dependencies. American hegemony ran not only on a similar exploitation of its domestic resource wealth, but also on an expansive international market for coal, oil, natural gas, and other strategic minerals developed by US transnationals and those from allied countries. It created the embedded liberal order that was the engine of the Great Acceleration.

Both the Soviet Union and the United States represented themselves as carrying forward universal missions, the empire of justice
versus the empire of liberty.[16] It was not ordained that the United States
would take up the burden of creating a Pax Americana after World
War II. Missionary ideals about free enterprise and anti-collectivism,
of spreading liberty and democracy, were one thing, but they could
find expression in being an example not an empire. Suspicion of big
government, and big military bureaucracies, ran deep in US political
culture. The vision that the United States had a world to save was promoted by national security elites within the US state, but it lacked a
popular rationale. Most importantly, it lacked a budget.

It managed to get both by anti-communism becoming the rhetorical center of a bipartisan coalition for economic expansion, at
home through growth and overseas through an empire of invitation.[17]
As Alan Wolfe argued, "economic growth offered a smooth and potentially harmonious future—instead of divisive, possibly ugly, and
certainly disruptive struggles over redistribution issues. Rapid economic growth, it was felt, could expand the pie sufficiently so that it
would not have to be cut in a different way."[18] The postwar politics
of growth was Fordist, a bargain between big business, big labor, and
big government, in which large corporations, like Ford and General
Motors, accepted collective bargaining and higher worker wages in
return for worker discipline and productivity on a mass-production
assembly line, with the state providing supportive welfare labor laws.
It was imagined that workers would be affluent enough to buy the
cars they were making, and that Fordist production was the formula
for a new affluent society.[19] The ecological element was overlooked:
everything depended on cheap and plentiful petroleum. The US
government helped with incentives for its extraction so automobile
manufacturing and new suburban settlements could be built upon
abundant oil. Fordism was, in environmental terms, an embedded coalition for burning massive amounts of carbon.

Anti-communism was crucial to the creation of this coalition because it rationalized converting the wartime US state into a permanent

national security state that would take up the burden of fighting for "freedom" across the globe. A crusade against communism also enabled politicians to pull together an electoral coalition of disparate interest groups around what was presented as an imminent threat to the American way of life.[20] A sense of geopolitical emergency loosened budget strings, justified international primacy, and legitimated a politics of growth that paid no attention to geo-ecological costs. The United States and its allies would outperform the Soviets on all fronts, especially the home front.

Geopolitics rationalized the extension of Marshall Plan aid to Western Europe to aid its recovery after World War II, tying together geopolitics, growth, and peace. All were underpinned by an intensified extraction and a broadened extension of hydrocarbon-based regimes of energy. An ideology of peace through military strength legitimized military Keynesianism as the de facto industrial policy in the United States. This underwrote a cold militarized peace across the developed world and active proxy wars across Africa, Asia, and the Americas. Fighting the Cold War in Asia, first in Korea and later in Vietnam, catalyzed economic recovery in Japan, Korea, and Taiwan. The clash of Cold War narratives helped set in motion a Great Acceleration across the globe.

Hydrocarbon fuels also underwrote the modernity of the Soviet Union and allowed it to earn considerable foreign exchange on international markets. Coal production made possible the breakneck electrification and industrialization of the Soviet Union with its massive steel and ferrous metal industrial complexes. Coal moved by rail, and later oil and natural gas pipelines bound the Soviet Republics together with a lattice of energy infrastructures. Controlled prices subsidized great industries and factories built across the union for political and ideological reasons. Despite having some of the largest oil and gas reserves in the world, the Soviet Union still imported hydrocarbons until the 1970s. This was changed by dedicated investment in Siberian oil and gas fields, stimulated by fear of energy scarcity under Soviet General Secretary Brezhnev.[21] By the mid-1970s the Soviet

Union was modernizing its mechanisms of control in Eastern Europe through new pipelines and exporting hydrocarbons for foreign exchange. Détente and German *Ostpolitik* enabled Soviet hydrocarbons to extend further to Italy and West Germany, setting up a consequential interdependence for over five decades.

Making all this possible were spaces that no single state power controlled but all exploited: the oceans and atmosphere of the planet. The Great Acceleration released enormous volumes of greenhouse gases which altered its chemical composition and physical properties. Some scientists had raised the issue of a potential global rise in temperature caused by a greenhouse effect generated by increasing levels of carbon dioxide and other gases in the atmosphere during the Cold War, and indeed framed it as a matter of national security for the United States in its competition with the Soviet Union.[22] Testifying before the US Congress in 1956, US Navy veteran and head of the Scripps Institution of Oceanography Roger Revelle commented that "we are making perhaps the greatest geophysical experiment in history" by burning such vast quantities of coal, oil and natural gas, thus releasing vast amounts of carbon dioxide into the air and oceans.[23] The following year, Revelle and his colleague Hans Suss published a scientific article which restated the point: "human beings are now carrying out a large-scale geophysical experiment" with the planet's atmosphere by burning fossil fuels at exponential rates.[24] A year earlier, their colleague Charles Keeling had established atmospheric carbon dioxide monitoring stations on Mauna Loa, Hawaii, and in Antarctica. The data he gathered started to make the atmospheric impact of the Great Acceleration visible on scientific instruments.

While geopolitical visions of space prevailed during the Cold War, the geo-ecological impacts of rising levels of greenhouse gases in the atmosphere were registering. More than a year before the fall of the Berlin Wall, Dr. James Hansen, Head of the Goddard Space Center of NASA, testified before the US Senate that "the earth is warmer in 1988 than at any time in the history of instrumental measurements." Data gathered from multiple observatory sites across the globe allowed him to add: "The rate of global warming in the past two decades is higher than at any earlier time in the record. The four warmest years in the past century all have occurred in the 1980s." This global warming, he argued, was driven by the greenhouse gas effect. The "change in the frequency of hot summers is large enough to be noticeable to the average person. So, we have already reached a point that the greenhouse effect is important. It may also have important implications other than for creature comforts."[25] With this in mind, the United Nations established the Intergovernmental Panel on Climate Change (IPCC) the same year.

While the Soviet Union did enormous environmental damage during its existence, no country comes close to the United States in terms of cumulative historical carbon dioxide emissions. According to a 2021 calculation that includes emissions from land use and forestry, the United States accounts for fully one-fifth of the cumulative carbon dioxide emissions in the world since 1850. China is a relatively distant second, with 11%, followed by Russia at 7%, Brazil at 5%, and Indonesia at 4%. Germany and the United Kingdom account for 4% and 3% of the global total, though this figure does not include their emissions overseas while they were colonial powers.[26]

These national totals are based on territorial carbon dioxide emissions, reflecting the geographic location where the emissions took place. Alternative measures, which might consider the degree to which territorial emissions are tied into affluent world markets—a lot of China's emissions, for example, are because its factories serve global markets—reveal how much high-consumption regions are responsible for the world's total carbon dioxide emissions. In per capita annual terms, those living in the United States remain the largest emitters of greenhouse gases in the world. In positioning itself as the vanguard of economic modernity and freedom, the US state has, at the same time, been at the vanguard of the destruction of the ecological space required for human flourishing on the Earth. The American century has been a highly toxic one for the planet. Liberal modernity has unleashed the material conditions not only of its own crisis but those of all life forms on the planet.

Civilizational Rescue and Hydrocarbon Peace in Post–Cold War Europe

The end of the Cold War in Europe in 1989 and the collapse of the Soviet Union created the possibility to build a new security order on the European continent. Already before the Soviet collapse, the Charter of Paris for a New Europe, adopted by most European countries along with the United States, Canada, and the Soviet Union in November 1990, set out some foundational principles for a Europe that would be whole and free. These included a commitment to democracy, prosperity through economic liberty, and equal security for all countries. States re-committed to respect the territorial integrity of other states. The phrase "sphere of influence" does not appear in the document, but language repudiating such a notion does: "With the ending of the division of Europe, we will strive for a new quality in our security relations while fully respecting each other's freedom of choice in that respect. Security is indivisible and the security of every participating State is inseparably linked to that of all the others."[27] Positive feelings covered over what would become a meaningful contradiction between the freedom of states to choose their own security relations and the idea of security as indivisible.

The security practices built around free choice for states created the conditions for the return of war on the European continent. Vladimir Putin's decision to launch a full-scale invasion of Ukrainian territory in February 2022 was the culmination of growing antagonism between the Russian Federation and the West over three decades. Behind the Charter of Paris was the presumption that Western states had cracked the formula for peace and prosperity in world affairs. Francis Fukuyama declared that the "end of history" was at hand because capitalist liberal democracies supposedly delivered prosperity and the conditions of human flourishing. Few were paying much attention to the geo-ecological costs, and hidden hierarchies, behind the prosperous facade of Western consumer capitalism and liberal modernity. The Charter was not an agreement negotiated between the parties to the Cold War to end the struggle, as the Soviet Union viewed it. Instead, the West's boosters claimed, it was the conceptual and ideological surrender of the Soviet Union. Its collapse just a year later seemed to confirm this.

What followed was a security order shaped by two geopolitical practices in tension with each other. The first was the drive to enlarge the sphere of the West by extending European Union and NATO membership toward the east into territories formerly under the direct or indirect control of Moscow. This drive came from a commitment to a civilizational mission of rescuing states that had suffered under Soviet tyranny and imperialism in the twentieth century. Once "captured nations" were being led to "freedom". The process by which this occurred was incremental and sometimes ad hoc but nevertheless consistent in its missionary justification through reference to civilizational values, economic modernity, and the transformative magic of democracy.

In April 2004, NATO conducted its largest expansion ever in admitting seven new member states—Estonia, Lithuania, Latvia, Slovakia, Slovenia, Bulgaria, and Romania—which took the US-led military alliance formed during the Cold War to the borders of the Russian Federation. In admitting these new members, NATO was also admitting states with deeply held antipathy toward Russia. Russia was the self-defining Other in their geopolitical cultures. In the Euro-Atlantic security order created by the European Union and NATO, there was no place for Russia.[28] The following month, the European Union's "big bang" enlargement admitted eight countries from the Baltics and Central and Eastern Europe—which for decades had been, as many described it, "under the Soviet yoke"—together with Cyprus and Malta. The sense that Europe was overcoming the divisions of the past was perceived differently by the national security elites in Moscow. Instead, they saw a Euro-Atlantic empire expanding to their border and insidiously turning neighboring countries against Russia.

The second geopolitical practice sought to bind Russia to Europe and create an interdependent "hydrocarbon peace." The peace achieved through growing the exploitation of hydrocarbons that was a material basis of the European Union, starting with the Coal and Steel Community of 1950, and extended to the Communist bloc by the *Ostpolitik* philosophy of "change through trade," remained central to West European, particularly German, thinking about peaceful relations with Russia. Exploiting hydrocarbons together was the pathway to peace, to binding former geopolitical antagonists together, France and Germany in the west, and Germany and Russia in the east. Of course, the considerable vested interests and capital accumulation opportunities were their own stimulus and fostered an "understanding" of Russia's security interests.

After the Soviet collapse, Russia in the late twentieth century emerged as a renewed oil power with the aid of joint ventures with Western powers and enterprising private firms. Putin's ascent to power saw the streamlining and consolidation of these hydrocarbon resources in the hands of favored loyal oligarchs and state-controlled companies, most prominently Gazprom.[29] World market desire, and especially European market demand, for hydrocarbon fuels controlled by the Russian state allowed the Putin administration to rebuild Russian state capacity, and rekindle its great power aspirations. Putin's strategy was a deliberate one, shaped by his appreciation of the importance of resource wealth, and strategic reserves, for state power.[30] Natural resource wealth accumulation created the material foundations for Putin's ideas about Russia's state security and geopolitical status to be translated into action.

Hydrocarbon energy infrastructures connecting Europe and Russia have long been contentious for geopolitical reasons.[31] The first Soviet pipelines delivering oil to the Eastern bloc and beyond to West Germany were opposed by the United States. After the Soviet collapse,

Western companies scrambled to make deals to develop hydrocarbon reserves in Siberia and the Caspian Sea. US oil companies employed many former government officials to lobby for their favored infrastructure projects and pipeline routes. The US state sought to shape how these projects evolved and championed pipeline projects that avoided Russian territory, reasoning that this gave suppliers more independence and European markets more suppliers.

The updated version of Europe's hydrocarbon peace, where Russia sold increasing quantities of natural gas to European Union consumers, was equally contentious. Nord Stream, a set of natural gas pipelines directly connecting Russia to Germany, was approved in September 2005 just before the end of the Social Democrat Gerhard Schröder's tenure as German chancellor. Schröder subsequently became head of the consortium of Russian and European companies that operated it. The Nord Stream pipelines, built by Gazprom and a consortium of European energy and construction companies, brought natural gas directly to Germany but diminished Ukraine's leverage as a transit country. A second set of pipelines, Nord Stream 2, began construction in 2011 and, despite being thrown into question by the events of 2014, was approved the next year. Having chosen to move away from nuclear power, Germany was receiving more than half of its natural gas from Russia just before February 2022. That alone amounted to 200 million euros in energy payments every single day to Russia.[32]

Putin's Hydrocarbon-Enabled Missionary Geopolitics

Vladimir Putin's decision to launch a full-scale invasion of Ukraine in February 2022 was the culmination of his two-decade effort to restore Russian power and status in international affairs after the collapse of the Soviet Union and the dramatic downturn in the economic fortunes of most Russians in the 1990s. It was clear from the outset that renewal and restoration were Putin's mission. What was not clear were the different strands of Putin's effort to revive Russia's standing and how the geo-economic and geopolitical could come into conflict with each other. It was also less than apparent how Putin and his team would conceptualize the task of modernizing Russia, whether they would look to a Western liberal model of the future or to more authoritarian models. What emerged over time was a model of the future that borrowed heavily from the Russian and Soviet past while building a crony political economy and propaganda media system that was firmly controlled by the Kremlin. Under Putin, Russia became a soft authoritarian petrostate, which derived its initial legitimacy from growth and modernization but shifted to national patriotic legitimacy strategies as incomes stagnated and crony capitalism deepened.

Oil revenues enabled Putin's authoritarian system and his geopolitical ambitions. Putin's dissatisfaction with the existing hierarchy of international power was apparent from early in his tenure. It found its first significant international expression in his Munich security conference address in February 2007. Russian leaders long viewed Russia as carrying a necessary civilizational role in its near abroad as an arbitrator of conflicts and peacekeeper between warring parties. This provided justification for Russian troop deployments in independent Moldova and Georgia, and for intervention by Russia in South Ossetia and Abkhazia in August 2008. Russian leaders and officials long stressed how they viewed Ukraine as a vital strategic interest. Any move to incorporate Ukraine into NATO would violate what the US ambassador to Russia and later director of the CIA in the Biden administration, William Burns, described as "the brightest of redlines for the Russian elite (not just Putin)."[33]

Putin's grievances accumulated in the subsequent years as a series of clashes, wars, and violent events increased tensions and conflict in Euro-Atlantic-Russian relations. His resentments about the US role in international affairs found expression in a set of important documents before the invasion of Ukraine. In December 2021, as it built up its military forces along the border of Ukraine, the Russian Federation published two draft treaties that expressed the type of security arrangements it desired. What is striking about these documents is how they view Russia–West relations as a struggle over spheres of influence, and propose to turn back the clock of post–Cold War history to solve this. Putin's achievement of a counter-hegemonic partnership with China gave him sufficient confidence to move ahead with his invasion of Ukraine.

A full explanation of the circumstances that led Putin to decide to invade Ukraine will be uncovered in time. The COVID-19 pandemic, which Putin spent in relative isolation and apparent fear of death, appears to have radicalized his views and personal sense of mission. But the arguments he presented justifying war were not new, but distillations of long-standing conceits. The first of these was that Ukraine was a territory that was not fully separable from Russia. Ukraine has long had significant symbolic meaning for Russia and Russians as the birthplace of Kievan Rus, the nucleus of what became the Russian state. Ukraine was conceived as a "brother nation" within the Tsarist empire and the Soviet Union. And Ukraine was a central location in the major collective trauma that was instrumentalized by the Putin government to legitimize its rule, the Great Patriotic War. Vladmir Putin gave expression to all these sentiments in the many rationales he provided for Russia's attitude toward Ukraine. Unusually for a world leader, he authored a lengthy essay on the history of Russian and Ukrainian relations that declared that both were "one people."[34] Ukraine thrived when in close alliance with Russia, while it suffered in opposition to it.

At odds with this sentiment was a second belief that parts of Ukraine were historic Russian territories that only by accidents of history ended up as part of the post-Soviet independent state of Ukraine. This was the driving conceit behind Russia's 2014 intervention that led to the annexation of Crimea, and to it sponsoring two de facto state entities—the Donetsk People's Republic and the Luhansk People's Republic—that were on their own terms economically unviable. After shifting local warlord leadership, the entities were taken under more direct proxy control by the Kremlin. An estimated $1

billion a year was transferred from the Russian treasury to these state-
lets so they could function as territorial instruments of Russia's goal
of shaping the geopolitical future of Ukraine.[35]

Creating a credible rationale for a new war proved difficult for
the Kremlin. The propaganda machine it had established in Russia
nevertheless worked overtime to generate a threat of "genocide" from
Ukraine against people in the Donbas. In February 2022, after a public
spectacle of cowed Kremlin advisers recommending the policy, Putin
recognized the separatist entities it had created as independent states
with territorial claims to all of the Donbas. In his speech justifying the
war, Putin began not with the supposed threat against people in the
Donbas, but with complaints about US hegemony and the post–Cold
War security order. The war Putin authorized was, in his own mind, a
crusade against the direction of history.

The Euro-Atlantic Civilizational Mission and Ukraine

The drive to expand NATO and the European Union to incorporate
the states between the European Union and the Russian Federation
dates back to the collapse of the Soviet Union. This cause proceeds
from the sense of a civilizational mission that has always existed
within the European Union and that NATO adopted explicitly after
the Cold War. Initially promising that NATO would advance "not
one inch" east of a unified Germany, the territorial slogan acquired
a new meaning: "not one inch" of the east was to be off limits to the
alliance.[36] NATO had an "open door," and membership was possible
regardless of the geographical location of the applying state. The ap-
plicant state alone was "free to choose," a phrase that resonated with
the ascendant neoliberalism in many Western states.

Various policies were put in place—like NATO's Partnership for
Peace (launched January 1994) and the European Union's Eastern
Partnership (launched May 2009)—to allow the development of

relations and a thickening of ties over time. Many Western security elites were reluctant to push an expansionist agenda too explicitly, fully aware of the potential for a zero-sum struggle over space. Others were cognizant of the hypocrisy of decrying spheres of influence while the US presided over its own. Yet a transatlantic advocacy coalition quickly developed for expansion that began to accumulate victories. The "big bang" expansions of NATO and the European Union in 2004 considerably strengthened this coalition as it extended the civilizational mission of Euro-Atlantic institutions.

The Atlantic Council think tank, funded by donations from major US corporations and Middle East petrostates, became an organizing center for expansionist advocacy within Washington, D.C. This had considerable success in creating a bipartisan group supportive of this within the US Congress.[37] Similar advocacy networks operated in Brussels. Diaspora organizations, professional lobbyists (often former officials and ambassadors), think tank advocates, and democracy-promotion organizations boosted political forces and candidates supportive of greater Euro-Atlantic integration. Together this transnational advocacy network created a robust discursive coalition for the expansion of Euro-Atlantic institutions eastward toward Russia. Predictably, this caused rising tension with Russia, most especially when NATO declared in Bucharest in April 2008 that Ukraine and Georgia would become members of the organization (while declining to offer them a membership action plan).

The Bucharest Declaration resonated rhetorically with the Atlanticist geopolitical culture first forged by Franklin Roosevelt and Winston Churchill in August 1941. American *lebensraum*, as Isaiah Bowman noted, was an order for open not closed space. No state should have a "veto" over Ukraine or Georgia's membership of NATO. The sovereign independence of states meant that they had the freedom to choose their own geopolitical orientation irrespective of geography. Spheres of influence belonged to a different time, or so it was imagined.

Needless to say, NATO's self-presentation as a military alliance whose expansion was a threat to no one was not convincing to Moscow's security elites. What they saw was a zero-sum geopolitical struggle for control over the geopolitical orientation of the states in-between Russia and NATO. Thus, at the same time as the agency of small states was celebrated, they were effectively forced to choose between two competing geopolitical blocks because of competition over this in-between space. The issue of geopolitical orientation became a divisive one in the domestic politics of these states.[38]

As US and EU leaders negotiated with Russia to diffuse the growing threat of a Russian invasion of Ukraine, they refused any restriction on NATO's "open door" policy. The prospect of Ukraine's membership in the alliance was not imminent but was publicly affirmed as desirable by all parties. In June 2017, Ukraine made NATO and EU membership its primary foreign policy goals, aspirations it added to the constitution in September 2019. Ukraine joined NATO's weapons procurement system in 2015 and made its first purchases through it in 2019. Ukraine and NATO intensified their relationship through expanding land and sea military exercises in the years prior to Russia's renewed invasion. In negotiations before the war, though, EU leaders did signal an openness to compromise with Russia on Ukraine's NATO ambition, as did President Zelensky.[39]

The subsequent war in Ukraine quickly became a proxy civilizational war between the collective West and the Russian state. To date, the war has left more than a hundred thousand killed and wounded on each side. A full accounting awaits the war's end. The war has become the largest in Europe since World War II and has mobilized a worldwide empire of weapons manufacture—from factories in Japan and Korea to Iran, Israel, and the United States—to supply the combatants.

Framing the war in civilizational terms, and casting the imperative of the West to respond in sacred terms, came easily to Western political leaders from the outset of the war as these scripts were already in use by enlargement advocates. The sacred, as noted earlier, is that which is beyond transactional rationality and cost-benefit calculations. It is an expression of the transcendent principles of the community, a non-negotiable moral belief.

Western civilizational discourse on the Ukraine war has revolved around three principles that were held to be of transcendent importance: state sovereignty, territorial integrity, and democracy. All were encompassed by the greatest floating signifier, "freedom." Russia sought to remove Zelensky from power and to install a puppet government in Ukraine that would change the country's Western geopolitical orientation. This violated the UN Charter which prohibited aggression by states against other states. Critics of Russia argued that its actions were motivated by a deep imperial antipathy against Ukrainian identity.

The scale of the 2022 invasion, however, significantly changed Western attitudes. Russia was blatantly challenging the territorial integrity of states on the European continent. Location and past history rendered the conflict of transcendent importance. US President Biden, who had deployed thousands of US troops to NATO's eastern flank before the war, spoke of how the United States had "a sacred obligation under Article 5 to defend each and every inch of NATO territory with the full force of our collective power."[40] It was an open question as to whether restoring Ukraine's territorial integrity was also a sacred obligation for NATO members. Biden described the war, in terms Roosevelt and Churchill pioneered, as part of "the great battle for freedom: a battle between democracy and autocracy, between liberty and repression, between a rules-based order and one governed by brute force."

It remains to be seen how Russia's war against Ukraine will end. Open-ended rhetoric by Western leaders signaled the commitment of Western states to Ukraine's cause in the war, but the longer the war endures the greater its costs. Currently those costs are viewed largely in geopolitical terms but, as always, there are many other costs.

Geo-Ecological Costs

The environmental costs of Russia's war against Ukraine are still accumulating and will endure for decades and more. The litany of crimes against the ecology of Ukraine itself is long. From the very outset, there was an acute danger of radiation. In the first few days of war, Russian forces took over the Chernobyl nuclear exclusion zone and even had its troops dig trenches in the radioactive soil of the surrounding "red forest." Russian forces seized the Zaporizhzhia nuclear power plant, the largest in Europe, in March 2022 after a fire fight. The area is close to frontline battle positions and has been shelled numerous times since. Grappling with electricity cuts, it has been forced to rely on backup generators to power its cooling systems.

Ukraine's energy infrastructure has suffered sustained attacks from Russian missiles and drones. Oil storage facilities have been destroyed, with resultant air pollution. Other missile attacks have started fires in shopping centers, apartment complexes, and factories. Air pollution levels across Ukraine have more than doubled as a result of the war. Groundwater systems have become contaminated, forcing certain communities to rely on deliveries of bottled water. The June 2023 destruction of the Kakhovka dam on the Dnipro river flooded thousands of acres of land including forests and villages.

The economic decline caused by war almost certainly resulted in reduced emissions in that field, but war and its consequences replaced them. One assessment put the greenhouse gas emissions for the first year of the war as equivalent to the total greenhouse gas emissions over the same period produced by the state of Belgium.[41] Any full assessment will have to wait until the war ends. The war reveals the security dilemmas of the age of climate change in a stark manner. It was made possible by the hydrocarbon power of the Russian state, and persists because of Russian hydrocarbon revenues from sales to India and China, among others. Ukraine's resistance is enabled by international allies which are high-emission states. The war itself, invasion and resistance, generates emissions that are, in Russia's case, profligate luxury emissions but are, in Ukraine's case, absolutely necessary and required for the state's survival.[42]

Russia's war has also poisoned a great variety of ecological regions and landscapes in Ukraine. Each bullet, grenade, mine, artillery shell, and missile is a remnant munition toxin in the soil and groundwater. Frontline fighting and the planting of explosive mines have contaminated large stretches of agricultural land. Nature reserves have become engulfed in the fighting. An estimated 280,000 hectares of forest have burned. The cost of environmental repair alone within Ukraine was calculated at $51 billion in early 2023.[43]

The geo-ecological costs of the war, of course, are not confined to Ukraine. Global commodity prices rose dramatically after the outbreak of war, with crude oil, natural gas, and coal prices soaring. Western sanctions were imposed immediately, including the cancellation of the Nord Stream 2 pipelines. Despite the sanctions, Russia had record hydrocarbon revenues in 2022 by shifting its export sales to China, Turkey, and India, though these were insufficient to cover Russia's mounting war costs.[44] Global grain and fertilizer prices rose dramatically as Russia blockaded Ukraine's Black Sea ports before a United Nations–mediated agreement allowed trade to resume until this collapsed in July 2023. The scarcity of grain affected millions in Africa, the Middle East, and Asia, pushing vulnerable populations to the brink of starvation and famine in some areas. Though the UN-sponsored grain export deal eased matters, the threat of starvation has endured as the war joined other factors, most especially extreme weather events and processes induced by climate change, in deepening food insecurity for millions of people in countries like Kenya, Lebanon, Pakistan, and Afghanistan.

Russia's war caused an increase in the price of hydrocarbons on world markets. Oil companies reaped recorded profits in 2022 and continue to actively invest in further hydrocarbon development infrastructure. Some companies, like Shell, have backed away from their public commitments to support a transition to clean energy sources.

The EU response to the war has unfolded over months in a series of sanction packages. While admirable in attempting to reduce Russia's revenues from hydrocarbon sales, the policies have also been a boom for the global natural gas (LNG) market. EU policies and contacts have incentivized investment in expensive LNG infrastructures across the world, thus locking in the burning of natural gas for decades to come.

Today Vladimir Putin's messianic war against Ukraine appears as a damaging blow against collective climate action by the international community. But there are some signs of hope too. The first is that Putin's war tore up the carbon peace coalition that underpinned European modernity after World War II. No longer does the European Union look to expansion of hydrocarbon trade as a positive foundation for a peaceful future. The second is that Putin's war has dramatized the importance of a speedy transition to clean sustainable energy regimes within the European Union and beyond. Renewable energy reduces geopolitical dependencies and disruption risks. It actualizes the promise of energy independence. The third is the possibility of a green reconstruction of Ukraine. International development agencies, the Ukrainian government, and nongovernmental organizations have all stressed this.[45]

No postwar reconstruction in history, however, has been environmentally sustainable, so realizing this aspiration will require a radical rethinking of existing technologies and practices. Ukraine will also have to build back resilient for climate change, which threatens the future fertility of its famous black soil.

War is the most dramatic form of geopolitical competition and it is understandable, amidst the contemporary struggles of people to resist invasion and flee to safety, that questions of climate change would retreat to the background. Immediate violent spectacles involving clear friends and enemies will always dominate slower dramas involving diffuse and occluded responsibility. While the geopolitical is always entangled in the geo-ecological, geopolitical cultures are primarily centered on state territories and populations. They give us a world that is territorially organized into states, some of whom are friendly and some of whom are threatening. They give us geopolitics as melo-drama and conspiracy, and missionary metanarratives of imaginary communities at the international level.

But Earth science is now presenting us with uncomfortable thoughts. Operating at a temporal and spatial scale well beyond that of any one geopolitical conflict, its narratives of climate emergency inevitably resize and rescale present-day geopolitics. Western liberals may see a grand clash between democracy and autocracy, with a pros-perous future to be won should liberal democracy prevail. Earth sci-ence qualifies that and poses some difficult questions. How much are the ideals of liberal modernity—the liberation of oppressed people, the spread of market democracy, the extension of human rights—reliant upon the presence of entrenched economic growth and energy-intensive forms of life? Are the celebrated ideals of modernity themselves superstructures built upon unsustainable economic prac-tices and therefore drivers of climate catastrophe?

A second uncomfortable thought is that the collective environ-mental consequences of geopolitical competition matters much more than who "won" or "lost" certain geopolitical struggles, even struggles like the Cold War. The Great Acceleration has significantly comprom-ised the planetary boundaries that have served humanity for hun-dreds of thousands of years. It is disconcerting to think that the "great liberation" of peoples and states after the end of the Cold War and the collapse of the Soviet Union may only be a momentary passing victory amidst a broader struggle that is being lost. But the fact that temperatures in Europe have increased at more than twice the global average over the past three decades—the highest of any continent in the world—is of greater material significance in the arc of human history than the fall of communism.[46] From the perspective of Earth science, the relative significance of which state is ascending in power and which is declining is a minor drama relative to a planetary envir-onmental crisis that threatens to radically change how humans live, or do not live, on Earth. The shared common spaces of the planet, most especially the Earth's atmosphere, are those that count not only in the long run, but in the here and now. They have been overlooked, seemingly invisible and unremarkable spaces, but they have made it possible for great powers to have geopolitical cultures and missions in the first place. They are now asserting an unwelcome disruptive materiality into our politics.

These points are disturbing to our ideals for they blur what we consider to be important differences between states, and they question the meaning of victory in geopolitical struggles. They are, for now, subversive truths. Instead, we remain gripped by geopolitical identities and cultures because they are what we have been socialized into and are exposed to on a daily basis. But stories about territorial identity and salvation alone do not hold us in their grip. So also do the military machines built to conquer the Earth and assert power across its territories. It is to these that we now turn.

6

Higher Further Faster

How do new technological infrastructures reshape geopolitical power? The question is formulated in classical geopolitical thought, but its dimensions are never fully elaborated. Ratzel wrote on how transcontinental railways bound the United States together and spurred its growth as a world power.[1] Mackinder echoes him in writing about how railways were "transmuting the conditions of land-power" in Eurasia and identifies spatial revolutions and the mobility of power as important questions in imperial thought.[2] Both note how technology changes territory and state power, but those changes are so broad, societal, and international that they are difficult to summarize. One figure who pursued the implications further than any other is the conservative German political theorist and prominent Nazi-era jurist Carl Schmitt.[3]

Schmitt, like the more infamous Karl Haushofer, was a major admirer of Halford Mackinder. The admiration is unusual in that England and Germany were major rivals in the inter-war period and then war-time enemy states. Recall also Mackinder's chauvinistic remarks on Prussians and German culture in *Democratic Ideals and Reality*. Yet, the same work elicits effusive praise from both of these German imperial nationalists (admittedly neither was Prussian). Schmitt's own writings are voluminous and legalistic, the output of a professional jurist and law scholar. He published two significant geopolitical works, a short book *Land and Sea*, first published in Nazi Germany in 1942, and a larger treatise, *The Nomos of the Earth*, written in Berlin between 1942

and 1945 but not published until 1950. In the preface to the latter
work, Schmitt acknowledges his indebtedness to geographers, "most
of all to Mackinder."[4] A "juridical way of thinking is far different from
geography." "Jurists," he explains, "have not learned their science of
matter and soil, reality and territoriality from geographers."

Refusing de-Nazification, Schmitt was banned from academic life
in postwar Germany. Yet he remained intellectually active and traveled regularly to Franco's Spain, where he was well received. In a
scripted radio dialogue from 1958, *Dialogue on New Space*, Schmitt
returns to the theme of an elemental clash between land- and sea-
power, citing Mackinder's *Democratic Ideals and Reality* again in the
discussion as a "brilliant text."[5]

Schmitt was a reactionary modernist, a figure who recognized the
tremendous power of technological and capitalist modernization and
sought to restrain it to preserve conservative ideals of harmony and
order.[6] His work is attentive to the relentless nature of modernity, to
its expression as exploitative capitalism and techno-scientific society,
and the entwinement of both with states seeking to leverage revolutions in military affairs to their advantage.

Schmitt's thought is an uncomfortable but helpful place to begin
considering geospatial revolutions and their relations to great power
militarism and the climate emergency. As in the previous chapters, I
want to pose questions about geopolitical modernity and its relations
to territoriality and the Earth. This chapter examines the idea of spatial revolutions and the hubris of domination and transcendence that
attend these.

Just as there are lines of connection between Ratzel, Mackinder,
Haushofer, and Schmitt, and beyond to postwar planning seminars
in the United States, there are also lines of connection between the
militaristic modernity of total war in Germany and the high frontiers
of Cold War American modernity. No figure embodies this more, of
course, than Werner von Braun (1912–1977), the German designer of
the V-2 rocket who later built the Saturn V rocket that enabled US
astronauts to plant an American flag on the moon.[7] Von Braun was

the patriotic German who became a patriotic American, a transatlantic rocket scientist whose fervent belief that humans must leave
the Earth and explore the solar system was the foundational creed
of his life's work. An enterprising salesman and evangelical Christian
in America, he channeled the tropes of both manifest destiny and *lebensraum* in presenting outer space as the last frontier to be conquered
by technologically advanced humans (now echoed by Elon Musk
and Jeff Bezos).[8] The desire of the US military-industrial complex
he worked within was to build rockets that go higher, further, and
faster.[9] That credo of the "rocket state," now institutionalized in the
military-industrial complexes of many world powers, has produced a
dangerously militarized international system. More broadly, as the rallying cry of a militaristic modernity at war against the material limits
of the Earth, it is deeply enmeshed in the practices that have created
the current climate crisis.[10]

In this chapter I begin by briefly introducing Schmitt on spatial
revolution. I then make the case for its reframing using the work of a
very different German thinker, the sociologist Ulrich Beck. Beck was
a pioneering thinker about how modernity was evolving and changing. His notion of "risk society" as a distinctive second modernity is
important in contextualizing geospatial revolutions. Finally, I briefly
note some geospatial revolutions in military affairs and how they have
intensified a military territorialization of the Earth. Yet, at the same
time, these processes have also produced greater scientific knowledge
about the Earth and about climate change. Like in previous chapters,
there are ambivalences, contradictions, and difficult moral dilemmas
in the story of geospatial revolutions.

Spatial Revolution as a Geopolitical Concept

Schmitt developed the notion of spatial revolution in his wartime
book *Land and Sea*, which he presents as a fable, around four themes.

In Schmitt's telling, acts of spatial revolution proceed from the leadership of charismatic individuals and powerful states. Alexander the Great, the Roman Empire in the first century, the remaking of Europe by the Crusades, and the voyages of Christopher Columbus: all are examples of heroic geographical expansionism. The world is remade by those who go out and act, who literally and figuratively sail past the old boundaries and create new ones. Spatial revolution is an expression of assertive masculinity, a thrusting into the world by those determined to seize virgin lands. Spatial revolution overthrows an old spatial order and bids to forge a new one. It can manifest in a violent episode of geopolitical transgression, a shock moment. In Schmitt's schema, spatial revolution is a fascist fantasy narrative, an implicit conceptual rationalization of German military aggression across Eurasia.

Spatial revolution is part of a mythic drama of earthly elements, most especially land and sea. He was enamored, like Mackinder, with the idea of the voyages of Columbus creating a new epoch in human affairs, and describes the expansion of European powers across the world's oceans as the first planetary spatial revolution. The twist in Schmitt's account is that the most important actor in advancing this spatial revolution is not Spain or Portugal or Holland, but England. It "was the English who finally overtook everyone, vanquished all rivals, and attained a world domination erected upon the domination of the oceans."[11] Schmitt's argument is that England grew in prosperity due to the plundering exploits of its pirate capitalists. The predatory capitalism they helped establish became institutionalized. Primitive capital accumulation flows enriched England. This capital helped spark the industrial revolution in Great Britain, which furthered its power and centrality in world affairs. From its initial "choice for the sea" in the seventeenth century came the sources of capital that powered it to supremacy on the oceans until the twentieth century. Given his appreciation of the role of force in international affairs, Mackinder may well have agreed.

Technological innovation is superficially engaged but nevertheless quite central conceptually in Schmitt's geopolitical thought. Schmitt was concerned with technology hastening the end of the spatial world order within which he lived. Technological innovations in military weapons production drove a spatial revolution in the location of warfare. In the past, warfare was largely fought across horizontal planes: "Despite the differences between land war and sea war that otherwise obtain in both types of war, there was a common plane, and the struggle was played out spatially in the same dimension, given that the warring parties faced each other on the same surface."[12] The introduction of submarines and aircraft as vehicles of warfare in the Great War displaced this dominant horizontal spatiality of battlefields on land and sea. Warfare acquired verticality, and new volumetric qualities. From the depths of the ocean and the vertex of the sky, states could wage war against their enemies. "The airplane flies over and drops its bombs; low-flying pilots dive down and then fly up and away; both execute their destructive function, then immediately leave the scene, with all that has befallen men and materials on the ground, whose fate is in the hands of the sovereign of the surface state."[13] In producing "an intensification of the technical means of destruction," modern air war produces a "disorientation" of space, law and sovereignty.[14]

Schmitt was writing in Berlin while he worked as an air raid warden amidst onslaughts of Allied bombing raids. Air war, he argued, could not be assimilated into existing laws of war. Air war undid any sense of clearly marked territorial demarcation of battlefields. "From a spatial perspective, the great transformation of war is demonstrated by the fact that, as regards airspace, it no longer is possible, as it was before, to speak of a theatre of war."[15] The object of air war was destruction as an end in itself.[16] The German experience with strategic bombing pushes Schmitt, at the end of *Land and Sea*, to suggest that the spatial revolution of his time is not just the triumph of the element of air but the element of fire unleashed by air power.[17]

Schmitt survived the bombing and occupation of Berlin. In the Cold War atomic age that followed, Schmitt's trepidations about "technologies of the future" only deepened. In his dialogue on power and space he wryly names the North American character "MacFuture."

This character allows Schmitt to voice his criticism of an ideology of "unencumbered technology" in the service of unbounded geographic expansionism that he saw as distinctly American. "As I see it," says MacFuture, "the true age of discoveries has only just now begun. ... How small the spaces were at that time, in the age of the so-called discoveries! How great, by contrast, are the spaces that today open themselves to us. Be they in the stratosphere or be they beyond the stratosphere in the universe."[18] Schmitt's skepticism about such boastfulness is evident in the response of his alter ego character, the old historian Altmann. He ends the dialogue with an appeal to the Earth: "I believe that the human shall awake one morning after a hard night threatened by atom bombs and similar terrors and shall gratefully recognize himself again as the son of the firmly grounded Earth."[19] We should not be fooled by Schmitt's contrast here, a technocratic United States against an organic Germany. The US military reached for the stars, after all, by using former Nazi scientists, like von Braun. Schmitt's firmly grounded Earth is more fascist myth than openness to the lively materiality of the planet.

Finally, Schmitt thinks that a spatial revolution is when the concept of space itself is fundamentally changed. Here Schmitt loosely connects the navigation achievements of Columbus (1451–1506) with the scientific theories of Copernicus (1473–1543). Both overthrew the spatial consciousness of their time (even if Columbus died without appreciating the change).[20] His assertion of the connections between geopolitical conquest and societal conceptions of space is sweeping:

> Each time when new lands and seas enter the field of vision of human collective consciousness by a new thrust of historical forces, by an unleashing of new energies, the spaces of historical existence undergo a corresponding change. Then there emerge new measures and directions of political-historical activity, new sciences, new orders, new life for new or reborn peoples. The expansion can be so deep and so surprising that not only qualities and measurements, not only the outermost human horizon, but even the structure of the concept of space itself is altered. Then one may speak of a spatial revolution.[21]

Schmitt argues that spatial revolutions produce new geographic pictures of the Earth, new conceptions of space that work their way into the everyday life of the world as a cultural community. He claims that "all domains of life, all forms of existence, all kinds of human creative force, art, science and technology partake in the new concept of space."[22] Spatial revolutions in classical geopolitics are thus systemic moments where the Earth is reimagined and remapped. With each spatial revolution comes a new image of the Earth, new ways of seeing and visualizing the world cartographically and otherwise.

Schmitt offers the most developed discussion of the concept of spatial revolutions in classical geopolitics. Yet, his moral failure was profound. *Land and Sea* is a poetic work of theory and history that is also a subtle work of propaganda and advocacy for the cause of Nazi Germany.[23] Implicitly, he suggests that Germany in the twentieth century is in a comparable historical position to England in the seventeenth.[24] While the great battles of the eastern and western fronts in Europe at the time he was writing do not make an appearance, they are in the background. And it is not difficult to see how Schmitt's concepts were usable propaganda for the heady aspiration of the Third Reich to remake the spatial order of the European continent, for Hitler's 'new order'.[25] Schmitt admires charismatic leaders who violently seize land and act boldly to unleash spatial revolutions. Indeed, it can be suggested that Schmitt sets up the Wehrmacht's *blitzkrieg* as a spatial revolution par excellence.[26] That Schmitt's elaborations of spatial revolution are colored by his political commitments, however, is standard fare in geopolitical writing.

Geospatial Revolutions and Risk Society

Schmitt's ideas on spatial revolution raise some central questions about the relations of geopolitics and technology to the Earth. Critical geographers have taken up these questions over the past two decades. I propose a reformulation of Schmitt's themes as a means of discussing some salient dynamics of geopolitics and technology that are crucial in understanding the contemporary condition and climate crisis. In doing so, I make two choices.

First, I have renamed the general research domain *geospatial revolutions* for a number of reasons. I want to break from Schmitt and the fascist subtext of his arguments. The prefix foregrounds the multiple *geos* that are important in geopolitics: the Earth as a dynamic system, great power competition, and geography more generally. Contemporary understandings of the geospatial as simply the combination of spatial software and geographic data forget the larger history behind Earth representation and spatial visualization. Geospatial revolution is not a narrow technoscientific matter. The geospatial is an important dimension of the contentious operation of geopolitics. As a felicitous phrase inspiring conceptual thought, it should not be the monopoly of data scientists.

Second, I want to enlist the conceptual arguments developed by the German sociologist Ulrich Beck to frame the discussion. Born near the Baltic Sea coast in the Pomeranian town of Stolp (now Słupsk, Poland) in May 1944, Beck's family fled the Red Army in the final days of the Third Reich to the city of Hanover. In 1986, Beck published *Risk Society: Towards a New Modernity* (English title translation from 1992), a groundbreaking work that appeared the same year as the Chernobyl disaster in the Soviet Union.[27] That disaster vividly illustrated Beck's arguments about the emergence of a generalized condition of global-risk society as a result of the runaway success of classical industrial modernity. It was not enough to recognize that there were multiple state versions of modernity, and implicitly organize these, as happened in the wake of Chernobyl, into a safe Western form and an unsafe Eastern variant. Rather, Beck argued, there already exists a rupture within modernity itself between a first classic industrial modernity and a second reflexive modernity. The defining event of that rupture was the Trinity test in the Jornada del Muerto desert, New Mexico, on July 16, 1945, that detonated the world's first atomic bomb. This rupture was caused by the emergence of risks manufactured by

modernization itself, anthropogenic risks without borders. This inaugurated a new round of modernization as technoscience came to
define the period after World War II. With the Great Acceleration of
this period came a great proliferation of technoscientific risk like the
radiation poisoning from Chernobyl.[28]

Beck's work elaborates this break and its social, political, and cultural implications, using ideal-type contrasts and distinctions. First, he
identifies two very different forms of modernizing logics. The first
in classical modernity is associated with the domination of nature
and the modernization of tradition. Classical modernity is organized
around the extraction of resources from the Earth and the production
of wealth through manufacturing and finance, with arguments within
it between different factions over the distribution of that wealth. This
process pollutes the Earth, exhausts resources, and exploits human
labor, but these outcomes are framed as acceptable externalities and
side effects of modernization. But as classical modernity both wid-
ens and deepens exploitation of the Earth through ever more refined
technoscientific mechanisms and processes, the risks produced by
classical modernization are more difficult to ignore and marginalize.

Reflexive modernity seeks to modernize the society created by
industrial modernity, a society that no longer struggles with scarcity
and hunger but with proliferating forms of risk which are increasingly insidious and invisible. It is the modernity that has to grapple
with the so-called side effects of first modernity, outcomes that can
no longer easily be put to the side because they are now everywhere.
Beck argues that in classical modernity concern for wealth production predominates over concern for risk production, whereas in reflexive modernity the relationship is reversed. "[O]ne historical type
of thinking and acting is relativized or overridden by another."[29] The
defining concern of reflexive modernization is how the risks and hazards systematically produced as part of modernization can be pre-
vented, minimized, contained, or disguised. Reflexive modernization
is not a rupture with the project of modernity itself but an upgraded
refinement of it, a second stage that seeks to manage the disruptive

and awkward consequences of classical modernity. Complicating matters is that both classical and reflexive modernizations are shadowed by counter-modernization projects that seek to restrain, stabilize, and anchor both modernizations around asserted fundamental hierarchies of gender, race, class, faith, and social status.

As the continuation and intensification of classical modernity, reflexive modernity deepens the processes of capitalist globalization, extraction, and space-time compression experienced in the early twentieth century. More and more regions and states are integrated into a global market economy. More land is appropriated for exploitation and commodification. Globalization thickens as rates of trade and foreign direct investment and densities of communications and travel increase.

This creates new forms of interdependence and entanglement. The need for access to abundant and cheap reserves of petroleum drove military strategies in World War II and helped shape its outcome. As noted, an abundance of coal and cheap petroleum literally fueled Pax Americana after World War II, and a way of life that was viewed as the pinnacle of modernity. High American modernity featured a suburban lifestyle that was made possible by widespread automobile ownership, itself enabled by a seemingly limitless supply of inexpensive gasoline. Hydrocarbons were the great geopolitical element of geospatial revolution, the prized resource, of the twentieth century.[30]

The second modernity of the post–World War II era featured continued space-time compression as deepening hydrocarbon use in air travel shrunk the globe further. The development of the civilian airline transportation industry enabled millions of people to move quickly across the globe with relative ease. Advances in telecommunications and computer technologies facilitated what over time became near-instantaneous broadcasts of events around the world.

As a global sense of place was emerging, so also was a growing sense of unease. Techno-scientific advances in chemistry and biology released new compounds into the planet's ecosystem, generating consequences that unfolded in slow but devastating ways. The promise of postwar modernity, the "better things for better living through chemistry" promise of Dupont Corporation, also produced polluted ecologies, forever toxins, and an atmosphere accumulating greenhouse gas emissions. The byproducts of the Great Acceleration of economic growth in the postwar period gathered in the atmosphere and incubated a climate crisis. That only became apparent as Revelle, Keeling and other Earth scientists presented their data. The more salient source of unease for those caught up within the geopolitics of the Cold War was the shadow of nuclear war. No previous hegemonic modernity faced such an existential prospect.[31]

Cold War Geospatial Revolutions in Military Affairs

In Schmitt, anxiety about the capacity of technology for earthly destruction is much more acute than it is with Mackinder. Innovative use of radio for state propaganda consolidated Nazi power in the 1930s, while combined arms *blitzkrieg* warfare secured its early military victories. But German air power and sea power proved insufficient in the face of Allied firepower. German cities suffered catastrophic losses as military bureaucratic momentum for strategic bombing prevailed.[32] At the end of his life, Schmitt warned about unencumbered technology encloses humans more than it liberates them.[33]

The use of atomic bombs on Japanese cities by the US military at the end of World War II was a culmination of classic modernization, and an event that inaugurated global-risk society. Nuclear weapon proliferation spurred the intensification of the geospatial revolutions in military affairs as the rocket state credo of higher, further, and faster took hold. What this meant in practice varied a great deal depending upon the national security bureaucracies created by the great powers to fight the Cold War. To simplify a more complex story, these privileged centers of weapons development and decision-making strived to militarize vertical space, to weaponize speed in military affairs, and to map the Earth and beyond as a battlespace. In doing so, they furthered a militarization of the various geo-ecological regions, or biomes, of the planet, like the deserts of the Middle East, the rainforests of Southeast Asia, and the ocean depths. Subject to militarization also were the very geo-ecological elements and processes that sustained life on the planet.

Territorializing Vertical Space

During World War II, the Allied powers developed radar as a means of identifying and tracking approaching enemy aircraft. From modest beginnings grew a military visualization technosphere that sought to render all moving objects as known coordinates on electronic displays. The technology gave expression to a desire to sense, target, and destroy if necessary. But building this dream of total surveillance and control was long, complicated, and expensive.

US detection of the first Soviet atomic bomb in August 1949, and realization that Soviet strategic bombers could launch a surprise attack on the US homeland via Arctic overflight, spurred the Truman administration into creating an air defense system to address the new threat. Out of this came the development of the Semi-Automatic Ground Environment (SAGE) computer-based control system for early warning radar. This was run by North American Air Defense Command (NORAD), created in 1958 as an effort to territorialize and securitize the airspace over the United States and Canada. In the early 1960s, NORAD held a series of military exercises that grounded civilian aviation from Florida to the Arctic Circle to simulate an air attack and potential defense. These Sky Shield exercises were presented as a success to the public, but revealed the significant shortcomings of air warning and defense systems in the face of a concerted attack by enemy strategic bombers.[34]

The advent of intercontinental ballistic missiles tilted the balance between offensive and defense decisively toward offensive weapons. The Sky Shield exercises were discontinued as the US military grasped that ballistic missiles were now the face of the nuclear threat. Security came from a dispersed triad of missile response options and ultimately from deterrence and mutually assured destruction, not superior defense. While air defense systems were upgraded, the US prioritized air offensive over defense until Ronald Reagan, seeking to diffuse political pressure from the anti-nuclear movement, presented missile defense as an imaginary shield against incoming hostile missiles. It worked rhetorically but not technically, spurring further defense appropriations as Reagan deepened the US commitment to the Soviet threat–driven military Keynesian growth politics launched at the outset of the Cold War.[35]

Developing early warning systems to detect submarines was even more challenging. Nevertheless, the US Navy sought to militarize the water surface and below through a series of initiatives and programs. Underwater acoustics became a major area of research, with both sensing enemy vessels and constructing stealthy submarines the motivation. The US Navy also sought to better understand undersea environments as potential battlespaces, and resource fields. To this end, it underwrote the creation of a complex network of listening devices on the ocean floor—SOSUS, the Sound Surveillance System—to detect the sounds of Soviet submarines prowling in the depths. It also funded an array of research on ocean environments that generated new scientific discoveries. The creation of an underwater infrastructure of transoceanic cables and hydrophones spurred the development of specialist equipment, vehicles, and knowledge in institutions like the Scripps Institution of Oceanography. As mentioned, its director in the 1950s and early 1960s, Roger Reville was among the first US scientists to warn about the dangers of human-driven climate change.

The US Navy also funded a series of sea laboratories to test the feasibility of humans living for extended periods of time in an underwater settlement.[36] Military motivations coexisted with universalist aspirations. The United Nations Conference on the Law of the Sea helped advance agreed-upon rules for the territorialization of maritime space—defining offshore jurisdiction—and exploitation of potential resources in the world's oceans, sea floors, and below.

Weaponizing Speed

The nuclear national security state spurred the development of ever faster weapon systems. The US state established the Strategic Air Command in 1946 to manage the delivery of nuclear weapons on aircraft. German V2 rocket technology was the foundation upon which the United States built its first rockets, while the Soviet Union advanced independently in the mid- to late 1950s. By the end of the decade, the first intercontinental missiles capable of carrying nuclear warheads were deployed. Improvements in speed and accuracy continued thereafter. By the early 1970s, it was widely acknowledged that both superpowers had the capacity to devastate each other's major cities. Seeking stable deterrence, both invested in creating a triad of nuclear missile launch platforms on land, sea, and air.

The capacity to deliver catastrophic blows to enemy heartlands was not the only structure of violence revolutionized by speed. The ability of states to project power across the globe with rapidity and agility—a concern of Mackinder from the Boer War onward—was transformed also.

The strategic importance of stable access to oil played a crucial role in the development of this capacity. The 1973 Yom Kippur War between Israel and Arab states triggered a geopolitical standoff between the superpowers and a hydrocarbon energy crisis. In response to both the significance of stable oil flows to world markets and growing instability in petroleum-producing states, the United States established a Rapid Deployment Force to give it the capacity to project military power quickly in crisis situations. In 1983 this was upgraded and formalized to become CENTCOM.[37] The United States now has eleven different combatant commands for rapid response to crises around the globe and in cyberspace.

Speed of a different kind, that of electromagnetic waves, enabled new forms of warfare during the Cold War and after. The ability of military machines to control and use the electromagnetic spectrum enabled them to see and strike targets from a distance. The capacity to deploy orbital sensors was crucial to the development of this type of power. It combined the permanent presence of satellites (and later loitering drones) with real-time transmission of the information gathered and near-instant processing of this information by visual display machines and human watchers. The militaristic vision, one that took decades to realize, was that what could be seen from above could be hit almost instantaneously by operators in control consuls thousands of miles away.

Technological transformations in the realm of transportation and communication revolutionized the experience of managing risk at the highest levels of the state. A year after the Cuban missile crisis, the United States and the Soviet Union established a direct teletype printer connection (the so-called hotline) for near instantaneous communications at any time of day between their respective leadership. This depended upon a transatlantic submarine copper coaxial cable system and wire telegraph circuit route via London-Copenhagen-Stockholm-Helsinki to connect Washington to Moscow. Justifying the move, the Kennedy administration declared: "This age of fast-moving events requires quick, dependable communication in times of emergency ... both governments have taken a first step to help reduce the risk of war by accident or miscalculation."[38] The innovation was an example of reflexive modernization, not anything like a full questioning of the Cold War militarism that had brought the superpowers to the brink of nuclear war, but a response to the catastrophic risk the crisis had laid bare, and an attempt to manage the real possibility of accidental nuclear war. Arms control agreements, painstakingly negotiated in the decades thereafter, built upon a shared technical recognition of the realities of global risk society.

Mapping the Earth, Picturing a Planet

The Cold War also drove a desire for greater geographic intelligence about the material surfaces of the Earth, and potential subterranean spaces.[39] For two decades the US Department of Defense and Central Intelligence Agency funded research on the development of a more accurate "figure of the Earth" at Ohio State University.[40] The work benefited from advances in camera optics, photo reconnaissance, and remote sensing made possible by new techno-scientific assemblages like the Corona spy satellites. Southern Arizona was turned into a geographic laboratory for the development of first-order geodesic measurements and accurate photo reconnaissance targeting. Photogrammetry, the deduction of the depth and dimensions of objects photographed remotely by airplanes or satellites, burgeoned as a precise techno-scientific form of geographic intelligence and became entwined with geodesy in the search for the precise positioning of points on the Earth's surface. Advances in computing power and electronic measuring devices furthered the work which yielded the first of a series of world geodetic system measurements, under the imprimatur of the US Department of Defense, in 1960. The use of geodetic satellites in the subsequent decades greatly refined the figure of the Earth and culminated in the 1980 Geodetic Reference System (GRS80).

A tragic incident from the Cold War—the shooting down of Korean Airlines Flight 007 when it wandered off course over the Soviet Union in 1983—triggered the controlled release of this satellite system, run by the US military, for worldwide civilian use as an aide to more accurate navigation. Using GRS80, this became the basis for the development of a global positioning system (GPS) set of standards and an associated navigation industry that grew rapidly in the subsequent decades. Computing power and electronics were revolutionizing other long-standing geographic practices as well. A complex confluence of factors went into the development of geographic information systems (GIS), the data management system for storing, integrating,

editing, analyzing, and displaying geographically referenced information. Part of the impetus came from missile navigation and the desire
of the US military to develop more sophisticated visualization of the
battlefields it faced in Vietnam to aid its counterinsurgency war there.

But modern geographic information techniques systems only came
together when advances in computing and spatial data visualization
concepts made it possible to convert data like aerial photography
and satellite images into standardized ortho-pixels. Computing was
quickly transforming cartography into spatial data management. To
manage the proliferating forms of geographic intelligence produced
by its various institutions, the US government created a separate
Defense Mapping Agency in 1972 to consolidate all military mapping
activities. This was subsequently folded into a larger National Imagery
and Mapping Agency, which was renamed and reorganized again in
2004 as the National Geospatial Intelligence Agency (NGA).

With an Earth profile shot from space as its seal, the motto of the
NGA is "Know the Earth … Show the Way … Understand the World."
NGA presents itself as delivering "world-class geospatial intelligence
that provides a decisive advantage to policymakers, warfighters, intelligence professionals and first responders." In Pax Americana, militarism, scientific discovery and humanitarianism blur easily into each
other.[41]

In 1966 the US government established a program called Earth
Resources Observation Satellites, which changed its name to Landsat
in 1975. The program launched its first satellite in 1972 and, unlike
the Corona system, it was a public program designed to use remote
sensing of the Earth for scientific purposes. Yet Cold War competition
was the backdrop for its launch, with Landsat designed to demon-
strate the superiority of US technology in geoimaging and to promote the ideal of sharing information about the Earth's surface and
its environment and natural resources. In 1979, the Landsat program
moved from NASA to the National Oceanic and Atmospheric Agency
(NOAA), and privatized in 1985 when the Earth Observation Satellite
Company (EOSAT), a partnership of Hughes Aircraft and RCA, was
selected by NOAA to operate the Landsat system under a ten-year

contract. But there were restrictions. The US national security establishment confined Landsat to imaging capabilities no better than 30 meters ground resolution. This restriction and growing competition from other states, especially after the Cold War, led to increasingly fine levels of resolution becoming available. Some states, like Israel, tried to restrict access to images of their terrain completely and were temporarily successful. Other states prohibited photographs of sensitive locations. Presently the ability of states to hide secret territories and sensitive complexes is under challenge from miniaturized drones and other technologies.

Schmitt was right in predicting expansion to outer space and the oceans' depths. It was in the upper atmosphere and beyond that the "higher, further, and faster" ethos found full expression. Predictably, the military dimensions of the work was occluded by destiny and mission talk. This was generated by a group of space exploration prosletizers in the United States who from the mid-1940s built their advocacy by drawing upon the mythology of the American frontier, the idea that the voids and desolate planets of the solar system were equivalent to the awe-inspiring lands of the American West. It was mythology all the way up, with idealized paintings of sublime natural landscapes in the West inspiring stylized paintings of Saturn, Mars, and the moon in the art of Chesley Bonestell (1888–1986). Bonestell teamed up with the exiled German science writer and rocket specialist Willy Ley in the late 1940s to write a series of popular works presenting the science of planetary exploration. Wernher von Braun and Walt Disney joined the club, with Disney producing a three-part television special on 'Man in Space' that platformed the German space proselytizers and illustrated their visions with compelling animation sequences. Disney's opening in July 1955 of its new theme park *Disneyland* in Anaheim California with a space-exploration centered *Tomorrowland* as a counterpoint to its *Frontierland* materialized the co-creative myth making.[42] America's future was off Earth.

Talk of answering the call of the 'final frontier' was the presentable side of myth. But 'exploration' was a polite word for conquest, domination and control, and 'man' an empty signifier to be filled by gun fighters forcing the American way of life forward. Outer space, Senator Lyndon Johnson of Texas explained, was "the ultimate position—the position of total control over Earth."[43] He was speaking in the wake of the passage of *Sputnik*, the first Soviet satellite, over US territory that year. Spurred by this and subsequent Soviet achievements in space travel, the United States began a series of space missions in the 1960s that attracted the attention of audiences across the world. Johnson's advocacy made Houston Texas a center of this activity.

The US race to the moon helped reframe the relationship of some humans to the Earth. This was facilitated by a series of famous photographic images of the Earth, pictures of the planet made possible only by the rockets sufficiently distant to allow a single image to capture all. Two images from the US space program proved particularly resonant.[44] The first, "Earthrise," was taken from Apollo 8 as it orbited the moon in December 1968. It shows the Earth as a delicate ball in partial shadow. The photograph is given perspective by the lunar surface in the foreground. It is an extraterrestrial image of the Earth, a seeming view from the moon. The second, the "Whole Earth," was taken four years later from Apollo 17 and pictured the globe as a blue planet of land and ocean.

In presenting a delicate blue ball in space, a lonely planet in a dark void of space, both pictures became icons of whole-Earth and one-world consciousness, as well as floating signifiers available for appropriation by various causes, projects, institutions, and actors. In their own way, these images advanced a geospatial revolution in consciousness, foregrounding planet Earth as a vulnerable singular unitary homeland of a humanity divided on the ground over parochial notions of home.

Military Technospheres: Intensified Territorialization and Targeting

The military technospheres created by world powers have placed unprecedented power in the hands of a few humans, and indeed, in certain instances, in the hands of a single person. Nuclear weapons

gave birth to a state-within-a-state apparatus with secretive production, storage, transportation, and control procedures. It also created
protocols for centralized decision-making by a supreme sovereign in
moments of perceived crisis and emergency. The risks associated with
such a concentration of power over global life are obvious.

Geospatial revolutions in sensing, surveillance, and mapping have
also enabled an intensification of the territorialization of state defense.
A good example of this is the emergence of air defense identification
zones (ADIZ). These are unilaterally declared security buffer zones in
airspace. They encompass not only the territorial airspace of a state—
the airspace above its land and twelve nautical miles from coastal
states—but extend to include the airspace adjacent to this sovereign
space also. Indeed, they often extend into the territorial airspace of
neighboring states and, in many cases, into international airspace. In
declaring an air defense identification zone, a country proclaims its
intention to identify, check, and locate all aircraft entering this created
geospatial zone. The goal is to check for the potential encroachment
of hostile military aircraft or other aerial vehicles toward the territorial airspace of the monitoring state. Radar systems and electromagnetic sensing capabilities enable the creation of ADIZs but, as zones
unrecognized under international law, they require international aviation communication standards and protocols to work without incident or the need for military enforcement.

The first air defense identification zone was declared by the United
States over the North American continent and adjacent waters in
December 1950. Thereafter the US established ADIZs for its allied
states in the Pacific and gradually handed control over to these states.
In the East China Sea, the ADIZs of Taiwan, China, and Japan all
overlap in certain places, while South Korea's overlaps with that of
China and Japan. The most contentious ADIZ is that of Taiwan, which
includes all of the Taiwan Strait and most of coastal mainland China.

The advent of ADIZs has produced a new language of territorial
conflict and contestation. Even though ADIZs are not equivalent
to the territorial airspace of states, a rhetoric of "violations" and

"incursions" is generated by their existence. So also are displays of non-recognition, deemed "right to fly" missions by states, as well as displays of enforcement, the scrambling jets in response to the appearance of military aircraft from rival states. Over the past decade, as tensions have risen between China, Taiwan, and the United States, ADIZs have generated a series of violation events that have further increased territorial anxieties. In October 2021, for example, a record number of Chinese military aircraft entered Taiwan's ADIZ, largely in the southwest corner.[45] Any incursion into the zone by Chinese fighter jets triggers Taiwan to deploy missile defense systems and scramble its military aviation. Irrespective of intention, there is a heightened potential for clashes and collisions.

Both China and Taiwan consider the Taiwan Strait, the 130-kilometer-wide body of water between Taiwan island and the coast of Fujian Province in China, part of their exclusive economic zone. In 1955 the US demarcated a median divide in the strait—the "Davis line," named after the US Air Force general who created it—in order to establish a tacit territorialization of the waterway and the airspace above it. This line was respected by both until mainland Chinese aircraft began regular encroachments in 1999. Ostensibly most of the strait is in international waters and airspace. To affirm this, the US military and allied states like Australia regularly fly surveillance missions in the area. In recent years, however, these have been challenged by mainland China which has acquired sufficient technical and military capacity to assert an exclusive claim to the space.[46] In June 2022, China's Foreign Ministry publicly declared that the Taiwan Strait is not international waters but "China's internal waters, territorial sea, contiguous zone and exclusive economic zone in that order."[47]

The area around Taiwan is only one of many regions featuring what the geographer Stephen Graham dubbed "vertical geopolitics."[48] The Israeli military has long sought to control not only the horizontalities of contested land but also its verticalities, its orbital space, skies, heights, and subterranean resources (like water aquifers) as it built out an ambitious architecture of occupation.[49] Palestinian groups and Lebanese militias have used tunnels to fight occupation.[50] The United States sought "full-spectrum dominance" in Afghanistan and Iraq, but faced resistance from militants using mountains, caves, tunnels, and the heights and depths of cities against them. Initially thought within the context of the US invasion of Iraq, and counterinsurgency warfare in urban space, the concept of vertical geopolitics has subsequently been extended to many other contexts and spaces.[51]

It is applicable also to contemporary incidents below the threshold of warfare that directly or indirectly involve great powers and their proxies. Security incidents surrounding underground cables and pipelines, data-transmission stations, low-Earth-orbit satellites, and high-altitude balloons are examples. The downing on February 4, 2023, of a high-altitude Chinese observation balloon that had flown across the Pacific and North American airspace by a US F-22 fighter jet on direct presidential orders is an example of how US-China competition extends to vertical space.[52] Indeed, the incident touched off a wave of territorial insecurity in the United States and Canada as NORAD adjusted its radar systems to detect smaller unidentified flying objects. Numerous harmless objects were destroyed at considerable expense. Seven months later, the US intelligence community determined that the Chinese balloon was not actually spying on US territory at all.[53] Most likely it was blown off course by high altitude winds. US-China relations were nevertheless set back by the incident, which underscored the territorial anxieties that accompany vertical geopolitics.

Geospatial revolutions in military affairs have also created unprecedented capacities for wealthy states to project violent force from remote distances. A famous declaration by former US Defense Secretary William J. Perry (who began his career as a Silicon Valley research scientist)—"once you can see the target, you can expect to destroy it"— is the credo of this global targeting capacity.[54] Seeing is destroying.[55] Or, at least, that is the aspiration within a military technosphere where objects in the world, including people and urban infrastructure, are all target coordinates.[56] Two weapon systems materialize this capacity in different ways: unmanned aerial vehicles (drones) and hypersonic weapons.

Drones come in many different forms but have the important capacity to endure in the sky while conducting real-time surveillance. Israel was the first state to turn drones into killing machines by outfitting them with missiles. The United States subsequently developed an entire fleet of killer drones, the grimly named Predator and Reaper machines, and used these extensively for target strikes in multiple countries as part of its Global War on Terror (GWOT).[57] Since 2001, US drone operators have killed thousands of suspected "terrorists" and innocent civilians in Afghanistan, Iraq, Pakistan, Somalia, Syria, and Yemen.[58] Drones have significantly transformed the space-time of warfare. Rather than a discrete territorial zone, the battlefield became more of a metaphor in a war conceptualized as civilizational and existential. As Derek Gregory and others have argued, the GWOT developed into an "everywhere war" that tied together drone operators sitting in windowless trailers on a Nevada military base with targeted strikes against suspected militants and their families in Waziristan or the deserts of Yemen.[59] It became a war that militarized airports, surveilled cyberspace, and securitized digital infrastructures and communications. It also became a "forever war," a war declared against a tactic rather than a singular group or state. There was no specified end to the fight, no moment when victory or defeat could be declared.

How revolutionary drones are as weapon systems in the conduct of warfare is a matter of debate.[60] Answering this requires specification of precisely what unmanned system is under discussion and in what context. Building reliable armed drones, for example, was a technological achievement that was not easy to replicate by other states.[61] A few companies, with significant state help and international components, finally succeeded. One Turkish assembled drone, the Bakhtar Bayraktar TB2, a medium-altitude long-endurance unmanned combat aerial vehicle, was a transformational weapons platform in the long-standing ground standoff between the Azerbaijani military and forces from the Nagorno-Karabakh Republic and Armenia in the fall of 2020.[62] Precision strikes guided by Turkish and Azerbaijani officials far from the contested front lines in Karabakh devastated Armenian defensive lines and strongpoints. By late September 2023, Azerbaijan's military offensive, blockade and renewed attack drove all of the Armenian residents of Nagorno-Karabakh from their homeland, over one hundred thousand people. The 'territorial integrity' doctrine of states facilitated this crime. But Azerbaijan's purchase of the latest killer drone platforms from Turkey and Israel to militarily dominate the airspace made it possible. Making that possible was Azerbaijan's wealth from its sale of hydrocarbons to world markets. Armenians like Ukrainians are direct victims of petrostate aggression.

Smaller drone systems enable on-the-fly surveillance and targeting. The Ukrainian army has employed a variety of these systems in its resistance against Russia's invasion. When integrated into broader networks (via Starlink), and able to draw upon other real-time intelligence data, these can be very effective at the tactical level. Small armed drones, such as the US Switchblade, can use the targeting intelligence for attacks on tanks and other military vehicles. The possible proliferation of these technologies to non-state actors, which is now occurring, has significant security implications across the world.

The development of hypersonic missiles—a speed of five or more times that of sound in air—has deepened insecurity between the great powers. These weapons differ from intercontinental ballistic missiles in that they combine speed with maneuverability over long distances. They also spend most of their flight time in the Earth's lower atmosphere, not in space. Hypersonic ballistic missiles have fins that enable maneuvers. Boost glide missiles rely on aerodynamic lift to stay aloft. Hypersonic cruise missiles, which are still in development, are designed to be powered throughout their flight by scramjet engines in a low-altitude flight path. The capacity for maneuvers in flight allows hypersonic missiles to respond to ground-based missile defense systems and to have, in theory, flexibility about their final target.

President Putin boasted of Russia's hypersonic missile capacities, in an address to the Duma that featured animation of warheads targeting the state of Florida, just days before the 2018 Russian presidential election.[63] The Russian military subsequently fired a series of these missiles at targets in Ukraine. China, for its part, tested two hypersonic missiles in the summer of 2021, demonstrating a globe-circling military capacity that reportedly left US military officials stunned because its capability surpassed that held by the Pentagon.[64]

Territorial Integrity First

The military-industrial complexes of great powers are embedded in border structures of modernity, and a capitalist global economy. They are, at once, engines of geo-spatial revolution and drivers of risk society. They have a mandate to produce state security and in pursuing this by hydrocarbon intensive means also produce pollution, toxicity and proliferating insecurities. They employ the language of universalism and humanitarianism to justify militarism and ecological imperialism. They have the capacity to destroy the Earth yet they also have created surveillance and monitoring systems that allowed humans to see the Earth from outer space. They also enabled, in sometimes roundabout ways, Earth science to develop as a field of study and more precise scientific measurements of the changing surface, ocean, and atmosphere of Earth. It is undoubtedly the case that the military-industrial complexes that lie at the heart of world powers today will play a critical role in how humans manage climate change. Military command structures already recognize this and have developed plans for how climate change will impact their missions.

Yet these military-industrial complexes are expressions of the modernity that has created the climate crisis. The rocket state accelerationist credo is an expression of the long-standing modern desire for human supremacy over the Earth, to dominate its spaces, and subordinate its elements to the will of human technological systems. These systems have long operated with no regard for the earthly extractions they demand, the fuels they burn, the waste they dump into the atmosphere, the ocean and the living spaces of the planet. They have for too long operated in a condition of exception to pollution monitoring because their mission was privileged above all others.

The ongoing rivalry between the militaries of the West, Russia, China, and India adds considerable instability to the international system at a time when trust and cooperation are needed to systematically address the emissions driving climate change. Deeply entrenched military-industrial complexes enjoy exceptional power because of their mission to secure the territorial integrity of the state and the safety of its people. They get to specify threats and how to address them. By design and definition, military bureaucracies do this relative to the military capabilities of rival powers. An "us-versus-them" territorial antagonism is built into the system's institutional design.

But, in geo-ecological terms, the territorial integrity of the state is a myth. It derives from the cartographic vision of territory as a container of space, a parcel of property, a grid that can be marked, fenced, and protected. It is an image of territory, territory on paper. The dynamics of solar radiation, atmospheric currents, and hydrological cycles cannot be stopped by border checkpoints or military weapons. An atmosphere loaded with greater amounts of greenhouse gases than any time in human history cannot be corralled and geofenced. To say that territories are geo-ecological is to say that they are bound

together by dynamic relationships and connections. It is to acknowledge that territories can never be independent. Territorial integrity
in geo-ecological terms is ineluctibly a question of planetary health.
And the territorial integrity of the Earth is under severe stress. It is to
this that I now turn.

7

Geopolitical Condition Red

Mackinder's belatedly famous 1904 address to the Royal Geographical Society featured a modified Mercator projection of the Earth within an oval-shaped framework.[1] The map is centered on the cross-continental landmass that Mackinder names in his address as Euro-Asia and labels the "pivot area" of world history. Africa, Australia, and two incomplete versions of the American hemisphere appear on the map's margins. Completely absent from the map are the Earth's polar regions. This is surprising because the British National Antarctic Expedition, led by Captain Robert Scott and co-organized by the very organization he was addressing, commanded considerable public attention at the time.[2] Indeed, Mackinder mentions Scott's expedition and an earlier one by the Norwegian Fridtjof Nansen in the Arctic in his opening remarks. But what was discursively acknowledged was not cartographically represented.

Mackinder's world map privileges a different story. It is designed to show the Earth's surface, with its uneven distribution of fertility and strategic opportunity, as a geo-ecological affordance for imperial ambition. To Mackinder, the map is a strategic warning. Should the German and Russian empires become allies, the balance of power would tilt in favor of the "pivot state," enabling its expansion into British-controlled regions, and the nightmarish possibility of an "empire of the world." To Henry Spencer Wilkinson, Mackinder's discussant that evening, the new geopolitical condition is one where "the world is an enclosed chess-board."[3] In the struggle for world power among imperial states, though, the polar regions are not on the board.[4]

Thinking of the Earth as a chessboard, not a planet, is a deep metaphorical habit in geopolitical thought. Climate breakdown, thus, is difficult to process. How ironic it is that the polar regions, once absent and invisible, are now the stuff of nightmares, genuine geographical pivots, among others, for present and future human history. Disappearing ice at both poles, as well as ice sheet instability in Greenland and Antarctica, haunts the future of coastal cities and settlements across the Earth. As I noted in the Introduction, should the Thwaites and adjacent Pine Island Glaciers in Antarctica disintegrate, this alone would raise sea levels by four feet (1.2 meters). More ominously, this would almost certainly be a prelude to the melting of the West Antarctic Ice Sheet itself, a process that would raise sea levels across the world by more than ten feet (3.3 meters). The rapidity of the disintegration of glaciers and ice sheets in the Antarctic ice-ocean system, of course, presents many uncertainties.[5] Change in complex systems is nonlinear and difficult to predict. But the last time the Earth experienced a comparable concentration of carbon dioxide in its atmosphere to today was 3–5 million years ago, when the temperature was 2–3°C warmer and the sea level was 10–20 meters higher than it is now.[6]

The Thwaites glacier has become a climate change celebrity territory in recent years, dubbed by the media as the "doomsday glacier."[7] But it is just one glacier among many in one region of a continent that is still largely separated from conventional geopolitical discussion. As Earth systems science has revealed over the past few decades, there are dozens of other vital planetary regions, biomes, and processes that shape the conditions of life on the planet as whole. Some are well known—the Amazon, the Arctic ice sheet, Greenland. Some are less recognized, such as the significance of thermohaline circulation in the oceans, but are emerging as subjects of considerable anxiety. All are exhibiting signs of instability and potential breakdown.[8]

The 2021 Intergovernmental Panel on Climate Change (IPCC) report underscored the perilous condition in which humanity finds itself in the early twenty-first century.[9] UN Secretary General António Guterres termed the report a "code red for humanity."[10] Indeed the color red, as a signifier of heat and danger, is increasingly ubiquitous in visualizations of global climatic change. Short video time-lapse animations, such as those produced by the US National Aeronautics and Space Agency (NASA), of global warming from 1880 to 2020 on a Robinson projection map of the Earth (including Antarctica!) show a planet increasingly turning a visual red.[11] Similar video animations projecting future temperature rises and fire weather days show the US continent, and other locations, as territories increasingly blanketed in red.[12] Global heating is visualized as the Earth becoming a red planet, no longer blue.

In seeking to describe a new post-Columbian epoch, Mackinder was interested in specifying the conditions of geopolitical practice facing British statesmen at the start of the twentieth century. The geopolitical condition is the big picture for the state strategist and practitioner; it describes the material conditions within which geopolitics is plotted, practiced, and pursued. Mackinder sought to describe the spatial condition of world politics, the emergent logic of great power competition, and the rising threats as he saw them.

Big picture geopolitical analysis is fraught with difficulties of many kinds—the unexamined situatedness of looking, the imperial fantasy of a global view, and so on—but it is a practice that is too important to leave to state strategists and practitioners alone. Democratic societies need vigorous debate on such matters. In this chapter I describe three features of our current geopolitical condition red, which all involve the intensifying interaction between climate change and geopolitics. As I have suggested throughout this book, the idea of *lebensraum* discloses the relationship between the geo-ecological and the geopolitical in unsettling ways. It is, however, fully appropriate for the contemporary moment because humans are facing a great dislocation and loss of living spaces as a consequence of climate change. This is the first feature—the condition of the Earth's terrestrial space—I want to describe. The second is the endurance of geopolitics in the face of the planetary emergency of climate change. The current form of competition between the great powers doubles down on extractive agendas and the defense of affluent ways of life while pursuing decarbonization and energy transition. The third is the way in which climate shocks are starting to unfold in world politics, and the potential this has for resurgent fascist spatial politics. Geopolitical condition red is geopolitics as the Earth transitions to a global surface temperature rise of 1.5 degrees Celsius (°C) above pre-industrial levels. It is a hot and dangerous condition.

Losing Living Space

In altering the chemical composition of the atmosphere through carbon fuel combustion and other activities, modern industrial civilization initiated a rupture in the climatic regime that made human flourishing and civilizations achievable, the geological epoch known as the Holocene. The Anthropocene is a manifest break from the relatively benign climatic conditions of the Holocene, the plus/minus 1°C climatic regime of the past eleven thousand plus years that allowed human civilizations to develop. It is also a dislocation that threatens the living spaces that humans have built in conquering the planet, the joined-up supply chains, economies, and technologies that have created a hierarchical global economy and state system.

Since the turn of the millennium, the ineluctable material realities of climate change have forced themselves upon human settlements across the globe. A 2021 study concluded that at least 85% of the world's population has been materially impacted by anthropogenic climate change in the form of disrupted weather patterns, heat waves, increased droughts, and flooding, as well as consequential crop failures.[13] Everyone in the world has experienced climate change, though that does not mean they comprehend it as such. It is a material force that foists itself upon humans no matter what they think.

Though modernity runs toward its own self-generated fantasies of the future (like colonizing Mars or the metaverse), these have sobering rivals in the temperature increase scenarios from Earth scientists.[14] The sixth IPCC Report presents five different climate futures that are modeled around variable levels of continued greenhouse gas emissions, from high-emission volumes to dramatically falling volumes. Within all, global surface temperatures will continue to increase until 2050 at least. Global heating levels will exceed 1.5°C soon, if they have not already done so, and are on course to surpass 2°C this century without a drastic reduction in emissions in this decade and continuing thereafter. Their summary is that, compared to 1850–1900, global surface temperatures between 2081 and 2100 are very likely to be higher by 1.0°C to 1.8°C even if drastic emission cuts are made, by 2.1°C to 3.5°C in their intermediate-emissions scenario, and by 3.3°C to 5.7°C under their high-emissions levels scenario. Put differently, the world is currently on course for global surface temperatures at or above 2.5°C higher than 1850–1900, a situation last seen on Earth over three million years ago and never experienced by humans.[15] The future of global heating promises to transport humans to a planetary climate regime that is unknown to us.

The IPCC Report, as a consensus government-approved document, may be too conservative (as past reports arguably were). Analysis by the Climate Action Tracker that accessed pledges made by states at the COP26 in Glasgow for 2030 estimated that even if these targets were met, the world is heading to heating of 2.4°C by the end of the century.[16] These pledges themselves are problematic, and sometimes performative and hollow.[17] The data behind the measurement of emissions may also be faulty and misleading.[18] The "real world action" scenario of the Climate Action Tracker is a rise of 2.7°C by 2100.[19] In sum, the future seems destined to be ruled by rising global temperatures and all that flows from that.

What this portends is a growing disjuncture between climate, ecologies, and settlements. As temperatures increase, droughts deepen, and extreme weather becomes more frequent, the ecological envelopes that have supported local flora and fauna for centuries start to shift. Old ecological systems come apart while new arrivals, including novel diseases, migrate inward. These changes stress human infrastructures and create conditions never before experienced by particular places and locations. The familiar becomes unfamiliar, the normal less present, the abnormal and uncanny more so.

There are many accounts of this process. One method that scientists have developed is climate analog mapping, a statistical and visualization technique that quantifies the similarity of a location's climate relative to the climate of another place and time. The technique is difficult because there are different emission scenarios and attendant climate models. Nevertheless, climate researchers have developed maps that seek to reveal current day analogs to the future climatic zones of certain locations, such as major urban areas. On study of the likely climate of Washington, D.C., in 2080, one where emissions are not mitigated and current policies largely prevail, shifts the climate similarity surface to around Greenwood, Mississippi.[20] The climate of the US capital becomes that of the Deep South, while its climate becomes more like the equator.

The general trend is a drift of mid-latitude climatic zones southward to more sub-tropical climatic zones. Mark Lynas characterizes it as follows: those who currently live in mid-latitude urban areas in the Northern Hemisphere are effectively "moving south by 20 km per year, which is about 54 metres per day, or 2.25 metres per hour. This in turn is just over half a millimetre a second, easy to see with the naked eye." He presents a striking metaphor to describe this process of spatial dislocation:

It is as if every major city—London, Moscow, Stockholm—were on a slow-moving giant conveyor belt, transporting them deeper and deeper towards the sub-tropics at the same speed as the second hand on a small wristwatch. This change in temperature will mainly be felt in terms of increasing heat, but moving outside a city's "normal" climate envelope will also alter species composition in the surrounding regions and lead to changes in water supply.[21]

Understood this way, climate change is a process of forced displacement. It decouples geo-ecological territories from the human superstructures built upon them: infrastructures, cultural landscapes, and political forms. It moves territories from their established historic locations toward novel positions and warped settings. Climate change is thus a concerted challenge to the idea of belonging to known places and spaces. To live in the Anthropocene is to live on territories that are moving and coming undone.

Climate analog mapping is a useful tool to help the general public translate what the abstractions of climate change may mean for the place where they currently live.[22] But these maps are focused largely on temperature and do not take into consideration the cascading implications of the many different manifestations of climate change. Also, in many instances, there is no reasonable analog to what future climate scenarios are possible, or even likely. Dislocation may be the emergent material reality of climate change, but the degree to which it becomes a pervasive experience depends on how quickly familiar referents disappear and life-support systems come under stress.

This threat to human life-support systems from climate change resonates with more classical geopolitical understandings of *lebensraum* as the spatial expression of Malthusian fears over land and food. Humans are a terrestrial species. While we utilize oceans and waterways, we live almost exclusively on dry land and require consistent access to drinking water and food. Land is the principal foundation for human livelihoods and well-being. Humans have come to dominate the Earth's land surface, and their land use practices affect more than 70% of the global ice-free land surface of the planet.[23] Land and water sustain the ecosystems that human societies depend upon to survive. The majority of the world's population remains directly dependent on freshwater access and lives within three kilometers of a body of freshwater. An estimated two billion people depend on subsistence agriculture for their livelihoods, and a further 120 million pastoralists depend upon animals who need regular food, water, and shelter.[24]

Intensified and expanded forms of agriculture have dramatically impacted hydrological and nitrogen cycles, as well as long-established biotic regions and ecosystems. Rising global consumption levels for food, feed, fiber, timber, and energy have driven unprecedented rates of land and freshwater use. Agriculture is currently estimated to account for 70% of global freshwater use.[25]

The expansion of land under agriculture and forestry across the globe has supported rising human population levels and the capacity of a majority of humans to live in urban regions. At the same time, the globalized expansion of food production has contributed significantly to rising greenhouse gas emissions, the loss of natural ecosystems—including old growth forests, savannahs, natural grasslands, and wetlands—and diminishing biodiversity. Globalized agricultural commodity chain production has driven deforestation and subsequent soil erosion and habitat transformation. Intensified cultivation, together with rising surface temperatures, has contributed to increasing levels of desertification across the globe.

A 2019 IPCC special report noted that a quarter of the Earth's ice-free land area is subject to human degradation.[26] Soil erosion from agricultural tillage is a particularly pronounced problem.[27] Rising surface temperatures and the extreme weather events associated with climate change only exacerbate land degradation, especially in coastal areas, river deltas, drylands, and permafrost regions. Declining glacier runoff threatens major river systems which are vital sources of freshwater for millions. Between 1961 and 2013, the annual area of drylands in drought has increased, on average by slightly more than 1% per year, with large inter-annual variability. About half a billion people live within areas which have experienced desertification.[28] Those most affected are in South Asia and East Asia, North Africa and sub-Saharan Africa, and the Middle East. But many other dryland regions, such as in northeastern Brazil, are also experiencing significant desertification.[29]

Climate change is an amplifier of existing stresses associated with human land use practices. A decline in reliably fertile agricultural land has serious implications for food-production levels. Extreme weather exacerbates this. The result is deepening food insecurity from both diminished local supplies and disrupted globalized food markets. Before the Russian invasion of Ukraine, the existing trajectory of greenhouse gas emissions suggested that serious crises in food production and distribution would hit in the next decade. The war across the fertile soils of Ukraine and Russia, the constricted flow of crops from ports to world markets, has accelerated this timetable.

The most ominous unsettling in the coming decades will be in areas where both heat stress and population numbers are increasing. Over the next fifty years, an estimated one to three billion people will find themselves outside the climatic conditions that have been the sustaining comfort zone of human civilization for the past six thousand years. This human climate niche has consisted of a relatively narrow subset of the existing climate zones across the surface of the Earth.[30] These are the temperature bands within which human populations tend to cluster. Research, combining human physiology, ecology, and historical population densities, identifies a primary peak niche around a mean annual temperature of 11°C to 15°C and a secondary peak around 27°C associated with monsoon climates largely found in South Asia.[31] In the absence of significant climate mitigation, "the temperature experienced by the average human is projected to change more in the coming decades than it has over the past six millennia."[32] The human climate niche that has sustained the flourishing of human civilizations is projected to move to higher latitudes because of global heating. At the same time, human population growth is projected largely at lower latitudes.

Research on the human costs of the emergent disjuncture between the existing human climate niche and coming surface temperature increases points to an expansion of places that will be hostile to human flourishing, and indeed increasingly uninhabitable.[33] With global temperatures currently on track to increase by 2.7°C by the end of the century, this would mean that two billion people would experience average annual temperatures above 29°C by 2100. The higher the emission scenarios, the higher the temperatures and the greater the numbers pushed beyond the human climate niche. More of the Earth becomes uninhabitable for permanent human settlement. People outside the human climate niche are burdened with increased mortality, lower productivity, impaired learning, lower crop yields, and greater infectious disease spreads.[34] Those countries most at risk currently are India, Nigeria, Indonesia, the Philippines, and Pakistan. Many people currently living there, and in other frontline areas, will respond by fleeing such oppressive climatic conditions north to mid-latitude countries. Climate change–driven migration has already begun.[35]

The injustice of this creeping climatic oppression is stark. Those most responsible for high greenhouse gas emissions are not those about to be pushed beyond the human climate niche. The "average future person exposed to unprecedented heat comes from a place where today per capita emissions are approximately half (56%) of the global average (or 52% in a world of 11.1 billion people)."[36] This is a disturbing condition, one where those less and least responsible for global heating are those most exposed to its effects. The manifest injustice of this justifiably supports claims of climate coloniality, of a world where rich countries generate high emission rates associated with affluent lifestyles and relative freedom, while millions of people in impoverished climate-vulnerable nations suffer the consequences.[37] Put differently, the process of globally maintaining the living spaces of the rich in the North hastens the unsustainability of the living spaces of most people in the South.

Climate change, thus, poses anew questions of *lebensraum* at a planetary scale. Powerful states may wish to emphasize their missionary ideals and occlude their emissionary practices, but the political question of who has caused the climate crisis and who suffers most from it is unavoidable. It is, in many ways, the foremost question in the Anthropocene.

Questions of climate justice are now integrated into the planetary boundaries research of Rockström and his collaborators, with emphasis on *safe and just* Earth system boundaries.[38] As they note, climate justice is a three-sided challenge, one that goes well beyond traditional liberal anthropocentric conceptions of justice.[39] The first is the question of inter-species justice and Earth system stability. Because of our ecological killing power, humans have a responsibility to nurture and sustain healthy ecosystems as the home of millions of non-human species as well as ourselves. Ecological justice is also in our own long-term interest. Second, humans have a responsibility to future generations to pass on to them a healthy and sustainable planet. We are massively failing in this. They also have a responsibility to confront the legacy of past injustice and provide reparations. Finally, humans have a responsibility to their own fellow humans alive today across the planet. Questions of climate injustice are entangled with questions of economic and racial hierarchy, with who gets to consume and pollute without limits, and who has to live with the consequences. Here questions of *lebensraum* become questions of what Achille Mbembe calls "necropolitics," political decisions structuring the conditions of life and death on the planet.[40]

The Persistence of Geopolitics

It is a powerful thing to know of a catastrophe ahead of time, to know that it is coming and that signs of it are all around. It is a powerful thing also to know that one's decisions today will have effects for thousands of years, that the stakes are not momentary and transitory but intergenerational and planetary, that they involve the survival of lifeforms on the planet and the world as humans have known it for thousands of years. What then is it, with this knowledge, to continue to operate as normal?

While knowledge of the parameters of the forthcoming climate catastrophe is now widespread across the world community,

contemporary world powers remain committed to territorial competition and economic growth, to protecting their own prosperity and
preserving their way of life into the future. As regions of the Earth, all
states share a common earthly fate, but their populations have never
demonstrated a capacity to subordinate their particular territorial
identity to a shared planetary one.

Addressing climate change requires an unprecedented collective
response on the part of the world's leading states, corporations, and
communities. It requires confronting some fundamental pillars of
modernity, such as capitalist economic growth and the "freedom" to
pollute without care. It requires an awareness of climate colonialism
and a commitment to climate justice. In the immediate term, it requires a commitment to phase out the use of coal, and to prohibit
funding for further oil exploration and extraction. But, with hydrocarbons still central to their military machines and global economic
structures and practices, all the leading world powers have refused to
do this.

Consequently, international affairs show recognition of climate
change as a pressing global problem that requires international diplomatic efforts to reduce emissions across the board. However, the existential threat from climate change is downscaled to its listing as just
one among many pressing global challenges. Rather than the material
reality of climate change inducing a profound questioning of modernity, and a call to create new collective global governance structures
fit to meet the existential challenge, climate change has been captured
by the practices of modernity and geopolitics. In modernity, climate
change becomes a new frontier in ecological modernization, a massive
stimulus to engineer at "scale and speed" a transition to clean energy
and a decarbonized net zero modernity. In geopolitics, the challenge
of climate change becomes a question of climate security and competition with rivals over energy-transition technologies and access to
rare-earth minerals. It becomes the rationale for a new scramble for
resources and capacities, from access to critical minerals to the ability
to manufacture solar panels and electric vehicles. Political rhetoric

has expanded to incorporate the climate crisis on the agenda, but the habits and practices of existing geopolitics endure.

This state of affairs produces a type of cognitive dissonance in public discourse. With evidence of climate change irrefutable, political discourse can clearly state the existential stakes involved in climate change while, at the same time, expressing confidence in slightly adjusted practices as the solution. Climate change is an emergency but it is also, as President Biden declared at the COP26 meeting in Glasgow in November 2021, an "incredible opportunity." In this schema, climate change means jobs: "We have the ability to invest in ourselves and build an equitable clean-energy future and in the process create millions of good-paying jobs and opportunities around the world."[41] Fossil fuel capitalism has brought the Earth to the precipice of catastrophe, but we are told that a shift to alternative fuels promises a bright green future.

This capture of climate change by existing discourse and practice is evident also in the latest US National Security Strategy document, published by the Biden White House in October 2022. It describes the 2020s as a decisive decade for America and the world and identifies two strategic challenges. The first is the great power competition faced by the United States and its allies from China and Russia, and the struggle to secure a world that is "free, open, secure and prosperous."[42] This is the long-standing universalist rhetoric of what Isaiah Bowman dubbed "American *lebensraum*." The second is a set of shared challenges that cross borders—climate change, food insecurity, communicable diseases, terrorism, energy shortages, and inflation. These, the document notes, are "not marginal issues that are secondary to geopolitics" but at the "very core of national and international security and must be treated as such."

Pursuing strategic competition seems to directly contradict the need for collaboration and collective security actions against transnational threats like climate change. But strategic competition is rendered virtuous because it advances a broader ecological modernization across the Free World. That there might be a contradiction between expanding economic prosperity and protecting the American way of life, on the one hand, and tackling the causes of climate change, on the other, is not recognized. US exceptionalism renders it an inherently virtuous power in global politics, so the historic vanguard of climate pollution can be re-imagined as the new frontier of climate solutions, leading the way to a greener world.

Since taking office in 2021, the Biden administration has ratched up US strategic competition with China. That competition was given considerable impetus by fear of a Chinese grand strategy to displace the United States in the Pacific, and to dominate the key industries of the future, like advanced computing, clean energy, digital infrastructures, and biotechnologies.[43] China's rare-earth metal export restrictions more than a decade ago inaugurated a ratcheting geopoliticization of minerals.[44] Supply chain difficulties during the Covid-19 pandemic heightened anxieties about vulnerabilities legitimated by globalization as a dominant ideology. Biden's administration has worked to forge a new "Washington consensus" around explicit industrial policy incentives and supply chain de-risking.[45] As of 2022, the United States had a list of fifty "critical minerals."[46] China's subsidized production of photovoltaic panels and electric vehicles has provoked protectionist sentiments in Western capitals, though many US corporations, like Apple and Tesla, have important production facilities in China.

In August 2022, the US Congress passed the CHIPS and Science Act that actively seeks to restrict China's access to the advanced microchip technologies driving artificial intelligence system development. It also seeks to incentivize the building on US territory of advanced microchip fabrication plants and to decouple Western infrastructure systems from Chinese supply chains. As noted earlier, the language of this policy effort underscores the spatial separatism behind it: the 'reshoring' of production in the United States, the 'friend-shoring' of supply chains, and the 'decoupling' of the production and trade networks binding the economies of China and the United States.

That same month, the US Congress passed a second major legislative package, the Inflation Reduction Act, that incentivizes not only a transition toward clean energy technologies across a series of sectors, but also a build-in-America industrial strategy. This impacted not only China, and Chinese companies seeking to sell to the US market, but member states of the European Union. This legislation places the imperative to fight climate change within strategic competition between the United States and China to dominate leading-edge technological systems and clean energy transition. The prospect of climate catastrophe is used to justify the ecological modernization of industrial policy and great power competition.

Multiple challenging difficulties flow from this. First, objectively, climate change is much more than a national security management challenge. The decisive decade, after all, does not shape the next century but thousands of years hereafter. Crucial time and resources are wasted by geopolitical competition and technological duplication. The sudden US obsession with "China-proofing" technological systems, for example, has demonstrably hurt US capacity to manage vulnerable ecosystems and climate change risks.[47] The short-term zero-sum world of geopolitics and geo-economics erodes opportunities for collaborative collective action at a critical juncture, jeopardizing the future for all.

That climate change is rhetorically acknowledged as not secondary to geopolitics is a modicum of progress. The Biden administration also commissioned the first ever national intelligence estimate on climate change and US national security upon entering office and authorized its public release.[48] But this report only confirms how thoroughly imprisoned the threat of climate breakdown is by geopolitics. The US national security state cannot think the crisis in any other way.

Second, there is a serious contradiction between protecting a way of life at the vanguard of producing the climate crisis and also seeking to address the causes of the climate crisis. Protected by existing discourse is one of the most fundamental of modernist commitments: economic growth. The idea of green growth or a Green New Deal does little to confront how growth as an ideology is part of the environmental crisis. It does, though, offer the possibility of significantly reducing greenhouse gas emissions, something that is worth pursuing to stave off the worst climate change outcomes. Because of the damage its model of development has already done to the planet's atmosphere, the United States has a much greater obligation to change than others.

Third, geopoliticizing climate change will likely limit collaborative efforts at the international level to address it. The existing cold war between the United States and China over Taiwan and the South China Sea is only exacerbated. Pragmatists argue that the only way to get meaningful climate change policies implemented is to wrap them in the flag of strategic competition, or the top line political challenge of the day (which is why Biden's climate policies are under an inflation-reduction banner). This is a compelling argument, but it sentences the political leadership of the United States to a multilevel game of political posturing and diplomacy, a bashing of China in the domestic arena and subtle diplomacy in the international arena. That the fate of significant climate action rests with deeply flawed US political structures does not bode well.

China, the United States, and India are currently the largest territorial emitters of greenhouse gases in the world with China accounting for 30% of the world's total, the United States 13.5%, and India 7.3%.[49] These are also the countries with the largest human populations—India surpassed China's population in March 2023—and together account for nearly 3.2 billion people, or 40% of the world's total population.[50] Without concerted efforts by these three countries, the prospect of keeping global surface temperature increases to less than 2°C is slim to nonexistent. Yet all three countries continue to use hydrocarbons to power their cities, industries, and transportation systems. Both India and China have inaugurated new coal-power plants in recent years, justifying their rising emissions by citing the need to "catch up" with the West's level of development and consumption.[51]

Territorial competition between all three, especially US-China and India-China competition, adds further legitimacy to the push for greater levels of national power. After Russia invaded Ukraine and Western countries moved to prohibit and restrict the sale of Russian oil and gas to Europe, both India and China took advantage of the situation to increase their purchases of Russian oil at favorable world prices. Oil sales between Russia and India were facilitated by the emergence of new shipping companies and "ghost fleets" moving oil in clandestine ways.

There is a risk, in using state territorial data for greenhouse gas emissions, of tacitly furthering the geopoliticization of the subject when other lenses are available. A class-consumption-based analysis effectively demonstrates how huge disparities in wealth within states and across the world are a structural part of the problem. One study calculated that the world's richest 1% are set to have per capita consumption emissions in 2030 that are still 30 times higher than the global per capita level compatible with the 1.5°C goal of the Paris Agreement, while the footprints of the poorest half of the world population are set to remain several times below that level.[52] It argued that tackling extreme inequality and targeting the excessive "luxury emissions" linked to the consumption and investments by the world's rich are the most effective way to reduce emissions.

While geopolitics still dominates the international arena, state elites are aware that they need to reduce their dependence on imported hydrocarbons and transition to cleaner sources. Both India and China have scaled up their renewable energy systems, especially solar power. Estimates suggest that China will install 154 gigawatts of solar capacity in 2023, and could reach 200 gigawatts a year thereafter.[53] To put this in perspective, the total US installed solar capacity at the end of 2022 was just 144 gigawatts. India, which gets 70% of its power from coal-powered electricity plants, is certainly behind, with around 65 gigawatts of total solar capacity, but is increasing capacity each year by larger amounts.[54] Its government seeks to emulate China's domestic solar energy achievements but it is currently emulating its prodigious burning of coal. With solar now the cheapest form of energy, doubling down on the burning of coal for power is a political choice by India's elites despite the country's acute climate vulnerability. Their emissions are likely to continue to rise while those of China may peak soon.

States, large and small, pursue climate diplomacy each year in the conference of the parties—COP—meetings. At COP26 in Glasgow in November 2021, the US climate envoy John Kerry and China's top climate diplomat, Xie Zhenhua, did commit to jointly work to "accelerate the transition to a global net zero economy."[55] Their efforts were undermined, as already noted, by Nancy Pelosi's visit to Taiwan in August 2022, which provoked China into breaking its climate dialogue with the United States. At COP26 both China and India objected to the aspiration to move away from coal production. The final declaration said that parties to the conference agree to "phase down," not "phase out," the unabated burning of coal.[56] Efforts the following year at COP27 in Egypt to have states commit to phase out fossil fuels (coal, oil, and natural gas) failed. COP 28 generated new weasel words — "transition away from fossil fuels in energy systems" — which obfuscated the core issue: the need to leave fossil fuels in the ground.[57]

While there are important emission reductions being made in many places, geopolitical competition still overwhelms collaborative climate action in the institutional life of major powers. Fighting cold wars against rival states is what the existing national security bureaucracies of world powers were designed to do. This mandate does not include addressing the unprecedented collective threat of a heating planet. Rallying against a territorial enemy is easier than rallying against nebulous climate change for politicians, for now at least.

A Climate Shock Moment?

In his 2020 climate fiction novel *The Ministry for the Future*, Kim Stanley Robinson depicts a harrowing climate catastrophe in India in which a sustained heat wave in Uttar Pradesh takes surface temperatures beyond that tolerable by human bodies, that is beyond a wet bulb temperature of 35°C. The resulting death of millions of people becomes a catalyst for change of government in India, and galvanizes the international community to come together to finally address the causes of climate change.

The global emergency of climate change has the potential to force the creation of a common front for survival among the world's states. Climate change is already a material reality that has intruded into the lives of billions across the planet. Despite what people think, this materiality will become increasingly oppressive and destructive to the habitats humans have created, to storied landscapes and familiar calendar year rituals. Will the tyranny of this ratcheting climatic change, and its cascading effects, force an unwelcome unification of humankind?[58]

While climate change has abundant tipping points in Earth system dynamics, we can imagine a tipping point in the human response to climate change. This might be a climate shock event or a series of such events which forces world leaders to treat climate as a planetary emergency to which everything else must be subordinated. This would be the climate pivot of history, the moment at which the competitive logic of great power geopolitics has to give way to the imperative of collective action by great powers to save human civilization from the ravages of climate breakdown. We can imagine this critical juncture as one where catastrophic events induced by climate change— wildfires, droughts, sea level rise, crop failures, mass heat wave deaths, uncontainable climate refugee flows—begin to crowd out the more traditional concerns about territorial security, economic prosperity, technological capabilities, and global primacy. At some point, these issues will begin to overwhelm the institutions and capacities of even the most resourced states in the world. Climate breakdown then becomes the predominant security issue across the world, and surviving it requires collective cooperation because the problem is global and systemic.

But it is questionable whether the world of states will ever get to this point—the point not of climate chaos, but of collective recognition of a shared story about what is happening. There is, after all, currently no shared "we" among the peoples of the world. It is a fact that *Homo sapiens* are a distinct species and that they share a common planetary home. From a planetary perspective, humans are objectively earthlings or, more precisely, terrestrials.[59] But it is also the case that there is no shared collective species identity or planetary home identity. A small cosmopolitan elite may identify as earthlings, but this identity has little traction politically. Indeed, putative universal identities—"man," "humanity," "civilization"—have a bad track record. Too often in human history the rhetoric of humanistic universalism has been a legitimation device for imperialism and actually existing hierarchy. "All mankind-ism" has long been a provincial and fraudulent universalism.[60] The political world is not one, and the manifest injustice of climate change suggests it will struggle to become one. Presently, there seems little prospect of a unified front against climate change.

Climate crisis presents a mobilization problem because the "enemy" is difficult to specify. Unlike great power geopolitics, the climate emergency has no clear territorial frontlines. It is an everywhere war, though there are clearly regions where it is already dramatically manifesting itself. While there are plenty of actors, corporations, and states to blame for the climate crisis, there is also a sense that responsibility is widespread and lies with a way of life, a mode of thinking, an economic system more than a transcendent enemy power. The climate crisis does not easily lend itself to the analogy of wartime mobilization, though many cite this. It has a serious action-response problem. Adopting certain policy measures and making certain sacrifices do not produce immediate, clear, and visible victories. Policy actions need to be adopted worldwide and not in a patchwork way, adhered to in certain areas but not others. The effects of painful energy transitions are not locally realized but planetary. The possibility for "free-rider" behavior, of a growing clash between anti-carbon and pro-carbon coalitions, and broad resentful backlash is high. Cognitive biases also present major problems, as wishful thinking tends to predominate when hard choices are required.

Further, there are many spoilers across the geopolitical land-scape who have vested interests in avoiding, misdirecting, refusing, and thwarting collective mobilization and action on climate change. Most obviously, these are transnational hydrocarbon producers, distributors, and sellers. These corporations are often state-controlled entities or are closely entangled with the ruling establishments of petrostates. This transnational network, this carbon-combustion complex, is deeply embedded in world powers and has managed to successfully thwart meaningful public policy initiatives to regulate and tax carbon combustion.[61] States and financial markets have long subsidized, supported, and funded the hydrocarbon industry. The fossil fuel energy infrastructure construction and maintenance industries are powerful allied interest groups. The carbon-combustion complex is also powerful in the developing world. State elites from petroleum-producing countries instrumentalize the language of anti-colonialism and modernization to argue that they have a "right" to use their hydrocarbons to develop. The developed world industrialized through carbon pollution; now it is their turn.[62]

The carbon-combustion coalition has created an informational system to advocate on its behalf and wage communication campaigns to distract, divide and disarm critics of the industry. The production of doubt over climate science findings was long a specialization of the hydrocarbon information lobby.[63] Today its tactics are subtler, but they amount to the same end, namely delaying actions to address the burning of coal, oil, and natural gas.[64]

In the face of clear material evidence for decades that continued hydrocarbon consumption will tip the planet into a dangerous new climatic regime, this consumption has nevertheless continued. Modernity has always supported narcissistic practices and attitudes, so this is hardly a surprise. But the grip of human self-absorption, and human supremacism, may be difficult to break as it plays to deeply embedded liberal conceits of independence and self-determination. Economic liberalism, and its associated ideas of an endlessly exploitable Earth, may only be exposed as a death cult after it is too late.

Obviously, a nuclear war between the great powers would greatly accelerate the coming crisis to human habitation on the planet. The resultant carnage would render territories at the center and in the vicinity of such an event uninhabitable. In addition, nuclear debris and radioactive fallout would circulate the globe, leaving an uncertain impact on the atmosphere and worldwide ecologies. A horrific occurrence such as this has the potential to trigger the collapse of one or more great powers.

Should nuclear war (hopefully!) be avoided, the material prospect given current emission trends and enduring practices is that the climate crisis will manifest itself as a series of rolling crises, breakdowns, and catastrophes. Bruno Latour terms what is in prospect as a process of "landing on Earth." The presumption that the delusions of reigning belief systems in politics, economics, religion, and "national security" will be exposed as the materiality of the climate crisis bites could be correct, but may not be. We cannot presume that the climate crisis will manifest itself in a way that is easily separated out from other crises and concerns. It is more realistic to assume that the climate crisis will manifest itself in hybrid and entangled forms, embedded within crises of public health, supply-chain breakdowns, energy-system outages, food-system failures, and infrastructural collapse. Absent nuclear war, there is unlikely to be one shared planetary existential moment for humans, an instance where people suddenly realize the magnitude of the crisis that is upon them and scramble to cooperate and survive as best they can. Rather, this is more likely to unfold as a series of geographically specific existential moments when people in certain territories encounter the material limits of living there. Such local and regional crises will likely ripple outward across the globe.

The cascading crises of climate breakdown will raise sharp questions of meaning and belonging as human living spaces are remade. Who narrates the crisis, and how? Will the worldwide scientific community be recognized as a source of authority, or will localized forms of knowing and framing triumph? Who will get to define the popular meaning of the crisis as it takes hold? It is realistic to expect the rise of salvation cults and messianic figures amidst the deepening crises. Renewed commitment to modes of concealment and escapism is also likely, perhaps more so than an intensification of eco-sabotage against fossil fuel infrastructures, companies, states, and leaders, though this is entirely within the realm of the possible, and already a matter of debate.[65]

Another major question concerns prevailing notions of national territory. Will love of country and its treasured places create a mobilizing national solidarity to address climate change?[66] Will exclusivist notions of territory predominate as the crisis unfolds, and will these, then, sanction harsh measures to defend the borders from migrants and those seeking refuge? We already see the emergence of practices consistent with an "armed lifeboat" vision of state territory, one where insider residents—whose high-emissions lifestyle may have disproportionately contributed to climate change—sanction violence against those fleeing stressed environments and seeking cooler ground and more resilient territory.[67] As the climate crisis takes hold, it could well trigger the rise of a new fascist politics and classical *lebensraum* dreams, with sharp bio-political hierarchies of privilege being asserted by force across geo-ecological spaces. A walled homeland would be at its center, with a privileged nation enjoying affluent living spaces. New colonies would be occupied and exploited to service these.[68] Beyond that would be wastelands and dumping grounds, sites for the containment of condemned and excluded peoples, exteriorized spaces for those already dead to the living.[69]

All the fundamental questions in such an "armed lifeboat" world are likely to be materialistic. How are food and water, basic material needs, to be obtained? Where is shelter to be found? From where does the energy needed to sustain significant human settlements come? It is reasonable to presume that states with high levels of social trust, greater levels of material wealth, developed infrastructure, and "good geography" will do better in conditions of stress and breakdown. However, no human society will remain unscathed as the geo-ecological territories of the Earth undergo wrenching change.

Conclusion

Uncharted Territory

Like many coastal settlements, the town of Norfolk, on the south-eastern shore of the US state of Virginia, is grappling with the consequences of rising tides. Across coastal territories seized in the early seventeenth century by English colonial enterprises, the sea is rising while the land is sinking.[1] Norfolk, though, is different from other coastal settlements because it is home to the largest naval complex in the world. It is the headquarters of the US Navy's Fleet Forces Command, a deep-water port facility serving aircraft carriers, battleships, and submarines, and an airport supporting hundreds of military aircraft. Altogether, this is the greatest concentration of naval power on the planet. Yet this enormous infrastructure, this awesome military power, cannot hold back the sea. Sewell's Point, the site of the Norfolk naval base, will be underwater by the end of this century, if not earlier.[2] The ocean will rise and the settler colonial empire that became a world superpower will fall, at the very least, back.

Climate change was once a coming storm, something in the distance but not yet upon us. No more. Climate change is here and unfolding in a world that is not ready for it. Large sections of the international community are aware of the seriousness of the crisis, yet the world's most powerful states, captured by their own territorial concerns, caught up in their own privileged narratives, and attached to existing hierarchies of power, have failed to stop the upward trajectory of greenhouse gas emissions. The first United Nations synthesis report on implementation of the Paris Climate Accords signed in December 2015 underscores the enormity of the challenge and the rapidly narrowing window to achieve it. To have any chance of holding average surface temperature increases to around 1.5°C, global greenhouse emissions must be reduced 43% by 2030 and 60% by 2035, compared to 2019 levels, and reach net zero by 2050 globally.[3] The world is far off track to realize this. Denouncing the persistent refusal to ban new hydrocarbon production in September 2023, UN Secretary General António Guterres described those involved as "planet wreckers." The "fossil fuel age," he declared, "has failed."[4] Yet all the major world powers are still encouraging investment in fossil fuel extraction and infrastructure, and still provide public subsidies for hydrocarbon fuel industries. The United States is first among the planet wreckers, accounting for more than one-third of planned global oil and gas expansion through 2050, followed by Canada and Russia.[5]

A constant refrain from the Earth scientists working on climate change is that the world will enter "uncharted territory" when it crosses the 1.5°C plus threshold of planetary global heating.[6] The metaphor is apt not simply for signaling that the world will become unrecognizable, but for presenting the climate crisis as a matter of losing one's sense of place, of not knowing where we are. As Bruno Latour has noted, the Earth, explored, charted, and conquered by modernity for five hundred years, "again appears—to the stupefaction of the rich enlightened portion of the human race—as terra incognita."[7]

Geopolitics is an important part of the story of the climate crisis. Commonly understood as great power competition, the geo-ecological affordances and costs of this game are still not widely recognized. Geopolitics rests on a primary exploitation and control of geo-ecological territories. Halford Mackinder's writings articulate it as a struggle for earthly power involving extractive resources, like coal, and colonial territories tasked to grow food for the metropole.

Mackinder helped express what was already established practice among world powers, namely treating the Earth as a competitive arena in which rival states struggled for territorial control, for resources, for power, position, and legitimacy. Ratzel rendered this pithily as the struggle for space, for *lebensraum* among world powers. Mackinder and Ratzel were both discursive entrepreneurs advocating a racialized geo-ecological imperialism to make their empires great.

Reformulating some ideas in Mackinder, I have identified three territorial practices associated with geopolitics in world politics. The first is the drive of world powers to control territories, starting with the territory they occupy as their own homeland, but extending also to neighboring territories, and resource-rich regions of the world. This inevitably leads to clashes between world powers over regions and places they deem vital to their security. The second is the practice of world powers creating missions for themselves in international affairs. This proceeds from a discursive territorialization of the globe into friend and enemy spaces, and the attribution of benign universalist intentions to oneself in contrast to rivals. The third is the territorialization of the Earth by the assemblages of the military-industrial complexes built by world powers. This has produced unprecedented knowledge about the Earth as a planet while, at the same time, translating it into a battlespace grid of targets. All these territorial practices have affective structures: anxiety and ambition about territorial control and power, national self-regard and missionary fervor, and dreams of technological supremacy and transcendence.

Geopolitics is one of many drivers of climate breakdown. Its territorial practices developed hand in hand with the expansion of capitalist relations of production to the ends of the Earth, evolving with advances in communications, transportation, and weapons technologies from the fifteenth century. Geopolitics has stimulated, extended, and protected the various forms of this mode of production since. It has also propelled states into cataclysmic world wars. And it has been its own source of justification for the expansion and intensification of high-emission forms of modernity.

Geopolitics, in sum, has always been entangled in other processes and systems, in capitalist political economies and heterogeneous networks of power. Its territorial practices are not exclusively its own, but rather institutionalized expressions of deep dispositions in modernity: the inanimacy of the Earth, human supremacy over all natural things, faith in a calling to colonize the planet, desire for exclusive control over land, for ordering through bordering. Entangled in the Great Transformation, the Great Acceleration, and the coming Great Dislocation is the story of great power competition.

Geopolitics is an unreliable narrator of the material world. It presents the globe as a chessboard when it is a planet, a passive and compliant arena for state action when the arena is full of dynamic processes and agencies of many kinds that exceed and transcend not only states but also humans. It recognizes that the stakes of geopolitical competition are sometimes geo-ecological, yet it does not extend this beyond anthropocentric and resource-centric vision. It ignores pollution and never provides real ecological costing of its schemas.[8] It draws metaphors from the natural world, but has them function to naturalize nationalist self-regard and aggression. Irrespective of whether world powers think of geopolitics as a struggle over earthly spaces or not, it has operated as such in material geo-ecological terms for centuries.[9]

Earthing geopolitics discloses its geo-ecological imperialism. No aspect of this is more consequential presently than the colonization of the Earth's atmosphere, and planetary ecosystems, by pollutants generated, for the most part, by affluent world powers. They have stolen the planet's carbon budget for themselves and left everyone suffering the consequences. I have argued that our contemporary condition is one where climate change is materially remaking the territories of the Earth, yet our societies are still caught in the grip of great power competition. The power of geopolitics to override and obscure the climate emergency in the everyday politics of states is its greatest current contribution to hastening climate catastrophe. Geopolitics remains necessary and virtuous to most, while climate action is desirable but burdensome. There is a strong refusal to see geopolitics as anti-thetical to climate action. We are far from a culture that views geo-politics as reckless great power narcissism in the face of a climate catastrophe. Yet it is precisely that.

It does not have to be this way. Geopolitics is not that old, and it is not inevitable. The three territorial practices that I have identi-fied in this book can all be constrained. First, global institutions and interstate agreements can reduce the anxiety of great powers over territorial disintegration, encroachments, and resource scarcities. Geopolitical competition can be moderated and de-escalated through agreements and creative diplomacy. This may require difficult com-promises. Second, great powers can and do cooperate when facing a common threat. Climate breakdown is a clear and present danger to international society, to the interstate system, and to human and non-human flourishing on the planet. It can and should be the basis for the reformulating of great power mission narratives around a common mission to save the Earth from the most catastrophic scenarios of cli-mate breakdown. Third, military-industrial technological systems can also be constrained by arms-control agreements and strong regula-tion of transformative military technologies. The scientific capacity of states can and should be redirected to building the systems and tech-nologies needed to establish climate resilience.

Imagining a post-geopolitics world is only part of the challenge. The fantasy of endless growth shared by all great powers needs to be abandoned. Capitalist modernity has to be restrained, not as a matter of ideology, but as a matter of responsible action in the face of per-sistent Earth-wrecking practices. Its dominance over contemporary human civilization is not inevitable. Many civilizations were never capitalist, while many aspects of contemporary life are not capitalist either. The dominant structures of capitalism can be reformed: de-growth alternatives and post-capitalist futures are already being im-agined.[10] The broad relationship of humans to the Earth could be restructured. Adaptation and recalibration are inevitable anyway, as radical change is coming no matter what. Whether human societies can organize and collaborate soon enough to avert the worst of the climate breakdown is the key question. Fatalism does not help.[11]

There are grounds for some optimism. Renewable power generation is surging across the world, and for the first time more investments are going into this sector than are going into oil.[12] Problems remain, especially as many of its power sources require considerable extractive demands upon the Earth, and generate their own emissions. But progress in this sector has been encouraging over the last decade. While the COP mechanism for climate diplomacy is failing to move decisively against hydrocarbon extraction, there are some high-ambition "coalitions of the willing" that are leading the way with emission-reduction innovation. It is possible that emissions may peak in the coming decade and start to decline, but the adjustment to the change already inevitable will be considerable. Finally, there is the possibility that climate change adaptation and resilience will become the source of a new shared mission in international politics. Many will be skeptical of this if it is led by high-polluting countries like the United States and China, but that should not get in the way of mobilizing behind this effort. The notion that the Earth is sacred is already widely shared, and could be the basis for a new planetary collective imagining of a sustainable future.

But we need to remain climate realists at this critical juncture, watching emissions, not promises. The current world order has proven itself painfully slow to respond to the climate threat. Resistance is entrenched. The UN Secretary General António Guterres puts the matter starkly: "Collective action or collective suicide. It is in our hands." Yet this may be more human-centric hubris. The new climate regime and its interaction with Earth system processes will ultimately determine our fate. Oceans are rising. And empires may fall sooner than we expect. A great dislocation is coming. Can we find a just course through it?

Acknowledgments

It is difficult to think of a lifetime as geologically significant. Yet, I have some material evidence from my own. I was born in rural Ireland when the parts per million (ppm) concentration of carbon dioxide in the Earth's atmosphere was 316. For all human prehistory and pre-industrial history that figure was around 280 ppm. Two years earlier my grandparents had replaced the horses on their farm with a small Massey Ferguson tractor. My uncle Eoin taught me how to drive that tractor at a relatively young age as he embarked on an ambitious modernization of the farm. I grew up working in our family store and was fortunate to have the opportunity to attend university. In my last days as a teenager I stepped onto an airplane for the first time and flew to the United States to begin graduate study. There I joined the fast lane of modernity, full of enormous cars, cheap gasoline, and affluence I had never before experienced.

Fast forward forty years. The global carbon dioxide concentration level is a record 419 ppm. The Ireland I left behind is now a wealthy country. There's an enormous industrial quarry on what used to be my grandparents farm. Flying from Dublin airport to the United States no longer feels like traveling to the future. But the runaway success of modernizing dreams, including the ease of flying across the North Atlantic ocean, has forced the Earth into a new geological age. This is hard to comprehend, a generation as a geological force, an Earth system rift in my own lifetime. My generation, I fear, is the last to experience living most of our years on a relatively stable planet. So let me acknowledge, at the outset, this disturbing materiality and how my generation's privileges and affluence have hastened the climate catastrophe future generations now face.

This book is written for a general audience. It began as an introduction to critical geopolitics and became, by degrees, a book about geopolitics and climate change. I am grateful to those who agreed to participate in a virtual book workshop when it was halfway between these: John Agnew, Simon Dalby, Gerry Kearns, Ian Klinke, John O'Loughlin, and Timothy Luke. John Agnew has for decades been a source of intellectual inspiration in how to think critically about space and politics. My longtime collaborator and friend, Simon Dalby, provided encouragement and the power of his example with his many works drawing connections between geopolitics and environmental change. Gerry and Ian made this book a lot easier by writing excellent biographies of Halford Mackinder and Friedrich Ratzel, respectively. I have known John O'Loughlin from my first days in the US. Happily, I could not have found a better mentor, advocate, collaborator, and friend. His positive energy and commitment to scholarship is extraordinary. Timothy Luke has been a supportive colleague, friend, and intellectual inspiration at Virginia Tech for many decades. I also want to remember Neil Smith (1954–2012), who wrote an indispensable biography of Isaiah Bowman, for encouragement back in the day at Rutgers University.

After the manuscript workshop, I decided I needed to rewrite large sections of the book. This took time, and was complicated by a global pandemic and other commitments. I want to thank my other research collaborators for their patience: Kristin Bakke, Karina Korostelina, Marlene Laruelle, and Gwendolyn Sasse. Thanks also to Luiza Bialasicwicz, Julie Newton, Sarah Wagner, and Julie Wilhelmsen. I would also like to acknowledge the help of a sabbatical semester at Virginia Tech and the understanding of my colleagues in the Government and International Affairs program at our campus in the Washington, D.C., metropolitan area. My PhD students helped with their questions and their own research projects. I am grateful to Emina Muzaferija for her help with the index of the book.

Anyone writing on climate change owes an enormous debt of gratitude to the thousands of Earth scientists across the world who have labored for decades to provide a detailed scientific account of a rapidly changing Earth. I count myself fortunate as a Geography undergraduate in Ireland to have had an inspiring climatology teacher in John Sweeney. John subsequently became part of the Intergovernmental Panel on Climate Change (IPCC) and a leading educator in Ireland on climate change and advocate for legislative changes to address Ireland's emissions. He was part of the IPCC team that was awarded the Nobel Peace Prize in 2007. Though Geography is highly specialized, and I gravitated toward political geography early, I have benefited from being part of a discipline that stretches across the physical and social science divide. I have also benefited from the many scholars using environmental history, feminism, science and technology studies, and political ecology to challenge the anthropocentrism of political theory, philosophy, religion, political economy, and international relations.

Finally, as I approached the last lap, my friend of more than three decades, Brendan Gleeson, former head of the Sustainability Institute at the University of Melbourne, agreed to give the final draft an editorial review. This was a great help in pushing me toward the finish line. Thank you, Brendan, for stepping in when I needed you. Also, once again I would like to thank Dave McBride for faith and patience and the production team at Oxford University Press for publishing my work.

The burden of the writing process was felt most by my family. Thanks to my sister and mother for unfailing love. I want to thank my daughters Sirin and Nives for their positivity and power. They have kept me happy amidst the negativities of our time. My wife has been not only supportive in a million everyday ways, but in the final months she also agreed to edit the manuscript. This book is dedicated to her.

Gerard Toal, Washington D.C, October 2023.

Notes

INTRODUCTION

1. For an account of China's dredging capacities, see Andrew Erikson and Kevin Bond, "Dredging under the Radar: China Expands South Sea Foothold," *National Interest*, August 26, 2015, https://nationalinterest. org/feature/dredging-under-the-radar-china-expands-south-sea-foothold-13701. For general background on China's neighborhood territorial disputes, see Bill Hayton, *The South China Sea: The Struggle for Power in Asia* (New Haven, CT: Yale University Press, 2014) and M. Taylor Fravel, *Strong Borders, Secure Nation: Cooperation and Conflict in China's Territorial Disputes* (Princeton, NJ: Princeton University Press, 2008).

2. The 3,200 acres figure is for the Spratlys only. See the Asia Maritime Transparency Initiative of the Center for Strategic and International Affairs in Washington, DC, at https://amti.csis.org/island-tracker/china/.

3. Speech by the Commander of the U.S. Pacific Fleet, Admiral Harry B. Harris Jr., to the Australian Strategic Policy Institute, Canberra, Australia, March 31, 2015.

4. China has signaled that it intends to declare an air defense identification zone over the islands that it built in the South China Sea but has not yet done so. The 1982 Law of the Sea Convention allows the first twelve miles of ocean surrounding the coastline of a sovereign territory to be claimed by that state. The United States does not accept that this applies to the new islands in the South China Sea and conducts freedom of navigation operations near the islands to assert this.

5. M. Taylor Fravel and Charles L. Glaser, "How Much Risk Should the United States Run in the South China Sea?" *International Security* 47, 3 (2022): 88–134.

6. For an overview of US reaction, see Ronald O'Rourke, "US-China Strategic Competition in South and East China Seas: Background

and Issues for Congress," *Congressional Research Service*, May 28, 2020, https://crsreports.congress.gov/product/pdf/R/R42784/.

7. Banyan, "A Chinese Lake," *Economist*, June 21, 2018.

8. The calculation of oil and gas reserves in terms of trillions of dollars is that of Trump administration National Security Adviser Robert O'Brien in a speech to the ASEAN.

9. James Borton, *Dispatches from the South China Sea: Navigating to Common Ground* (Irvine: Universal, 2022), p. xiii.

10. Sam Ellis, "Why China Is Building Islands in the South China Sea," *Vox.com*, February 17, 2017. https://www.vox.com/videos/2017/2/17/14642818/china-south-china-sea-us-islands.

11. On the history of the nine-dash line, see Hayton, *The South China Sea*. On China's expansive geo-body, see William A. Callahan, *China: The Pessoptimist Nation* (Oxford: Oxford University Press, 2009).

12. Richard Bernstein and Ross Munro, *The Coming Conflict with China* (New York: Vintage, 1997); Graham Allison, *Destined for War: Can America and China Escape Thucydides's Trap?* (Boston: Houghton Mifflin Harcourt, 2017).

13. Banyan, "China Is Resorting to New Forms of Bullying in the South China Sea," *Economist*, October 3, 2019. https://www.economist.com/asia/2019/10/03/china-is-resorting-to-new-forms-of-bullying-in-the-south-china-sea.

14. Stephen Chen, "Can a New Graphene Coating Save the Chinese Military from Rusting Away in the South China Sea?," *South China Morning Post*, July 1, 2019. https://www.scmp.com/news/china/science/article/3016480/can-new-graphene-coating-save-chinese-military-rusting-away.

15. Borton, *Dispatches from the South China Sea*.

16. Steve Mollman, "The South China Sea's Untapped Oil and Natural Gas Are Back in Focus," *Quartz*, July 27, 2017, https://qz.com/1037896/south-china-seas-untapped-oil-and-natural-gas-back-in-focus.

17. David Wallace-Wells, *The Uninhabitable Earth: Life after Warming* (New York: Tim Duggan Book, 2019)

18. Scott Kulp and Benjamin H. Strauss, "New Elevation Data Triple Estimates of Global Vulnerability to Sea-Level Rise and Coastal Flooding," *Nature Communications* 10 (2019), https://www.nature.com/articles/s41467-019-12808-z.

19. The term *terraforming* was initially used in science fiction to describe the fantasy of deliberately modifying the atmosphere, temperature, surface topography, and ecology of planets to be similar to the environment

of Earth. Since then, the term has come to describe the process of organizing the Earth to serve the requirements of modernity. See Amitav Ghosh, *The Nutmeg's Curse: Parables for a Planet in Crisis* (Chicago: University of Chicago Press, 2021).

20. Stuart Elden, "Foreword," in K. Peters, P. Steinberg, and E. Stratford, eds., *Territory Beyond Terra* (London: Rowman and Littlefield, 2018).

21. For an account of this, see the many volumes of Immanuel Wallerstein's world-system analysis.

22. Peter Taylor, *The Way the Modern World Works: World Hegemony to World Impasse* (Chichester, UK: Wiley, 1996).

23. Ulrich Beck, *Risk Society: Towards a New Modernity* (London: Sage, 1992); *World Risk Society* (Cambridge: Polity, 1999); *World at Risk* (Cambridge: Polity, 2009).

24. Timothy Mitchell, *Carbon Democracy* (London, Verso, 2011), p. 260.

25. Johan Rockström and Owen Gaffney, *Breaking Boundaries: The Science of Our Planet* (New York: DK, 2021).

26. Intergovernmental Panel on Climate Change, *Climate Change 2021: The Physical Science Basic* (hereafter IPCC, 2021).

27. World Meterological Organization, *State of the World's Climate 2022*, p. ii.

28. Damien Carrington, "Oceans Were the Hottest Ever Recorded in 2022, Analysis Shows," *Guardian*, January 23, 2023, https://www.theguardian.com/environment/2023/jan/11/oceans-were-the-hottest-ever-recorded-in-2022-analysis-shows ; Oliver Milman, "Hottest Ocean Temperatures in History Recorded Last Year." *Guardian*, January 11, 2022, https://www.theguardian.com/environment/2022/jan/11/oceans-hottest-temperatures-research-climate-crisis.

29. World Meterological Organization, *State of the World's Climate 2022*, p. ii.

30. IPCC 2018 Summary for Policymakers, p. 7, in *Global Warming of 1.5°C: An IPCC Special Report on the Impacts of Global Warming of 1.5°C above Pre-industrial Levels and Related Global Greenhouse Gas Emission Pathways, in the Context of Strengthening the Global Response to the Threat of Climate Change, Sustainable Development, and Efforts to Eradicate Poverty* (Cambridge: Cambridge University Press, 2018), pp. 3–24.

31. Chris Mooney, "A Greenland Glacier's Rapid Melting May Signal Faster Sea Level Rise," *Washington Post*, May 8, 2023, https://www.washingtonpost.com/climate-environment/2023/05/08/sea-level-rise-greenland-glacier-melt/.

32. Rockström and Gaffney, *Breaking Boundaries*, p. A1.

33. The IPCC 2018 Report estimated a global mean sea level rise (relative to 1986–2005) of between 0.26 to 0.77 meters by 2100 under the 1.5°C global warming scenario.

34. IPCC 2021, p. 29.

35. IPCC AR6 Synthesis Report, March 2023, p. 13.

36. Ibid, p. 9.

37. IPCC AR6 Synthesis Report, March 2023, p. 11.

38. Neil Smith, *Uneven Development: Nature, Capital and the Production of Space* (Oxford: Blackwell, 1984)

39. Tom Perreault, Gavin Bridge, and James McCarthy, eds., *The Routledge Handbook of Political Ecology* (London: Routledge, 2020).

40. Naomi Klein, *This Changes Everything: Capitalism vs. the Climate* (New York: Simon Schuster, 2014).

41. This quote is widely used by a number of critics. For its origins, see Fredric Jameson, *The Seeds of Time* (New York: Columbia University Press, 1994), xii.

42. G. Supran, S. Rahmstorf and N. Oreskes, "Assessing ExxonMobil's Global Warming Projections." *Science* 379, no. 153 (2023), eabk0063, online January 13, 2023.

43. Oliver Milman, "'Monster Profits' for Energy Giants Reveal a Self-Destructive Fossil Fuel Resurgence." *The Guardian*, February 9, 2023, https://www.theguardian.com/environment/2023/feb/09/profits-ene rgy-fossil-fuel-resurgence-climate-crisis-shell-exxon-bp-chevron-totalenergies.

44. Tom Wilson. "Saudi Aramco Cashes in on 2022 Oil Boom with Record $161bn in Profits." *Financial Times*, March 13, 2023, p. 3..

45. Lynn White Jr., "The Historical Roots of Our Ecologic Crisis," *Science* 155, no. 3767 (1967): 1203–1207.

46. Bruno Latour, *We Have Never Been Modern* (Cambridge, MA: Harvard University Press, 1993).

47. Vaclav Smil, *How the World Really Works* (New York: Viking, 2022).

48. Ibid, p. 47

49. Sally Weintrobe, *Psychological Roots of the Climate Crisis* (New York: Bloomsburg, 2021).

50. Adam McKay, director, *Don't Look Up*, Netflix, 2021.

51. In this book I favor the term "world power" where I can, mindful of its genealogy as an aspirational status of rival empires in the late nineteenth century. British, US, and German ideas of "world power" (*Weltpolitik*) are open about its ecological motivations and demands. See Matthew Spencer, *The Atlantic Realists* (Stanford, CA: Stanford University Press,

2022), 18–49 Thinking of large state power geo-ecologically is more precisely materialistic than substituting "great power" with "full-spectrum power." See Phillips O'Brien, "There's No Such Thing as a Great Power: How a Dated Concept Distorts Geopolitics," *Foreign Affairs*, June 29, 2023, https://www.foreignaffairs.com/ukraine/theres-no-such-thing-great-power.

52. A good example of the military Keynesianism associated with this is AUKUS, a 2021 trilateral security pact between Australia, the United Kingdom, and the United States to build next-generation nuclear submarines in Australia.

53. Uri Friedman, "The New Concept Everyone in Washington Is Talking About," *The Atlantic*, August 6, 2019.

54. Walter Russell Mead, "The Return of Geopolitics: The Revenge of the Revisionist Powers," *Foreign Affairs* 93, no. 3 (2014): 69–79.

55. Jakob Grygiel and A. Wess Mitchell, *The Unquiet Frontier: Rising Rivals, Vulnerable Allies, and the Crisis of American Power* (Princeton, NJ: Princeton University Press, 2017).

56. Elbridge Colby and A. Wess Mitchell, "The Age of Great-Power Competition: How the Trump Administration Refashioned American Strategy," *Foreign Affairs* 99, no. 1 (2020): 118–124, 126–130.

57. White House, *National Security Strategy of the United States*, December 2017, p. 25, https://nsarchive.gwu.edu/document/16478-white-house-national-security-strategy.

58. *Summary of the 2018 National Defense Strategy of the United States*, p. 2, https://dod.defense.gov/Portals/1/Documents/pubs/2018-National-Defense-Strategy-Summary.pdf.

59. Daniel Lippman, Lara Seligman, Alexander Ward, and Quint Forgey, "Biden's Era of 'Strategic Competition,'" *Politico*, October 5, 2021; Cornell Overfield, "Biden's 'Strategic Competition' Is an Unclear, Confusing Term," *Foreign Policy*, October 13, 2021.

60. The White House, *National Security Strategy*, October 2022, p. 2, https://www.whitehouse.gov/wp-content/uploads/2022/10/Biden-Harris-Administrations-National-Security-Strategy-10.2022.pdf.

61. Michael Klare, "Geopolitics Will Cost Us Our Planet." *The Nation*, October 11, 2021, https://www.thenation.com/article/world/geopolitics-will-cost-us-our-planet/. Klare's logic is compelling, but the notion that it is "our planet" is part of the problem.

62. Simon Dalby, *Pyromania: Fire and Geopolitics in a Climate-Disrupted World* (Newcastle: Agenda Publishing, 2023).

63. Gavin Bridge and Philippe Le Billion, *Oil*, 2nd edition (Cambridge: Polity, 2017).

64. Daniel Yergin, *The Prize* (New York: Free Press, 1991).

65. John Morrissey, *The Long War: Centcom, Grand Strategy, and Global Security* (Athens: University of Georgia Press, 2017); Robert Vitalis, *Oilcraft: The Myths of Scarcity and Security That Haunt U.S. Energy Policy* (Stanford, CA: Stanford University Press, 2020).

66. The Abrams battle tanks have gas turbine engines whose fuel consumption depends on specific configuration and use.

67. Constantine Samaras, William J. Nuttall, and Morgan Bazilian, "Energy and the Military: Convergence of Security, Economic and Environmental Decision-Making," *Energy Strategy Reviews* 26 (2019): 1–11.

68. Michael Klare, *All Hell Breaking Loose: The Pentagon's Perspective on Climate Change* (New York: Metropolitan, 2019).

69. Neta C. Crawford, *The Pentagon, Climate Change, and War* (Cambridge, MA: MIT Press, 2022).

70. Oliver Belcher, Patrick Bigger, Ben Neimark, and Cara Kennelly, "Hidden Carbon Costs of the Everywhere War: Logistics, Geopolitical Ecology, and the Carbon Bootprint of the U.S. Military," *Transactions of the Institute of British Geographers* 45, no. 1 (2020): 65–80. For an attempt to create a global audit of the carbon bootprint of military institutions, see https://militaryemissions.org/

71. The carbon-combustion complex is the "interlinked fossil fuel extraction, refinement, and combustion industries, financiers, and government 'regulatory' agencies that defend fossil fuel use in the name of employment, growth and prosperity." See Naomi Oreskes and Erik M. Conway, *The Collapse of Western Civilization* (New York: Columbia University Press, 2014), pp. 54–55.

72. Daniel Yergin, *The New Map: Energy, Climate and the Clash of Nations* (New York: Penguin, 2020).

73. The seminal article making this argument within Anglo-American Geography is John Agnew, "The Territorial Trap: The Geographical Assumptions of International Relations Theory," *Review of International Political Economy* 1 (1994): 53–80. For the latest scholarship, see the academic journals *Political Geography* and *Geopolitics*.

CHAPTER 1

1. Macron undertook the overseas trip on July 25–28, 2021. For a record of official activities, see: https://www.elysee.fr/emmanuel-macron/deplacement-du-president-emmanuel-macron-en-polynesie-francaise.

2. For details on the French testing, using military archives files and three-dimensional modeling, see the March 9, 2021, report by the French investigative website Disclosure in association with INTERPRT, a research collective, and Princeton University's Science & Global Security program. They identified 193 tests at the nuclear atolls of Moruroa and Fangataufa until 1996. Between 1966 and 1974, the military carried out 46 open-air explosions that Macron acknowledged were "not clean." See Sébastien Philippe, Tomas Statius, *Toxique: Enquête sur les essais nucléaires français en Polynésie* (Paris, PUF, 2021).

3. The representation of Tahiti as an erotic idyll was tied to Gauguin's efforts to fund his travel there and sell his paintings, exertions that largely failed in his lifetime. See Nancy Mowll Mathews, *Paul Gauguin, An Erotic Life* (New Haven, CT: Yale University Press, 2001).

4. According to Disclosure, only 63 Polynesian civilians have been compensated for radiation exposure since the tests ended in 1996. Approximately 110,000 people, almost the entire population of French Polynesia at the time, were exposed, with leukemia, lymphoma, and other cancers subsequently rife in the population.

5. Speech by President Emmanuel Macron from Papette, July 28, 2021, https://www.elysee.fr/front/pdf/elysee-module-18162-fr.pdf.

6. Leslie Blume, "Trinity Nuclear Test's Fallout Reached 46 States, Canada and Mexico, Study Finds." *New York Times*, 20 July 2023. The US passed a Radiation Exposure Compensation Act in 1990 and expanded it in 2000. Still many exposed groups were overlooked and actively campaign for recognition.

7. Colin Waters et al., "Can Nuclear Weapons Fallout Mark the Beginning of the Anthropocene Epoch?" *Bulletin of the Atomic Scientists* 71, no. 3 (2015): 46–57; Gary Hancock, Stephen G. Tims, L. Keith Fifield, and Ian T. Webster, "The Release and Persistence of Radioactive Anthropogenic Nuclides," in C. N. Waters, J. A. Zalasiewicz, M. Williams, M. Ellis, and A. M. Snelling, eds., *A Stratigraphic Basis for the Anthropocene* (London: Geological Society, 2014), 265–281.

8. Kate Brown quotes Dr. Robert Gale declaring: "A nuclear accident anywhere in the world is everywhere in the world." Kate Brown, *Manual*

For Survival: A Chernobyl Guide to the Future (New York: Norton, 2019), p. 247.

9. Jan Zalasiewicz, Colin N. Waters, Mark Williams, and Colin P. Summerhayes, eds., *The Anthropocene as a Geological Time Unit: A Guide to the Scientific Evidence and Current Debate* (Cambridge: Cambridge University Press, 2019).

10. The term "General Winter" is a personification of the climatic conditions that severely impeded the military invasions of Russia by Napoleon and Nazi Germany.

11. Klaus Dodds, *Geopolitics: A Very Short Introduction*, 2nd edition (Oxford: Oxford University Press, 2014), p. 1; Colin Flint, *Introduction to Geopolitics*, 3rd edition (London: Routledge, 2017).

12. John E. Kieffer, *Realities of World Power* (New York: David McKay, 1952), p. 9.

13. David G. Haglund, "The New Geopolitics of Minerals," *Political Geography Quarterly* 5, no. 3 (1986): 221–240.

14. Sven Holdar, "The Ideal State and the Power of Geography: The Life-Work of Rudolf Kjellén." *Political Geography* 11 (1992): 307–323. Ian Klinke and Mark Bassin, "Introduction: *Lebensraum* and Its Discontents." *Journal of Historical Geography* 61 (2018): 53–58; Gerry Kearns, *Geopolitics and Empire: The Legacy of Halford Mackinder* (Oxford: Oxford University Press, 2009).

15. Robert Seager II, *Alfred Thayer Mahan: The Man and His Letters* (Annapolis, MD: Naval Institute Press, 1977).

16. Ola Tunander, "Swedish-German Geopolitics for a New Century: Rudolf Kjellén's 'The State as a Living Organism.'" *Review of International Studies* 27 (2001): 451–463.

17. On the factors that influence the popularity of new words, see Alan Metcalf, *Predicting New Words: The Secrets of Their Success* (New York: Houghton Mifflin Harcourt, 2004).

18. "History Revisited," *New York Times*, July 4, 1903, p BR8. The article is a discussion of Emil Reich, "A New View of the War of American Independence," *The North American Review* 177, no. 560 (1903): 31–44.

19. Hans Weigert, *Generals and Geographers: The Twilight of Geopolitics* (New York: Oxford University Press, 1942).

20. Holger H. Herwig, *The Demon of Geopolitics: How Karl Haushofer "Educated" Hitler and Hess* (Lanham, MD: Rowman and Littlefield, 2016).

21. Mark Bassin, "Race Contra Space: The Conflict between German Geopolitik and National Socialism," *Political Geography Quarterly* 6, no. 2 (1987), 115–134; Trevor J. Barnes and Christian Abrahamson, "Tangled

Complicities and Moral Struggles: The Haushofers, Father and Son, and the Spaces of Nazi Geopolitics," *Journal of Historical Geography* 47 (2015): 64–73.

22. Barnes and Abrahamsson, "Tangled Complicities and Moral Struggles."

23. See chapter 4 of my *Critical Geopolitics: The Politics of Writing Global Space* (Minneapolis: University of Minnesota Press, 1996).

24. "Germany's Brain Truster," *Life*, November 20, 1939, 62–66.

25. Neil Smith, *American Empire: Roosevelt's Geographer and the Prelude to Globalization* (Berkeley: University of California, 2003).

26. Isaiah Bowman, "Geography versus Geopolitics," *Geographical Review* 34 (1942)

27. Richard Hartshorne, "Political Geography," in P. James and C. Jones, eds., *American Geography: Inventory and Prospect* (Syracuse, NY: Syracuse University Press, 1954), pp. 211–214.

28. Henry Luce, "The American Century," *Life*, February 17, 1941.

29. Bowman stated this in 1940, a year prior to Luce's essay, to his colleagues in the Council on Foreign Relations. See Smith, *American Empire*, pp. 27–28, 319.

30. Gearóid Ó Tuathail, "Spiritual Geopolitics: Fr Edmund Walsh and Jesuit Anti-Communism," in Klaus Dodds and David Atkinson, eds., *Geopolitical Traditions: A Century of Geopolitical Thought* (London: Routledge, 2000), pp. 187–210; David Ekbladh, "Present at the Creation: Edward Mead Earle and the Depression-Era Origins of Security Studies," *International Security* 36, no. 3 (2011–2012): 107–141; Or Rosenboim, *The Emergence of Globalism: Visions of World Order in Britain and the United States, 1939–1950* (Princeton, NJ: Princeton University Press, 2017); Stephen Wertheim, *Tomorrow the World: The Birth of U.S. Global Supremacy* (Cambridge, MA: Belknap Press, 2020).

31. Susan Schulten, *The Geographical Imagination in America, 1880–1950* (Chicago: University of Chicago Press, 2001); Timothy Barney, *Mapping the Cold War: Cartography and the Framing of America's International Power* (Chapel Hill: University of North Carolina Press, 2015).

32. Both geopolitics and grand strategy have a similar genealogy in the English language, emerging from the dilemmas of the British Empire and given justification by World War II.

33. Leslie W. Hepple, "The Revival of Geopolitics," *Political Geography Quarterly* 5 (1986): S21–S38; Alan Henrikson, "The Moralist as Geopolitician," *The Fletcher Forum* 5, no. 2 (1981): 391–427.

34. Greg Grandin, *Kissinger's Shadow: The Long Reach of America's Most Controversial Statesman* (New York: Picador, 2015).

35. Published in 1968 before he became a general, the book reproduces the theory of the state as an organism (as well as containing factual errors like confusing Washington state and Washington, DC). See Leslie W. Hepple, "Metaphor, Geopolitical Discourse and the Military in South America," in James S. Duncan and Trevor J. Barnes, eds., *Writing Worlds: Discourse, Text and Metaphor in the Representation of Landscape* (London: Routledge, 1992), pp. 136–154.

36. Justin Vaisse, *Zbigniew Brzezinski: America's Grand Strategist.* (Cambridge, MA: Harvard University Press, 2018).

37. Tom Kunz, "The Geopolitics of Jay-Z," *New York Times,* July 20, 2009.

38. Ulrike Jureit, "Mastering Space: Laws of Movement and the Grip on the Soil," *Journal of Historical Geography* 61 (2018): 81–85.

39. The German geographer Oscar Peshel (1826–1875), who preceded Ratzel as the chair of geography at Leipzig, used the phrase in 1874 to refer to the relations between people and the Earth. See Klinke and Bassin, "Introduction"; Ian Klinke, *Life, Earth, Colony: Friedrich Ratzel's Necropolitical Geography* (Ann Arbor: University of Michigan Press, 2022), chapter 4.

40. Friedrich Ratzel, "Lebensraum: A Biogeographical Study (translated by Tul'si [Tuesday] Bhambry) [1901]," *Journal of Historical Geography* 61 (2018): 59–80.

41. Ibid, p. 60. The surface area of Earth is closer to 510 million square kilometers, 29% taken up by land, while the remaining 71% is covered by water.

42. Thomas Malthus, *An Essay on the Principle of Population and Other Writings* (Penguin, 2015); Alison Bashford, *Global Population: History, Geopolitics and Life on Earth* (New York: Columbia University Press, 2014).

43. Ibid, p. 73.

44. Ibid, p. 73. surface area of Earth is closer to 510 million square kilometers, 29% taken up by land, while the remaining 71% is covered by water.

45. Tul'si (Tuesday) Bhambry, Translator's Introduction to "Lebensraum: A Biographical Study [1901]." *Journal of Historical Geography* 61 (2018): 59.

46. Klinke, *Life, Earth, Colony.*

47. Smith, *American Empire*, p. 327.

48. Robert Strausz-Hupé, *Geopolitics: The Struggle for Space and Power* (New York: Putnam, 1942); *The Balance of Tomorrow: Power and Foreign Policy in the United States* (New York: Putnam, 1945).

49. Henry Kissinger, *White House Years* (New York: Little Brown, 1979), p. 914.

50. Hedley Bull, "Review: Kissinger: The Primacy of Geopolitics," *International Affairs* 56, no. 3 (1980): 484–487.

51. Kissinger, *White House Years*, p. 915.

52. Ibid, p. 1063.

53. Ibid, p. 31.

54. Edmund J. Walsh, *Total Empire: The Roots and Progress of World Communism* (Milwaukee: Bruce Company, 1951). On geopolitics as a radical Right tradition of international relations thought see Jean-François Drolet and Michael Williams, "The radical Right, realism, and the politics of conservatism in postwar international thought," *Review of International Studies* 47, no. 3 (2021): 273–293.

55. G. Ó Tuathail, "The Effacement of Place? US Foreign Policy and the Spatiality of the Gulf Crisis," *Antipode* 25 (1993): 4–31; Andrew Bacevich, *The New American Militarism* (New York: Oxford University Press, 2013).

56. See the *Oxford English Dictionary*, 3rd edition (Oxford: Oxford University Press, 2012).

57. Emil Reich, *Handbook of Geography: Descriptive and Mathematical*, 2 volumes (London: Duckworth and Son, 1908).

58. Clarence J. Glacken, *Traces on the Rhodian Shore: Nature and Culture in Western Thought from Ancient Times to the End of the Eighteenth Century* (Berkeley: University of California Press, 1967).

59. See also Daniel Deudney, *Dark Skies: Space Expansionism, Planetary Geopolitics, and the Ends of Humanity* (New York: Oxford University Press, 2020), pp. 270–276.

60. Ratzel was an active member in various associations that had overlapping membership, such as the German Colonial Society (established 1887), the Pan-German League (established 1891), and German Navy League (established 1898). A fulcrum of conservative-nationalist opinion, not to mention racist and anti-Semitic sentiments, such associations attracted criticism from liberal political forces and figures. Rival powers and neighboring states were also concerned about the popularity of such revisionist ideas within a dynamically industrializing German state.

61. Kearns, *Geopolitics and Empire*, p. 53.

62. For a German Communist perspective on geopolitics first published in 1929, see Karl Wittfogel, "Geopolitics, Geographical Materialism and Marxism," translated by G. L. Ulmen, *Antipode* 17 (2006): 21–71.

63. Yves Lacoste, "An Illustration of Geographical Warfare: Bombing the Dikes of the Red River, North Vietnam," *Antipode* 5, no. 2 (1973): 1–13. See also Gavin P. Bowd and Daniel W. Clayton, "Geographical

Warfare in the Tropics: Yves Lacoste and the Vietnam War," *Annals of the Association of American Geographers*, 103, no. 3 (2013): 627–646.

64. Yves Lacoste, *La géographie, ça sert, d'abord, à faire la guerre* (Paris: Maspero, 1976).

65. I was unaware of his work for decades. See Claude Raffestin, *Pour une geographie du pouvoir* (Lyons: ENS edition, [1980] 2019). Juliet Fall, "Lost Geographers: Power Games and the Circulation of Ideas within Francophone Political Geographies," *Progress in Human Geography* 31, no. 2 (2007): 195–216; Juliet Fall and Stéphane Rosiére, "On the Limits of Dialogue between Francophone and Anglophone Political Geography," *Political Geography* 27 (2008): 713–716.

66. Richard Peet, *Modern Geographical Thought* (Oxford: Blackwell, 1998).

67. This was within radical geography. Beyond it, Saul Cohen kept the wartime tradition of thinking geopolitically alive within Cold War US political geography. See Saul Cohen, *Geography and Politics in a World Divided* (New York: Random House, 1963). A second edition was published a decade later by Oxford University Press.

68. The expression *critical geopolitics* was coined by the British political geographer and journal editor Peter Taylor, who used it in 1984 in the review process for my first journal article. It was subsequently the title of my PhD dissertation at Syracuse University. See Gearóid Ó Tuathail, "The Language and Nature of the New Geopolitics: The Case of US-El Salvador Relations," *Political Geography Quarterly* 5 (1986): 73–85.

69. Simon Dalby, *Creating the Second Cold War: The Discourse of Politics* (London: Pinter, 1990). The initial Committee on the Present Danger was created in 1951. A third iteration was created in 2004 and a fourth in 2019.

70. Mary Louise Pratt, *Imperial Eyes: Travel Writing and Transculturation* (New York: Routledge, 1992)

71. I should have been more precise in describing this as human geo-power, everything from engineering to cartography to forceful terraformation through grand modernist schemes. Like geopolitics, the neologism geo-power proved attractive and was adopted by others to refer to the non-human and the dynamics of the Earth system, the opposite of the meaning I had laid out. Elizabeth Grosz, *Chaos, Territory, Art: Deleuze and the Framing of the Earth* (Durham, NC: Duke University Press, 2008).

72. For this point, see Pierre Charbonnier, *Affluence and Freedom: An Environmental History of Political Ideas* (Cambridge: Polity, 2021), p. 32.

73. Tzetan Todorov, *The Conquest of America: The Question of the Other* (New York: HarperPerennial, 1984); James Der Derian and Michael J. Shapiro,

eds., *International/Intertextual Relations: Postmodern Readings of World Politics* (Lexington: Lexington Books, 1989); David Campbell, *Writing Security* (Minneapolis: University of Minnesota, 1992).

74. Edward Said, *Orientalism* (New York: Vintage, 1979)

75. My own thinking on this was influenced by attending a series of summer workshop courses in 1983 on Marxism and Culture at the University of Illinois that featured figures like Stuart Hall, Henri Lefebvre, Frederic Jameson, and Gayatri Chakravorty Spivak. It became the basis for Cary Nelson and Lawrence Grossberg, eds., *Marxism and the Interpretation of Culture* (Champaign: University of Illinois Press, 1988). For popular geopolitics see, inter alia, Klaus Dodds, "The 1982 Falklands War and a Critical Geopolitical Eye: Steve Bell and the If . . . Cartoons," *Political Geography* 15 (1996): 571–592; Joanne P. Sharp, *Condensing the Cold War: Reader's Digest and American Identity* (Minneapolis: University of Minnesota, 2000); Marcus Power and Andrew Crampton, eds., *Cinema and Popular Geo-Politics* (London: Routledge, 2007); Jason Dittmer and Tristan Strum, *Mapping the End Times: American Evangelical Geopolitics and Apocalyptic Visions* (Farnham, UK: Ashgate, 2010); and Jason Dittmer, *Captain America and the Nationalist Superhero* (Philadelphia: Temple University Press, 2013).

76. See Klaus Dodds, Merje Kuus, and Joanne Sharp, eds., *The Ashgate Research Companion to Critical Geopolitics* (Farnham, UK: Ashgate, 2013).

77. For critiques and reflections see, "Review Symposium: Gearóid Ó Tuathail, (1996) *Critical Geopolitics: The Politics of Writing Global Space* (Minneapolis: University of Minnesota Press)," *Political Geography* 19 (2000): 345–396; Martin Müller and Paul Reuber "Empirical Verve, Conceptual Doubts: Looking from the Outside in at Critical Geopolitics," *Geopolitics* 13 (2008): 458–472; F. Ciută and Ian Klinke, "Lost in Conceptualization: Reading the 'New Cold War' with Critical Geopolitics," *Political Geography* 29 (2010): 323–332; Simon Dalby, "Recontextualising Violence, Power and Nature: The Next Twenty Years of Critical Geopolitics?" *Political Geography* 29 (2010): 280–288. For my response to critiques, see Gerard Toal, "Una reflexión sobre las críticas a la Geopolítica Crítica," *Geopolítica(s): Revista de estudios sobre espacio y poder* 12, no. 2 (2021), 191–206, https://doi.org/10.5209/geop.78616; Gerard Toal et al., "Intervention: Critical Geopolitics/critical geopolitics 25 Years On," *Political Geography* 90, October (2021) https://doi.org/10.1016/j.polgeo.2021.102421.

78. Robert W. Cox, "Social Forces, States, and World Orders: Beyond International Relations Theory," *Millennium* 10, no. 2 (1981): 126–155.

79. Robert W. Cox, *Production Power and World Order* (New York: Columbia University Press, 1987); Peter Taylor, *Britain and the Cold War: 1945 as Geopolitical Transition* (London: Pinter, 1990); John Agnew and Stuart Corbridge, *Mastering Space: Hegemony, Territory and International Political Economy* (London: Routledge, 1995); See also the later texts John Agnew, *Geopolitics: Re-visioning World Politics* (London: Routledge, 1998); John Agnew, *Geopolitics: Re-visioning World Politics*, 2nd edition (London: Routledge, 2003); and John Agnew, *Hegemony: The New Shape of Global Power* (Philadelphia: Temple University Press, 2005).

80. Lorraine Dowler and Joanne Sharp, "A Feminist Geopolitics?" *Space and Polity* 5, no. 3 (2001): 165–176.

81. The community of political geographers was also very small relative to large disciplines like political science. The later development of constructivism as a theory of international relations was built on some of the same foundations as critical geopolitics.

82. Terrence W. Haverluk, Kevin M. Beauchemin, and Brandon A. Mueller, "The Three Critical Flaws of Critical Geopolitics: Towards a Neo-Classical Geopolitics," *Geopolitics* 19 (2014): 19–39; Phil Kelly, "A Critique of Critical Geopolitics," *Geopolitics* 11 (2006): 24–53; Vicki Squire, "Reshaping Critical Geopolitics? The Materialist Challenge," *Review of International Studies* 41 (2015): 139–159.

83. Robert Kaplan, *The Revenge of Geography* (New York: Random House, 2012); Tim Marshall, *Prisoners of Geography* (New York: Scribner, 2015).

84. Toby Ord, *The Precipice: Existential Risk and the Future of Humanity* (New York: Hachette, 2020).

85. Charbonnier, *Affluence and Freedom*.

86. See Simon Dalby, "Political Geography and Climate Change: Introduction to a Virtual Special Issue of Political Geography on Climate Change and Political Geography, November 2015–February 2016," *Political Geography* 50 (2016) 71–73.

87. This literature is now too extensive to cite fully. See, among others, Jairus Grove, *Savage Ecology: War and Geopolitics at the End of the World* (Durham, NC: Duke University Press, 2019); Sanjay Chaturvedi and Timothy Doyle, *Climate Terror: A Critical Geopolitics of Climate Change* (New York: Palgrave Macmillan, 2015); Shannon O'Lear, Simon Dalby, eds., *Reframing Climate Change: Constructing Ecological Geopolitics* (London: Routledge, 2016).

88. See Simon Dalby, *Environmental Security* (Minneapolis: University of Minnesota Press, 2002) and *Security and Environmental Change* (Cambridge: Polity, 2009).

89. Simon Dalby, *Anthropocene Geopolitics: Globalization, Security, Sustainability* (Ottawa: University of Ottawa Press, 2020), p. 10.
90. Ibid, p. 10.
91. Ibid, p. 70.
92. See, for example, also Bruno Latour, *Facing Gaia: Eight Lectures on the New Climatic Regime* (Cambridge: Polity, 2017); Bruno Latour, *Down to Earth: Politics in the New Climatic Regime* (Cambridge, Polity, 2018); Philip Conway, "Back Down to Earth: Reassembling Latour's Anthropocenic Geopolitics," *Global Discourse* 6 (2016): 43–71; Marc Usher, "Terra Incognita," *Progress in Human Geography* 44 (2019): 1019–1046.
93. Latour, *Down to Earth*, p. 41.

CHAPTER 2

1. Obituary, "H.J. Mackinder, 66 [*sic*], Noted Geographer," *New York Times,* March 8, 1947, p. 13. Mackinder was actually 86 when he died. The two celebrated works are Halford J. Mackinder, "The Geographical Pivot of History," *Geographical Review* 23 (1904): 421–444, and Halford J. Mackinder, *Democratic Ideals and Reality* (London: Constable and Company, 1919).
2. "The Father of Geopolitics," *New York Times*, March 9, 1947, p. E8.
3. See W. H. Parker, *Mackinder: Geography as an Aid to Statecraft* (Oxford: Clarendon Press, 1982), p. 147.
4. See Gearóid Ó Tuathail, *Critical Geopolitics: The Politics of Writing Global Space* (Minneapolis: University of Minnesota Press, 1996). The journalistic habit of searching for the "brain" behind a state leader endures and presents various geopoliticians as gray cardinals exerting power behind the scenes.
5. Edward Mead Earle, "Introduction," in Mackinder, *Democratic Ideals and Reality* (New York: Henry Holt), p. xxi.
6. Major George Fielding Eliot, "Foreword," in Mackinder, *Democratic Ideals and Reality*, pp. vii–xi.
7. Timothy Barney, *Mapping the Cold War: Cartography and the Framing of America's International Power* (Chapel Hill: University of North Carolina Press, 2015).
8. So far there have been three biographies of Mackinder. Besides Kearns and Parker (note 3) see Brian Boulet, *Halford Mackinder: A Biography* (College Station: Texas A & M University Press, 1987).
9. Amitav Acharya and Barry Buzan, *The Making of Global International Relations* (Cambridge: Cambridge University Press, 2019).

10. On Mackinder's project as the cultivation of a way of seeing, see chapter three of my book *Critical Geopolitics* (Minneapolis: University of Minnesota Press, 1996), pp. 75–110.

11. Halford J. Mackinder, "The Physical Basis of Political Geography," *Scottish Geographical Magazine* 6 (1890): 78–84.

12. Halford J. Mackinder, "Geography and History," letter to the editor, *The Times*, February 9, 1905, p. 6.

13. Halford J. Mackinder, "The Human Habitat," *The Scottish Geographical Magazine* 47, no. 6 (1931): 321–335 (see pp. 323–324).

14. Ibid., p. 324.

15. Ibid., p. 331. Famously, this phrase was first used by Herbert Spencer (1820–1903) and only later adopted by Charles Darwin as an alternative description of the process of natural selection. The phrase resonated with the Malthusian expression Darwin used from the outset: "struggle for existence." Both phrases were central to the ideology of social Darwinism, the belief that social groups were in existential struggles with each other, and that those who ruled were superior and deserving.

16. Halford Mackinder, "What London Thinks," letter to the editor, *The Times*, September 8, 1908, p. 6..

17. For a discussion see Kearns, *Geopolitics and Empire*, pp. 107–112.

18. Halford J. Mackinder, "On the Scope and Methods of Geography," *Proceedings of the Royal Geographical Society and Monthly Record of Geography* 9, no. 3 (1887): 141–174. Quote is on p. 142.

19. Mackinder, "Pivot," p. 422.

20. James Bryce, "Geography in Its Relation to History," *Proceedings of the Royal Geographical Society and Monthly Record of Geography* 8, no. 3 (1886): 193–198.

21. Mackinder, "Pivot," p. 422.

22. Mackinder, *Democratic Ideals*, p. 8.

23. Mackinder, "Finance Bill," *Hansard*, May 18, 1916, p. 1726.

24. Mackinder, "Habitat," pp. 332–333.

25. Halford J. Mackinder, "Man-Power as a Measure of National and Imperial Strength," *National and English Review* 14 (1905): 143.

26. Malthus, *Essay on the Principle of Population*, p. 29.

27. Halford Mackinder, *Britain and the British Seas* (London: William Heinemann, 1902), p. 343.

28. Halford Mackinder, *The Nations of the Modern World: An Elementary Study in Geography* (London: George Philip and Son, 1911), p. 270.

29. Mackinder, "Canadian Preference," *Hansard*, February 8, 1911, p. 325.

30. Mackinder's speculations elicited laughter in Parliament at this time. He responded that those members who laugh have not the imagination to see that from small beginnings still under Britain's control, great things may come. Ibid., p. 326.

31. Mackinder, "Imperial Conference," *Hansard*, April 19, 1911, p. 996.

32. Mackinder, "Debate on the Address," *Hansard*, February 23, 1910, pp. 315–323.

33. Ibid., p. 322; also see Mackinder, "Colonial Preference," *Hansard*, July 21, 1910, p. 1474.

34. Mackinder, *Democratic Ideals*, p. 208.

35. Ibid., p. 193.

36. Mackinder, *Democratic Ideals*, p. 199.

37. Halford Mackinder, *Our Own Islands: An Elementary Study in Geography* (London: George Philip and Son, 14th edition, 1914), p. 5.

38. Halford Mackinder, *The Modern British State: An Introduction to the Study of Civics* (London: George Philip and Son, 2nd edition, 1922), p. 67.

39. Halford Mackinder, *The World War and After* (London: George Philip and Son, 1924), pp. 238–239.

40. Ibid., p. 217.

41. Ibid., p. 217.

42. Mackinder, "Vote of Credit," *Hansard*, November 10, 1915, p. 1239.

43. Mackinder, "Man-Power."

44. Mackinder, *Democratic Ideals*, p. 128.

45. Mackinder, "Finance Bill," *Hansard*, May 21, 1919, p. 465.

46. Mackinder, "Navy Estimates," *Hansard*, July 22, 1921, p. 921.

47. In 1915 Mackinder worried about German expansion into eastern Europe. He viewed the vast wealth potential and enormous resources of Russia as an important asset in the fight against Germany. Mackinder, "Vote of Credit," *Hansard*, November 10, 1915, p. 1239.

48. Ibid., p. 11.

49. Mackinder, "Man-Power."

50. Mackinder, "Debate on the Address," *Hansard*, February 23, 1910, p. 319.

51. Ibid., p. 323.

52. Ibid., p. 24.

53. Mackinder, *Democratic Ideals*, p. 38.

54. See the discussion of "space perception" in Friedrich Ratzel, *Politische Geographie* (Leipzig: Derlag von Oldenburg, 1897). Klinke argues that spatial ideas were ultimately "second-order phenomena" to Ratzel. Klinke, *Life, Earth, Colony*, p. 105.

55. Mackinder, *Democratic Ideals*, pp. 40–41.

56. Ibid., pp. 200–201. For further on this argument, see my *Critical Geopolitics*, pp. 75–110.

57. Mackinder, *Democratic Ideals*, p. 27.

58. Ibid., p. 29.

59. Ibid., p. 28.

60. The word "revolution" is used three different ways in *Democratic Ideals and Reality*. The most common manner is to describe eventful historical moments, like the English, French, and Russian revolutions. The second is to describe significant changes in the mentality of people about the world and the relation of spaces within it. The third is to describe how technology transforms spatial relations irrespective of what people think about it.

61. Mackinder, "The Physical Basis of Political Geography," p. 79.

62. Mackinder, "Geographical Pivot," p. 427.

63. Ibid., p. 432.

64. Ibid., p. 434.

65. Mackinder, *Democratic Ideals*, pp. 147–148.

66. Ibid., p. 12.

67. Ibid., p. 96.

68. Ibid., p. 84.

69. "MPs Trip on R.36," *The Times*, June 18, 1921, p. 7. Mackinder's friend, Lord George Curzon (1859–1925), former viceroy of India, was part of this trip.

70. "Reprieve for Airships? August 1 the Last Day; Sir H. Mackinder's Appeal," *The Times*, July 5, 1921, p. 11.

71. Halford J. Mackinder, "Far Australasia," letter to the editor, *The Times*, July 5, 1921, p. 11..

72. "Reprieve for Airships? R33 Continental Voyage" and "Airships Safe and Swift," *The Times*, July 7, 1921, p. 10 and Sir Trevor Dawson, letter to the editor, "Reprieve for Airships? War and Commercial Uses. Financial Success Assured," *The Times*, July 11, 1921, p. 11.

73. "The Fate of R.38," *The Times*, August 25, 1921, p. 9.

74. Mackinder, *The World War and After*, p. 277.

75. Ibid., p. 285.

76. Mackinder served as chair of the committee from 1920 to 1945 (in title), the only paid position. One historian attributed the achievements of the committee to Mackinder's "tireless energy (despite his age), his meticulous attention to detail, and his visionary dedication to the imperial ideal" (p. 212). See Kevin Burley, "The Imperial Shipping Committee," *Journal of Imperial and Commonwealth History* 2, no. 2 (1974): 206–225.

77. Halford J. Mackinder, "Steamship Speeds. Economic Times to Australia. Imperial Committee's Conclusions," *The Times*, November 3, 1926, p. 15. He argued that the ocean ferries between Southampton and New York are subsidized by the "millionaires of America who pay high fares for great speed and luxury," whereas there are few rich people among the six million Australians.
78. Halford J. Mackinder, "The Geographical Pivot of History," *Geographical Review* 23 (2004): 421–444.
79. Ibid., p. 421.
80. Ibid., p. 422.
81. Halford J. Mackinder, "The Round World and the Winning of the Peace," *Foreign Affairs* 21, 4 (1943): 604.
82. C. Kruszewski, "The Pivot of History," *Foreign Affairs* 32 (1954).
83. Gerry Kearns, "Topple the Racists 2: Decolonising the Space and the Institutional Memory of Geography," *Geography* 106, no. 1 (2021): 4–15.
84. For a discussion of Mackinder's influence in Russia, see Charles Clover, *Black Wind, White Snow: The Rise of Russia's New Nationalism* (New Haven, CT: Yale University Press, 2016).
85. Mackinder, "Geographical Pivot," p. 438.

CHAPTER 3

1. Mackinder, *Democratic Ideals and Reality*, p. 150.
2. Ibid., pp. 161–162.
3. Torbjorn Knutsen, "Halford J. Mackinder, Geopolitics and the Heartland Thesis," *The International History Review* 36, no. 5 (2014): 835–857.
4. Mackinder, "Vote of Credit," *Hansard*, November 10, 1916, p. 1238.
5. Quoted in Carl Schmitt *Land and Sea: A World-Historical Meditation.* Translated by Samuel Garrett Zeitlin (Candor, New York: Telos Press, 2015), p. 73. The original source is Sir Walter Raleigh, "A Discourse of the Invention of Ships, Anchors, Compass, &amp c.," *The Works of Sir Walter Raleigh, Kt.* (Oxford: University Press, 1829, reprinted 1965), vol. 8, p. 325.
6. Eric Ellis, *The Anthropocene: A Short Introduction* (New York: Oxford University Press, 2018), pp. 10–11.
7. James C. Scott, *Against the Grain: A Deep History of the Earliest States* (New Haven, CT: Yale University Press, 2017), p. 40.
8. David Graeber and David Wengrow, *The Dawn of Everything: A New History of Humanity* (New York: Farrar, Straus and Giroux, 2021), p. 119.

9. Ratzel described *lebensraum* and *ecumene* as equivalent, but technically the latter referred only to the known inhabited Earth and not habitable parts unknown, of which there were many. Klinke, *Life, Colony, Death,* chapter 4.

10. Much of the literature within Geography is at pains to disassociate human territoriality from biological drive or aggressive instinct, but it is quite comfortable making universal generalizations thereafter based on the parochial experience of Europe in the world. See Robert Sack, "Human Territoriality: A Theory," *Annals of the Association of American Geographers* 73 (1983): 55–74. More generally, see David Storey, *Territories: The Claiming of Space.* Third edition (London: Routledge, 2024).

11. Dominic D. P. Johnson and Monica Duffy Toft, "Grounds for War: The Evolution of Territorial Conflict," *International Security* 38, no. 3 (Winter 2013/14): 9.

12. Such arguments are justifications for Darwinian versions of realism. See Bradley A. Thayer, "Bringing in Darwin: Evolutionary Theory, Realism, and International Politics," *International Security* 25, no. 2 (2000): 124–151; Azar Gat, "So Why Do People Fight? Evolutionary Theory and the Causes of War," *European Journal of International Relations* 15: 571–599; and Richard Ned Lebow, "You Can't Keep a Bad Idea Down: Evolutionary Biology and International Relations," *International Politics Review* 1 (2013): 2–10.

13. Dominic D. P. Johnson and Monica Duffy Toft identify a series of proximate mechanisms by which human territoriality finds expression: the endowment effect, loss aversion, emotional attachment to homeland, sacralizing land, and the "first owner" bias. "Correspondence: Evolution and Territorial Conflict," *International Security* 39, no. 3 (Winter 2014–2015): 198.

14. Dominic D. P. Johnson and Monica Duffy Toft, "Bringing 'Geo' Back into Politics: Evolution, Territoriality and the Contest over Ukraine (with comment)," *Cliodynamics* 5 (2014): 87–122.

15. Scott, *Against the Grain,* p. 118.

16. Graeber and Wengrow, *The Dawn of Everything,* pp. 276–327.

17. Scott, *Against the Grain,* p. 119.

18. Carl Schmitt, *The Nomos of the Earth* (New York: Telos, 2006), p. 42.

19. Jean Gottman, *The Significance of Territory* (Charlottesville: University of Virginia Press, 1973); Stuart Elden, *The Birth of Territory* (Chicago: University of Chicago Press, 2013); Charles Maier, *Once Within Borders* (Cambridge, MA: Belknap Press, 2016).

20. Carl Schmitt, *Land and Sea* (Candor, NY: Telos Press, 2015).

21. Jane Jacobs, *Systems of Survival* (New York: Random House, 1992).

22. Gottman, *Significance*, p. 14.

23. António Ferraz de Oliveira, "Territory and Theory in Political Geography, c. 1970s–90s: Jean Gottmann's *The Significance of Territory*," *Territory, Politics, Governance* 9, no. 4 (2021): 553–570.

24. For a sense of the extensive debate within the field of geography on territory and territoriality, see John Allen, "Three Spaces of power: Territory, Networks, plus a Topological Twist in the Tale of Domination and Authority," *Journal of Power* 2, no. 2 (2009): 197–212; Alexander Murphy, "Entente Territorial: Sack and Raffestin on Territoriality," *Environment and Planning D: Society and Space* 30 (2012): 159–172; David Storey, *A Research Agenda for Territory and Territoriality* (Cheltenham, UK: Edward Edgar, 2020).

25. Franck Billé, Somatic States: *On Cartography, Geobodies, Bodily Integrity* (Durham: Duke University Press, 2024).

26. Agnew, *Geopolitics: Re-visioning World Politics*, pp. 15–34. See also Jordan Branch, *The Cartographic State: Maps, Territory, and the Origins of Sovereignty* (Cambridge: Cambridge University Press, 2014); Ayesha Ramachandran, *The Worldmakers: Global Imaging in Early Modern Europe.* (Chicago: University of Chicago Press, 2015).

27. J. C. Sharman, *Empires of the Weak* (Princeton: NJ Princeton University Press, 2019).

28. See Immanuel Wallerstein's four-volume set, *The Modern World-System* (Berkeley: University of California Press).

29. Julian Go, *Patterns of Empire* (New York: Cambridge University Press, 2011).

30. Dipesh Chakrabarty, *The Climate of History in a Planetary Age* (Chicago: University of Chicago Press, 2021).

31. William Connolly, *Facing the Planetary: Entangled Humanism and the Politics of Swarming* (Durham, NC: Duke University Press, 2017).

32. Elizabeth Kolbert, *The Sixth Extinction: An Unnatural History* (New York: Henry Holt, 2014).

33. Sonja Sengupta, "Can Nations Be Sued for Weak Climate Action? We'll Soon Get an Answer," *New York Times*, March 29, 2023, https://www.nytimes.com/2023/03/29/climate/united-nations-vanuatu.html.

34. Charbonnier, *Affluence and Freedom*, pp. 66–71; Latour, *Facing Gaia*, pp. 266–292.

35. Pierre Charbonnier, "'Where Is Your Freedom Now?' How the Moderns Became Ubiquitous," in B. Latour and P. Weibel, eds., *Critical*

Zones: The Science and Politics of Landing on Earth (London: MIT Press, 2020), 76–79.

36. For a creative upscaling of classical geopolitical narratives into IR theory, see Daniel Deudney, "Geopolitics as Theory: Historical Security Materialism," *European Journal of International Relations* 6 (2000): 77–107.

37. Phil Kelly, *Classical Geopolitics: A New Analytical Model* (Stanford, CA: Stanford University Press, 2016).

38. See also Saul Cohen, *Geopolitics of the World System* (Lanham, MD: Rowman and Littlefield, 2003).

39. Kelly, to his credit, has sought to cultivate this. See Phil Kelly, "A Critique of Critical Geopolitics," *Geopolitics* 11 (2006): 24–53.

40. Pierre Bourdieu, *The Field of Cultural Production* (New York: Columbia University Press, 1993), Neil Fligstein and Doug McAdam, *A Theory of Fields* (New York: Oxford University Press, 2012).

41. Julian Go, "Global Fields and Imperial Forms: Field Theory and the British and American Empires," *Sociological Theory* 26, no. 3 (2008): 206.

42. The understanding of spatial landscapes as the product of layers of previous investment that have sedimented together to give localities distinctive identities was a popular metaphor within British economic geography in the 1980s. See, for example, Doreen Massey, *Spatial Divisions of Labour: Social Structures and the Geography of Production* (London: Macmillan, 1984).

43. These are the titles of chapters three and four of *Democratic Ideals and Reality*. Also Charles de Montesquieu, *The Spirit of the Laws* (Cambridge: Cambridge University Press, 1989).

44. See the discussion in de Oliveira, "Territory and Theory in Political Geography, (note 23).

45. The concept of geopolitical codes derives from Alexander George's notion of the "operational code" of leaders as adopted by John Lewis Gaddis to refer to presidential administrations, and subsequently extended almost beyond recognition to refer to the practices of states. See Alexander George, *The Operational Code: A Neglected Approach to the Study of Political Leaders and Decision-Making* (Santa Monica: Rand Corporation, 1967); John Lewis Gaddis, *Strategies of Containment: A Critical Appraisal of Postwar American National Security Policy* (New York: Oxford University Press, 1982), p. ix; Peter Taylor, *Political Geography: World-Economy, Nation-State and Locality* (London: Longman, 1989); Peter Taylor, *Britain and the Cold War: 1945 as Geopolitical Transition* (London: Pinter, 1990); Colin Flint, *Introduction to Geopolitics*, 3rd edition (London: Routledge, 2016).

46. The concept of strategic culture was first developed by the British strategist and Mackinder evangelist Colin Gray. See Alastair Iain Johnston, "Thinking about Strategic Culture," *International Security* 19, no. 4 (Spring 1995): 32–64.

47. The notion is not strictly confined to modern states. Entities that make claims to sovereignty over a certain territory create geopolitical cultures. Thus, unrecognized states like Transnistria, terrorist groups like Al-Qaeda, military alliances like NATO, and multi-state unions like the European Union can have geopolitical cultures. What is crucial is their claim to rule part of the Earth, even if that claim is not realized or pooled in practice.

48. Gertjan Dijkink, *National Identity and Geopolitical Visions: Maps of Pride and Pain* (London: Routledge, 1996).

49. An imaginary is a concept with its origins in psychoanalytic theory, particularly the work of Jacques Lacan. It has become a commonsense term for a shared taken-for-granted or unconscious concept about the world. A geographical imaginary, thus, refers to an unconscious spatial ordering of the world. As with the concept of imagination more broadly, I am using the term *geopolitical imaginary* to describe a particular class of geographical imaginaries, those that operate as sense-making devices to organize and spatialize politics among states.

50. See the work that appears in the journal *Geopolitics* and *Political Geography*. Also see, inter alia, Gerard Toal and Carl Dahlman, *Bosnia Remade* (Oxford: Oxford University Press, 2011); Bojan Savić, "Where Is Serbia? Traditions of Spatial Identity and State Positioning in Serbian Geopolitical Culture," *Geopolitics* 19, no. 3 (2014): 684–718; Laurence Broers, *Armenia-Azerbaijan: Anatomy of a Rivalry* (Edinburgh: Edinburgh University Press, 2019).

51. Susan Smith and Rachel Pain, eds., *Fear: Critical Geopolitics and Everyday Life* (London: Routledge, 2008); Sara Smith, "Intimate Geopolitics: Religion, Marriage, and Reproductive Bodies in Leh, Ladakh," *Annals of the Association of American Geographers* 102, no. 6 (2012): 1511–1528.

52. John O'Loughlin and Gerard Toal, "The Geopolitical Orientations of Ordinary Belarusians: Survey Evidence from Early 2020," *Post-Soviet Affairs* 38 (2022): 43–61.

53. John O'Loughlin, Gerard Toal, and Kristin M. Bakke, "Is Belarus in the Midst of a Generational Upheaval?," *Global Voices*, September 17, 2020, https://globalvoices.org/2020/09/17/is-belarus-in-the-midst-of-a-generational-upheaval/.

54. On the "intermestic" and other hybrid concepts foregrounded by globalization, see Timothy W. Luke, "Placing Power/Siting Space: The Politics of Global and Local in the New World Order," *Environment and Planning D: Society and Space* 12 (1994): 613–628. See also Campbell Craig and Fredrik Logevall, *America's Cold War: The Politics of Insecurity* (Cambridge, MA: Belknap Press, 2009), p. 10.

55. David Cadier, "The Geopoliticisation of the EU's Eastern Partnership," *Geopolitics* 24, no. 1 (2019): 71–99.

56. In doing so, they were echoing the Belarussian opposition candidate Sviatlana Tsikhanouskaya. See https://twitter.com/JoeBiden/status/1296107655723921415; Michael Birnbaum and Isabelle Khurshudyan, "On Belarus, E.U. Plans Sanctions but Tries to Avoid Conflict between Russia and the West," *Washington Post*, August 19, 2020, https://www.washingtonpost.com/world/europe/belarus-eu-sanctions-election/2020/08/19/f3788fb2-e21e-11ea-82d8-5e55d47e90ca_story.html.

57. "Lavrov: Foreign Players Seek to Impose Their Own Rules on Belarus," *Belta News*, August 19, 2020, https://eng.belta.by/politics/view/lavrov-foreign-players-seek-to-impose-their-own-rules-on-belarus-132698-2020/.

58. See Duncan Bell, *The Idea of Greater Britain: Empire and the Future of World Order, 1860–1900* (Princeton: Princeton University Press, 2007).

59. Duncan Bell, *Dreamworlds of Race: Empire and the Utopian Destiny of Anglo-America* (Princeton, NJ: Princeton University Press, 2020).

60. Srdjan Vucetic, *The Anglosphere: A Genealogy of a Racialized Identity in International Relations* (Stanford: Stanford University Press, 2011).

61. Marlene Laruelle, "The 'Russian World': Russia's Soft Power and Geopolitical Imagination," *Center for Global Interests Papers*, May 2015.

62. Patrick Jackson, *Civilizing the Enemy* (Ann Arbor: University of Michigan Press, 2006).

63. Emma Hutchison, *Affective Communities in World Politics* (Cambridge: Cambridge University Press, 2016).

64. MacLeish quoted in David Reynolds, *From Munich to Pearl Harbor* (Chicago: Ivan Dee, 2001), p. 96.

65. Ibid.

66. Frank Costigliola, *Roosevelt's Lost Alliances: How Personal Politics Helped Start the Cold War* (Princeton, NJ: Princeton University Press, 2013).

67. "The Atlantic Charter." August 14, 1941, https://www.nato.int/cps/en/natohq/official_texts_16912.htm.

68. Smith, *American Empire*, Part IV.

69. "Atlantic Charter."

70. Carl Schmitt, *Land and Sea: A World-Historical Meditation* (Candor, NY: Telos Press, 2015), p. 46. Throughout, Schmitt uses the terms "England" and "the English," even referring to England as an island, not exactly a reassuring grasp of geography from a legal scholar.

71. Karl Marx and Friedrich Engels, *The Communist Manifesto* (New York: International Publishers, 2014).

72. Marshall Berman, *All That Is Solid Melts into Air* (New York: Verso, 1983); David Harvey, *The Condition of Postmodernity* (Oxford: Wiley Blackwell, 1991).

73. Ian Klinke, "Chronopolitics: A Conceptual Matrix," *Progress in Human Geography* 37 (2012): 673–690.

74. Mackinder, *The World War and After*, p. 278.

CHAPTER 4

1. NATO, Bucharest Summit Declaration, April 3, 2008, https://www.nato.int/cps/en/natolive/official_texts_8443.htm.

2. Michael Hechter, *Internal Colonialism: The Celtic Fringe in British National Development, 1536–1966* (Berkeley: University of California Press, 1977).

3. Ian Lustick, *Unsettled States Disputed Lands* (Ithaca, NY: Cornell University Press, 1993).

4. All quotations are from the speech by Halford Mackinder to the Scottish Unionist Association as reported in *The Glasgow Herald*, January 20, 1922, p. 10.

5. Anders Stephanson, *Manifest Destiny: American Expansion and the Empire of Right* (New York: Hill and Wang, 1995); Greg Grandin, *The End of the Myth* (New York: Metropolitan Books, 2019); A. G. Hopkins, *American Empire: A Global History* (Princeton, NJ: Princeton University Press, 2018).

6. Daniel Immerwahr, *How to Hide an Empire: A History of the Greater United States* (New York: Farrar, Straus and Giroux, 2019).

7. Carlotta Gall and Tom de Waal, *Chechnya: Calamity in the Caucasus* (New York: New York University Press, 1999).

8. Crisis Group, *Chechnya: The Inner Abroad* (Brussels: Crisis Group, 2015). https://www.crisisgroup.org/europe-central-asia/caucasus/russianorth-caucasus/chechnya-inner-abroad

9. Olga Vendena, "Social Polarization and Ethnic Segregation in Moscow," *Eurasian Geography and Economics* 43 (2002) 3: 216–243.

10. Owen Lattimore, *Pivot of Asia: Singkiang and the Inner Frontiers of China and Russia* (Boston: Little Brown, 1950).

11. Brandon Barbour and Reece Jones, "Criminals, Terrorists, and Outside Agitators: Representational Tropes of the 'Other' in the 5 July Xinjiang, China Riots," *Geopolitics* 18 (2013): 95–114.

12. James Millward, "The Uighurs' Suffering Deserves Targeted Solutions, Not Anti-Chinese Posturing," *The Guardian*, July 27, 2020.

13. John Sudworth, "China's Hidden Camps." *BBC News*, October 24, 2018, https://www.bbc.co.uk/news/resources/idt-sh/China_hidden_camps. See also Sarah Tynen, "State Territorialization through *Shequ* Community Centres: Bureaucratic Confusion in Xinjiang, China," *Territory, Politics, Governance* 8, no. 1 (2020): 7–22.

14. Associated Press, "China Cuts Uighur Births with IUDs, Abortion, Sterilization," June 29, 2020, https://apnews.com/269b3de1af34e17c1941a514f78d764c.

15. Joanne Smith Finley, "Why Scholars and Activists Increasingly Fear a Uyghur Genocide in Xinjiang," *Journal of Genocide Research* 23 (2021): 348-370.

16. Benno Weiner, *The Chinese Revolution on the Tibetan Frontier* (Ithaca, NY: Cornell University Press, 2020).

17. Laura Hughes, "Britain Opens Door to Citizenship for 300,000 Hong Kong Residents," *Financial Times*, May 29, 2020.

18. Richard W. Maass, *The Picky Eagle: How Democracy and Xenophobia Limited US Territorial Expansion* (Ithaca, NY: Cornell University Press, 2020).

19. Joseph Masco, *The Nuclear Borderlands: The Manhattan Project in Post-Cold War New Mexico* (Princeton, NJ: Princeton University Press, 2006).

20. Matthew Farish, "The Lab and the Land: Overcoming the Arctic in Cold War Alaska," *Iris* 104 (2013): 1–29.

21. Yarimar Bonilla, "The Coloniality of Disaster: Race, Empire, and the Temporal Logics of Emergency in Puerto Rico, USA," *Political Geography* 78 (2020): 1–11.

22. Comprehensive Nuclear Test Ban Treaty Organization, "The Soviet Union's Nuclear Testing Programme," https://www.ctbto.org/nuclear-testing/the-effects-of-nuclear-testing/the-soviet-unionsnuclear-testing-programme.

23. Kate Brown, *Plutopia: Nuclear Families, Atomic Cities, and the Great Soviet and American Petroleum Disasters* (New York: Oxford University Press, 2013).

24. Marlene Laruelle, *Russia's Arctic Strategies and the Future of the Far North* (New York: M. E. Sharpe, 2014).

25. The idea of natural borders, of course, is deeply problematic. See Juliet Fall, "Artificial States? On the Enduring Geographical Myth of Natural Borders." *Political Geography* 29 (2010): 140–147.

26. Caroline Humphrey and Franck Billé, *On the Edge: Life along the Russia-China Border* (Cambridge, MA: Harvard University Press, 2021).

27. John J. Mearsheimer, *The Tragedy of Great Power Politics* (New York: Norton, 2001), pp. 114–128; John Mearsheimer, "Why the Ukraine Crisis Is the West's Fault: The Liberal Delusions That Provoked Putin," *Foreign Affairs* 93, no. 5 (2014): 77–84, 85–89.

28. Carl Schmitt, *The Nomos of the Earth in the International Law of Jus Publicum Europaeum* (New York: Telos Press, 2007), p. 281.

29. James Monroe, Text of the 1823 address to Congress.

30. Jay Sexton, *The Monroe Doctrine: Empire and Nation in Nineteenth-Century America* (New York: Hill and Wang, 2012).

31. Carl Schmitt, "The Grossraum Order of International Law with a Ban on Intervention for Spatially Foreign Powers: A Contribution to the Concept of Reich in International Law," in Carl Schmitt, *Writings on War*, translated and edited by Timothy Nunan (Oxford: Polity Press, 2011), p. 83.

32. Claudio Minca, Rory Rowan, *On Schmitt and Space* (London: Routledge, 2016); John O'Loughlin and Herman Van Der Wusten, "Political Geography of Panregions," *Geographical Review* 80, no. 1 (1990): 1–20.

33. Mark Mazower, *Hitler's Empire: How the Nazis Ruled Europe* (New York: Penguin, 2008); Jeremy Yellen, *The Greater East Asia Co-Prosperity Sphere: When Total Empire Met Total War* (Ithaca, NY: Cornell University Press, 2020).

34. Lloyd Gardner, *Spheres of Influence: The Great Powers Partition Europe, From Munich to Yalta* (Chicago: Elephant Paperbacks, 1994).

35. Paul Keal, *Unspoken Rules and Superpower Dominance* (London: Macmillan, 1983).

36. Megan Black, *The Global Interior: Mineral Frontiers and American Power* (Cambridge: Harvard University Press, 2018).

37. Toal, *Near Abroad*, pp. 80–87.

38. Andrew Kramer, "Russia Claims Its Sphere of Influence in the World," *New York Times*, August 31, 2008.

39. Amatai Etzioni, "Spheres of Influence: A Reconceptualization," *The Fletcher Forum of World Affairs* 39, no. 2 (2015): 117–132; Susanna Hast, *Spheres of Influence in International Relations: History, Theory and Politics* (London: Routledge, 2016); Filippo Costa Buranelli, "Spheres of Influence as Negotiated Hegemony—The Case of Central Asia,"

Geopolitics 23, no. 2 (2018): 378–403; Van Jackson, "Understanding Spheres of Influence in International Politics," *European Journal of International Security* 5 (2020): 255–273.

40. Roger Morehouse, *The Devils' Alliance: Hitler's Pact with Stalin, 1939–1941* (New York: Basic Books, 2014).

41. Campbell Craig and Fredrik Logevall, *America's Cold War: The Politics of Insecurity* (Cambridge, MA: Belknap Press, 2009).

42. See Vineet Thakur and Peter Vale, *South Africa, Race and the Making of International Relations* (Lanham, MD: Rowman and Littlefield, 2020).

43. Halford J. Mackinder, "The Great Trade Routes," *The Institute of Bankers* 12 (1900). Mackinder gave a series of four lectures on the theme to the Institute of Bankers in London in the last months of 1899.

44. I owe this word to my colleague and co-author Timothy Luke. See Timothy W. Luke and Gearóid Ó Tuathail, "Global Flowmations, Local Fundamentalisms, and Fast Geopolitics: 'America' in an Accelerating World Order," in Andrew Herod, Susan Roberts, and Gearóid Ó Tuathail, eds., *An Unruly World? Globalization, Governance and Geography* (London: Routledge, 1998), pp. 72–94.

45. John A. Thompson, *A Sense of Power: The Roots of America's Global Role* (Ithaca, NY: Cornell University Press, 2015).

46. President Carter, "State of the Union Address," January 23, 1980.

47. Daniel Yergin, *The Prize: The Epic Quest for Oil, Money, and Power* (New York: Simon & Schuster, 1991), p. 140.

48. John Morrissey, *The Long War: Centcom, Grand Strategy, and Global Security* (Athens: University of Georgia Press, 2017).

49. Henry Farrell and Abe Newman, "Weaponized Interdependence: How Global Economic Networks Shape State Coercion," *International Security* 44 (2019): 42–79.

50. Marieke de Goede and Carola Westermeier, "Infrastructural Geopolitics," *International Studies Quarterly* 66 (2022): 1–12.

51. Chris Miller, *Chip War: The Fight for the World's Most Critical Technology* (New York: Scribner, 2022).

52. Catherine Tatiana Dunlop, *Cartophilia: Maps and the Search for Identity in the French-German Borderland* (Chicago: University of Chicago Press, 2015).

53. The disputed section is a 550-mile stretch through the Himalayas that was demarcated by a treaty in 1914 involving Britain, India, and Tibet. Chinese state representatives never accepted the demarcated border line, named the McMahon line after the British colonial official that first drew it.

54. *BBC News*, "Galwan Valley: China and India Clash on Freezing and Inhospitable Battlefield," June 17, 2020, https://www.bbc.com/news/world-asia-india-53076781. Jeffrey Gettleman, "Caught between Indian and Chinese Troops, at 15,000 Feet," *New York Times*, July 11, 2020, https://www.nytimes.com/2020/07/11/world/asia/india-china-border-ladakh.html.

55. Mackinder, *Democratic Ideals and Reality*, p. 161. Mackinder's map was crudely drawn and conceptualized. He named a section of space as Ukraine but not as a separate state. His map labels what became Yugoslavia as Great Serbia.

56. James Fairgrive, *Geography and World Power* (London: University of London Press, 1915), p. 329.

57. Timothy W. Snyder, *Bloodlands: Europe between Hitler and Stalin* (New York: Basic Books, 2010).

58. Gary Bertsch, Cassady Craft, Scott Jones, and Michael Beck, eds., *Crossroads and Conflict: Security and Foreign Policy in the Caucasus and Central Asia* (New York: Routledge, 2000); Donald Rayfield, *Edge of Empires: A History of Georgia* (London: Reaktion Books, 2012).

59. Alexander Cooley, *Great Game, Local Rules: The New Great Power Contest in Central Asia* (New York: Oxford University Press, 2012);

60. Cohen, *Geopolitics of the World System*, p. 43. The terms "crush zone" and "shatterbelt" are sometimes used interchangeably. See Kelly, *Classical Geopolitics*, p. 185.

61. Nicholas Spykman, *The Geography of the Peace* (New York: Harcourt, Brace, 1944)

62. Franck Billé, "Auratic Geographies: Buffers, Backyards, Entanglements," *Geopolitics* 11 April 2021.

63. Peter Trubowitz, *Politics and Strategy: Partisan Ambition and American Statecraft* (Princeton, NJ: Princeton University Press, 2011).

64. Anssi Passi, *Territories, Boundaries and Consciousness: The Changing Geographies of the Finnish-Russian Border* (London: Wiley, 1997).

65. Karen McVeigh, "High Seas Treaty: Historic Deal to Protect International Waters Finally Reached at UN," *The Guardian*, March 4, 2023.

66. Text of the Outer Space Treaty of 1967, available at https://history.nasa.gov/1967treaty.html.

67. Peggy Hollinger and Clive Cookson, "Europe Envisages Sending Astronauts to the Moon in Space Agency's Own Craft," *Financial Times*, June 6, 2023.

68. Adam Satariano, Scott Reinhard, Cade Metz, Sheera Frenkel and Malika Khurana, "Elon Musk's Unmatched Power in the Stars," *New York Times*, July 28, 2023, https://www.nytimes.com/interactive/2023/07/28/business/starlink.html.

69. Wendy Whitman Cobb, "Russian Anti-Satellite Weapon Test: What Happened and What Are the Risks?," *The Conversation*, November 16, 2021.

70. Kenneth Chang, "'Nothing Short of Amazing': NASA Mars Helicopter Makes Longest Flight Yet," *New York Times*, April 25, 2021.

71. James Amos, "China Releases Videos of its Zhurong Mars Rover," *BBC News*, June 27, 2021.

72. See https://emiratesmarsmission.ae/.

73. Jackie Wattles, Manveena Suri and Vedika Sud, "India becomes the fourth country ever to land a spacecraft on the moon." *CNN*, August 24, 2023, https://www.cnn.com/2023/08/23/world/chandrayaan-3-lunar-landing-attempt-scn/index.html

74. Synthesis Report of the IPCC Sixth Assessment Report (AR6), March 20, 2023, p. 25.

75. Vladimir Putin's annual news conference, December 23, 2021, http://en.kremlin.ru/events/president/news/67438.

76. Speech of Xi Jinping, General Secretary of the Central Committee of the Communist Party of China, President of China to the Democratic National Construction Association and the Federation of Industry and Commerce, March 6, 2023, http://www.news.cn/politics/leaders/2023-03/06/c_1129417096.htm.

CHAPTER 5

1. Lowe writes that an "economy of affirmation and forgetting" structures liberal ways of understanding. This "economy civilizes and develops freedom for 'man' in modern Europe and North America, while relegating others to geographical and temporal spaces that are constituted as backward, uncivilized, and unfree." See Lisa Lowe, *The Intimacies of Four Continents* (Durham: Duke University 2015), p. 3. See also Charbonnier, *Affluence and Freedom*, pp. 58–63.

2. The origin of this creed is usually credited to Immanuel Kant's 1795 essay on perpetual peace. For an incisive discussion of how modern conceptions of peace are embedded in ecological unsustainability see Pierre Charbonnier's forthcoming book on war ecology (Paris: La

Découverte, 2024). I am grateful to Pierre for sharing the first chapter of this welcome new book with me.

3. Benjamin Barber, *Jihad versus McWorld* (New York: Ballantine Books, 1996). See the large literature on 'democratic peace theory' within International Relations starting with Michael W. Doyle, "Kant, Liberal Legacies, and Foreign Affairs." *Philosophy and Public Affairs*, 12, no. 3 (1983): 205–235.

4. Mackinder, *The World War and After*, pp. 238–239.

5. David Campbell, *Writing Security* (Minneapolis: University of Minnesota Press, 1992).

6. Anija Curanović, *The Sense of Mission in Russian Foreign Policy* (New York: Routledge, 2021), p. 3.

7. Agnew, *Geopolitics*, chapter three.

8. Patrick Porter, *The False Promise of Liberal Order: Nostalgia, Delusion and the Rise of Trump* (Cambridge: Polity, 2020).

9. Teju Cole, "The White Savior Industrial Complex," *The Atlantic.* March 21, 2012, https://www.theatlantic.com/international/archive/2012/03/the-white-savior-industrial-complex/254843/.

10. On civil religion in the United States see Robert Bellagh, *Beyond Belief: Essays on Religion in a Post-Traditional World.* (Berkeley: University of California Press, 1991). On civil religion in US foreign policy see Walter McDougall, *The Tragedy of U.S. Foreign Policy: How America's Civil Religion Betrayed the National Interest* (New Haven: Yale University Press, 2016).

11. Philip Tetlock, "Thinking the Unthinkable: Sacred Values and Taboo Cognitions," *Trends in Cognitive Sciences* 7, no. 7 (2003): 320–324.

12. W. Steffen, W. Broadgate, L. Deutsch, O. Gaffney, and C. Cornelia, "The Trajectory of the Anthropocene: The Great Acceleration," *The Anthropocene Review* 2, no. 1 (2015): 81–98.

13. Figures from https://ourworldindata.org/greenhouse-gas-emissions.

14. For data on the great acceleration, see http://igbp.net website.

15. J. R. McNeill and Peter Engelke, *The Great Acceleration: An Environmental History of the Anthropocene since 1945* (Cambridge, MA: Belknap Press, 2014), p. 5.

16. Odd Arne Westad, *The Global Cold War* (Cambridge: Cambridge University Press, 2007).

17. Geir Lundestad, "Empire by Invitation? The United States and Western Europe, 1945–1952," *Journal of Peace Research* 23, no. 3 (1986): 264–277.

18. Alan Wolfe, *America's Impasse: The Rise and Fall of the Politics of Growth* (Boston: South End Press, 1981), p. 10.

19. Fordism as a futuristic model of capitalism was most influentially elaborated by Antonio Gramsci. See Stefan Link, *Forging Global Fordism: Nazi Germany, Soviet Russia, and the Contest over the Industrial Order* (Princeton, NJ: Princeton University Press, 2020).

20. Elaine Taylor May, *Homeward Bound: American Families in the Cold War Era* (New York: Basic Books, 2008).

21. Marshall Goldman, *Petrostate: Putin, Power and the New Russia* (New York: Oxford University Press, 2008).

22. Joshua P. Howe, ed., *Making Climate Change History: Documents from Global Warming's Past* (Seattle: University of Washington Press, 2017).

23. Roger Revelle, Testimony before the House Committee on Appropriations, February 8, 1956, in Howe, *Making Climate Change History*, p. 63.

24. Roger Revelle and Hans E. Suess, "Carbon Dioxide Exchange between Atmosphere and Ocean and the Question of an Increase of Atmospheric CO_2 during the Past Decades" (1957), in Howe, *Making Climate Change History*, p. 57.

25. Congressional Testimony of Dr. James Hansen to the U.S. Senate Committee on Energy and Natural Resources, June 23, 1988, https://www.sealevel.info/1988_Hansen_Senate_Testimony.html.

26. Simon Evans, "Analysis: Which countries are historically responsible for climate change?" *Carbon Brief*, October 5, 2021, https://www.carbonbrief.org/analysis-which-countries-are-historically-responsible-for-climate-change/.

27. Charter of Paris for a New Europe, Paris, 1990, at https://www.osce.org/files/f/documents/0/6/39516.pdf.

28. William H. Hill, *No Place for Russia: European Security Institutions since 1989* (New York: Columbia University Press, 2018).

29. Goldman, *Petrostate*; see also Alexander Etkind, *Russia Against Modernity* (Cambridge, Polity, 2023).

30. Putin earned a graduate degree in "economic science" with a dissertation on the subject of raw materials and strategic planning. However, there is considerable doubt as to how much this was an original work by Putin. See Fiona Hill and Clifford G. Gaddy, *Mr Putin: Operative in the Kremlin* (Washington, DC: Brookings Institution Press, 2013), pp. 222–223.

31. On the climate change case against pipelines, see Andreas Malm, *How to Blow Up a Pipeline* (London: Verso, 2021).

32. Kathrin Bennhold, "The Former Chancellor Who Became Putin's Man in Germany," *New York Times*, April 23, 2022, https://www.nytimes.

com/2022/04/23/world/europe/schroder-germany-russia-gas-ukra ine-war-energy.html.

33. William J. Burns, *The Back Channel* (New York: Random House, 2020), p. 233.

34. Vladimir Putin, "On the Historical Unity of Russians and Ukrainians," July 12, 2021, available at kremlin.ru.

35. This is an estimate, as the actual subsidies to each "republic" are secret. For a discussion, see Thomas de Waal and Nikolas Twickel, *Beyond Frozen Conflict: Scenarios for the Separatist Conflicts of Eastern Europe* (London: Rowman and Littlefield International, 2020), p. 93.

36. Mary E. Sarotte, *Not One Inch: America, Russia and the Making of the Post-Cold War Stalemate* (New Haven, CT: Yale University Press, 2021).

37. The United Arab Emirates was a major donor to the Atlantic Council in 2021. Qatar also provided significant funding in the past. Other major donors include Amazon, Facebook, Goldman Sachs, the Rockefeller Foundation, and UK Foreign, Commonwealth & Development Office. See https://www.atlanticcouncil.org/in-depth-research-reports/rep ort/2021-annual-report-honor-roll-of-contributors/.

38. Mitchell Orenstein, *The Lands In-Between* (New York: Oxford University Press, 2019); Scott Radnitz, *Revealing Schemes: The Politics of Conspiracy in Russia and the Post-Soviet Region* (New York: Oxford University Press, 2021).

39. Kathrin Bennhold and Anton Troianovski, "Germany's Chancellor Meets with Putin as the Tone of the Crisis Shifts." *New York Times*, February 15, 2022, https://www.nytimes.com/2022/02/15/world/eur ope/germanys-chancellor-prepares-to-meet-with-putin-as-the-tone-of-the-crisis-shifts.html.

40. The White House, "Remarks by President Biden on the United Efforts of the Free World to Support the People of Ukraine, March 26, 2022, The Royal Castle in Warsaw, Poland," https://www.whitehouse.gov/ briefing-room/speeches-remarks/2022/03/26/remarks-by-president-biden-on-the-united-efforts-of-the-free-world-to-support-the-peo ple-of-ukraine/.

41. Lennard de Klerk et al., *Climate Damage Caused by Russia's War in Ukraine*, June 1, 2023, https://climatefocus.com/wp-content/uploads/ 2022/11/clim-damage-by-russia-war-12months.pdf.

42. John Feffer, "Russia's Invasion of Ukraine Is Also an Assault on the Planet," *Foreign Policy in Focus*, June 5, 2023, https://www.commondre ams.org/opinion/russia-s-invasion-of-ukraine-also-assault-on-planet.

43. Svitlana Andrushchenko, "How to Make Russia Pay for War Damage to the Environment," *Financial Times*, April 13, 2023, p. 17.

44. Anastasia Stognei, "Moscow's Record Oil and Gas Revenues Fail to Cover War Cost," *Financial Times*, January 11, 2023, p. 17. On Russia's fossil fuel exports, see https://energyandcleanair.org/financing-put ins-war/.

45. https://ceobs.org/joint-statement-plan-to-address-the-environmen tal-impact-of-war-in-ukraine/.

46. World Meteorological Organization, *The State of the Climate in Europe 2021*. Report available at https://public.wmo.int/en/our-mandate/clim ate/wmo-statement-state-of-global-climate/Europe.

CHAPTER 6

1. Friedrich Ratzel, *Sketches of Urban and Cultural Life in North America*, translated and edited by Steward A. Stehlin (New Brunswick, NJ: Rutgers University Press, 1988).

2. Mackinder, "Geographical Pivot," p. 434.

3. Schmitt has long been termed the Third Reich "crown jurist." After initially backing Hitler's dictatorship, he was marginalized by Nazi party factional politics. Joseph Bendersky, "The Expendable Kronjurist: Carl Schmitt and National Socialism, 1933–36." *Journal of Contemporary History* 14, no. 2 (1979): 309–328.

4. Schmitt, "Author's Foreword," *The Nomos of the Earth*, p. 37.

5. Carl Schmitt, *Dialogues on Power and Space* (Cambridge: Polity, 2015), p. 61.

6. Jeffrey Herf, *Reactionary Modernism: Technology, Culture, and Politics in Weimar and the Third Reich* (Cambridge: Cambridge University Press, 1984).

7. Michael J. Newfeld, *Von Braun: Dreamer of Space, Engineer of War*, (New York: Vintage, 2008).

8. David Beers, "Selling the American Space Dream," *The New Republic*, December 7, 2020; Daniel Deudney, *Dark Skies: Space Expansionism, Planetary Geopolitics, and the Ends of Humanity* (New York: Oxford University Press, 2020); Catherine Newell, *Destined for the Stars: Faith, the Future and America's Final Frontier* (Pittsburg: University of Pittsburg Press, 2019); Mary-Jane Rubenstein, *Astrotopia: The Dangerous Religion of the Corporate Space Race* (Chicago: University of Chicago Press, 2022).

9. A 2014 series of *Captain Marvel* comic books uses the catchphrase "higher, further, faster, more." It became a three-word tagline in a

Superbowl trailer for the Walt Disney Company 2019 film *Captain Marvel*.

10. The idea of the "rocket state" is in Thomas Pynchon's *Gravity Rainbow* (New York: Penguin, 1973). See also Dale Carter, *The Final Frontier: The Rise and Fall of the American Rocket State* (London: Verso, 1988).

11. Schmitt, *Land and Sea*, p. 46.

12. Schmitt, *Nomos of the Earth*, p. 319.

13. Ibid., p. 320.

14. Ibid., pp. 320–321.

15. Ibid., pp. 318–319.

16. Ibid., p. 316.

17. Schmitt, *Land and Sea*, p. 91.

18. Schmitt, *Dialogues on Power and Space*, p. 77.

19. Ibid., p. 82.

20. Tzvetan Todorov, *The Conquest of America: The Question of the Other* (New York: HarperPerennial, 1984).

21. Schmitt, *Land and Sea*, p. 49.

22. Ibid., p. 59.

23. Samuel Garrett Zeitlin, "Propaganda and Critique: An Introduction to Land and Sea," in Carl Schmitt, *Land and Sea*, pp. xxxi–lxix. Schmitt was a marginal figure in the Nazi power structure during World War II. Various sources confirm his enthusiasm for Hitler's initial policies up to the Nazi-Soviet pact, which he viewed as legally valid. He considered Operation Barbarossa to be a mistake. See Zeitlin's discussion, pp. xl–xli.

24. Gopal Balakrishnan, *The Enemy: An Intellectual Portrait of Carl Schmitt* (London: Verso, 2000), p. 242.

25. Mark Mazower, *Hitler's Empire: How the Nazis Ruled Europe* (New York: Penguin, 2008), pp. 576–581.

26. Oliver Simons, "Carl Schmitt's Spatial Rhetoric," in Jens Meierhenrich and Oliver Simons, eds., *The Oxford Handbook of Carl Schmitt* (New York: Oxford University Press, 2016), pp. 776–802.

27. Beck, *Risk Society*.

28. The phrase "manufactured risks" is associated with the work of the British sociologist Anthony Giddens, whereas the phrase "anthropogenic risk" is associated with geologists and ecologists.

29. Beck, *Risk Society*, p. 19.

30. Timothy Mitchell, *Carbon Democracy: Political Power in the Age of Oil* (London: Verso, 2011).

31. Taylor, *The Way the Modern World Works*.

32. Michael S. Sherry, *The Rise of American Air Power* (New Haven, CT: Yale University Press, 1987).

33. Schmitt, *Dialogues on Power and Space*, p. 80.

34. Jim Davitch, "A Shield in the Sky: The Vertical Geopolitics of Transcontinental Air Defense," PhD dissertation, Virginia Tech, May 2023.

35. Francis Fitzgerald, *Way Out There In the Blue: Reagan, Star Wars and the End of the Cold War* (New York: Simon and Schuster, 2001); Columba Peoples, *Justifying Ballistic Missile Defence: Technology, Security and Culture* (Cambridge: Cambridge University Press, 2009); Alan Wolfe, *The Rise and Fall of the Soviet Threat* (Boston: South End Press, 1984)

36. Naomi Oreskes, *Science on a Mission: How Military Funding Shaped What We Do and Don't Know about the Ocean* (Chicago: University of Chicago Press, 2021); Rachel Squire, *Undersea Geopolitics: Sealab, Science and the Cold War* (Lanham, MD: Rowman and Littlefield, 2021).

37. Morrissey, *The Long War*.

38. "Kennedy Hails the Measure," *New York Times*, June 21, 1963, p. 2.

39. Parts of this section draw upon my essay "Battlefield" in John Agnew and David Livingstone, eds., *The Sage Handbook of Geographical Knowledge* (Los Angeles: Sage, 2011), pp. 217–226.

40. John Cloud, "Crossing the Olentangy River: The Figure of the Earth and the Military–Industrial–Academic-Complex, 1947–1972," *Studies in History and Philosophy of Science Part B: Studies in the History and Philosophy of Modern Physics* 31 (2000): 371–404.

41. See the NGA website: https://www.nga.mil/.

42. See Newell's superb account of this story in *Destined for the Stars*.

43. Lyndon B. Johnson, *The Vantage Point: Perspectives of the Presidency, 1963–1969* (New York: Holt, Reinhart and Winston, 1971), p. 276.

44. Denis Cosgrove, "Contested Global Visions: One-World, Whole-Earth, and the Apollo Space Photographs," *Annals of the Association of American Geographers* 84 (1994): 270–294.

45. *BBC News*, "Record Number of China Planes Enter Taiwan Air Defence Zone," October 5, 2021, https://www.bbc.com/news/world-asia-58794094.

46. Demetri Sevastopulo and Kathrin Hille, "China Vows to 'Crush' any Attempt by Taiwan to Pursue Independence," *Financial Times*, June 12, 2022, https://www.ft.com/content/342d53cf-4a88-4a01-85be-017b1 db57693.

47. Jill Goldenziel, "China Claims to Own the Taiwan Strait. That's Illegal," *Forbes*, June 28, 2022, https://www.forbes.com/sites/jillgoldenziel/2022/06/28/china-claims-to-own-the-taiwan-strait-thats-illegal/.

48. Stephen Graham, "Vertical Geopolitics: Baghdad and After," *Antipode* 36 (2004): 12–23; Stuart Elden, "Secure the Volume: Vertical Geopolitics and the Depth of Power," *Political Geography* 34 (2010): 35–51.

49. Eyal Wiezman, *Hollow Land: Israel's Architecture of Occupation*. (London: Verso 2007).

50. Ian Slesinger, "A Cartography of the Unknowable: Technology, Territory and Subterranean Agencies in Israel's Management of the Gaza Tunnels," *Geopolitics* 25 (2020): 17–42.

51. Peter Adey, *Aerial Life* (Oxford: Wiley-Blackwell 2010); Alison J. Williams, "Re-Orientating Vertical Geopolitics," *Geopolitics* 18 (2013): 225–246.

52. For an impressive open-source reconstruction of the balloon's journey, see Muyi Xiao, Ishaan Jhaveri, Eleanor Lutz, Christoph Koettl, and Julian E. Barnes, "Tracking a Chinese Balloon from Space," *New York Times*, March 20, 2023, https://www.nytimes.com/interactive/2023/03/20/science/chinese-space-balloon-incident.html.

53. David Martin, "The Bizarre Secret Behind China's Spy Balloon," *CBS News*, September 17, 2023, https://www.cbsnews.com/news/the-bizarre-secret-behind-chinas-spy-balloon/

54. From 1954 to 1964 William Perry served as director of Sylvania Electronic Defense Laboratories in California. This quote is from when Perry served (1977–1981) as under secretary of defense for research and engineering in the Carter administration. It was his one-sentence summation of the advances in precision missiles and saturation weaponry at the time. It is cited in the preface to the English edition of Paul Virilio, *War and Cinema: The Logistics of Perception* (London: Verso, 1989), p. 4.

55. Derek Gregory, "From a View to a Kill: Drones and Late Modern War," *Theory, Culture and Society* 28 (2011): 188–215; A. J. Williams, "Enabling Persistent Presence? Performing the Embodied Geopolitics of the Unmanned Aerial Vehicle Assemblage," *Political Geography* 30 (2011): 381–390.

56. Rey Chow, *The Age of the World Target: Self-Referentiality in War, Theory, and Comparative Work* (Durham, NC: Duke University Press, 2006), p. 27.

57. Jeremy Scahill, *Dirty Wars: The World Is a Battlefield* (New York: Nation Books, 2013).

58. For one source on the figures, see https://www.newamerica.org/international-security/reports/americas-counterterrorism-wars/.

59. Derek Gregory, "The Everywhere War," *Geographical Journal* 177 (2011): 238–250; Hugh Gusterson, *Drone: Remote Control Warfare* (Cambridge, MA: MIT Press, 2017); Lisa Park and Caren Kaplan, eds., *Life in the Age of Drone Warfare* (Durham, NC: Duke University Press, 2017).

60. Antonio Calcara, Andrea Gilli, Mauro Gilli, Raffaele Marchetti, and Ivan Zaccagnini, "Why Drones Have Not Revolutionized War," *International Security* 46, no. 4 (2022): 130–171.

61. Andrea Gilli and Mauro Gilli, "The Diffusion of Drone Warfare? Industrial, Organizational, and Infrastructural Constraints," *Security Studies* 25 (2016): 50–84.

62. Stephen Witt, "The Turkish Drone That Changed the Nature of Warfare," *New Yorker*, May 9, 2022, https://www.newyorker.com/magazine/2022/05/16/the-turkish-drone-that-changed-the-nature-of-warfare.

63. Vladimir Putin, Presidential Address to the Federal Assembly, March 1, 2018.

64. Dmitri Sevastopolu, "China Conducted Two Hypersonic Weapons Tests This Summer," *Financial Times*, October 20, 2021, https://www.ft.com/content/c7139a23-1271-43ae-975b-9b632330130b.

CHAPTER 7

1. The map was created by Bernard Vernon Darbishire, a Welsh cartographer who studied under Mackinder at Oxford University and later became a professional cartographer. He established a company in partnership with Stanford of London to produce and sell maps. Darbishire also taught cartographic design and drawing at the School of Geography at Oxford. This explains the double credit on the map. Darbishire is best known for his *War Atlas* published by Oxford University Press in 1915.

2. This expedition, also known as the *Discovery* expedition, was between 1901 and 1904.

3. Mackinder, "Geographical Pivot," p. 438.

4. The polar regions at the outset of the twentieth century were arenas of state competition for prestige and position. The ability of states to set aside competition and cooperate in these regions has waxed and waned. At numerous points in the twentieth century, the polar regions became highly contested zones of struggle. Today, Antarctica and its surrounding seas are very much within the sights of resource-seeking states. See Sanjay Chaturvedi, *The Polar Regions: A Political Geography* (Chichester, UK: Wiley, 1996); Klaus Dodds, *Geopolitics in Antarctica* (Chichester, UK:

Wiley, 1997); Klaus Dodds and Mark Nutall, *The Scramble for the Poles* (Cambridge: Polity, 2016).

5. Instability does not mean collapse, and there is some geophysical research that suggests that Thwaites may be more resilient than feared. See J. N. Bassis, B. Berg, A. J. Crawford, and D. I. Benn, "Transition to Marine Ice Cliff Instability Controlled by Ice Thickness Gradients and Velocity," *Science* 372, no. 6548 (2021): 1342–1344; Matthew J. Hoffman, Xylar Asay-Davis, Stephen F. Price, Jeremy Fyke, and Mauro Perego, "Effect of Subshelf Melt Variability on Sea Level Rise Contribution from Thwaites Glacier, Antarctica," *Journal of Geophysical Research: Earth Surface* 124 (2019): 2798–2822.

6. World Meteorological Organization Secretary General Petteri Taalas, cited in Rob Pichera, "CO_2 Levels in the Atmosphere Reach a 3 Million-Year High, Putting the World 'Way off Track' on Climate Goals," *CNN*, October 25, 2021, https://www.cnn.com/2021/10/25/world/emissions-climate-greenhouse-gas-bulletin-wmo-intl/index.html.

7. Angela Fitz, "'Doomsday Glacier,' Which Could Raise Sea Level by Several Feet, Is Holding on 'by Its Fingernails,' Scientists Say," *CNN*, September 6, 2022, https://edition.cnn.com/2022/09/05/world/thwaites-doomsday-glacier-sea-level-climate/index.html.

8. Damien Carrington, "Gulf Stream Could Collapse as Early as 2025, Study Suggests," *The Guardian*, July 25, 2023, https://www.theguardian.com/environment/2023/jul/25/gulf-stream-could-collapse-as-early-as-2025-study-suggests.

9. Intergovernmental Panel on Climate Change, *Climate Change 2021: The Physical Science Basis.* Working Group I contribution to the Sixth Assessment Report of the Intergovernmental Panel on Climate Change, August 2021. Available at www.ipcc.ch.

10. Secretary-General's statement on the IPCC Working Group 1 Report on the Physical Science Basis of the Sixth Assessment, August 9, 2021, https://www.un.org/sg/en/content/secretary-generals-statement-the-ipcc-working-group-1-report-the-physical-science-basis-of-the-sixth-assessment.

11. There are a series of these videos. See Video: Global Warming from 1880 to 2020, https://climate.nasa.gov/climate_resources/139/video-global-warming-from-1880-to-2020/; and Lori Perkins, Global Temperature Anomalies from 1880 to 2020, January 14, 2021, https://svs.gsfc.nasa.gov/cgi-bin/details.cgi?aid=4882.

12. For an example, see the temperature forecast map for the United States in Bonni Cohen and Jon Shenk, directors, *An Inconvenient Sequel:*

Truth to Power (Paramount Pictures, 2017). For a typical red fire weather day map, see Maanvi Singh and John Upton, "Northern California Sees More and More 'Fire Weather' Days, Data Shows," *The Guardian*, November 9, 2021, https://www.theguardian.com/us-news/2021/nov/09/northern-california-wildfires-fire-weather-climate.

13. Max Callaghan et al., "Machine-Learning-Based Evidence and Attribution Mapping of 100,000 Climate Impact Studies," *Nature Climate Change* 11 (2021): 966–972.

14. See Deudney, *Dark Skies*; Rubenstein, *Astrotopia*.

15. Intergovernmental Panel on Climate Change, *Climate Change 2021: The Physical Science Basic*, SPM-17.

16. Climate Action Tracker, "Despite Glasgow Climate Pact 2030 Climate Target Updates Have Stalled," June 2022, https://climateactiontracker.org/documents/1051/CAT_2022-06-03_Briefing_MidYearUpdate_DespiteGlasgowTargetUpdatesStalled.pdf.

17. Chris Mooney, Juliet Eilperin, Desmond Butler, John Muyskens, Anu Narayanswamy, and Naema Ahmed, "Countries' Climate Pledges Built on Flawed Data, Post Investigation Finds," *Washington Post*, November 7, 2021, https://www.washingtonpost.com/climate-environment/interactive/2021/greenhouse-gas-emissions-pledges-data/.

18. Much of Europe Union's emissions reductions are achieved by burning biomass instead of coal and then not counting the resulting greenhouse gases, which can be comparable to those from coal. See Michael Birnbaum, "E.U.'s Big Climate Ambitions Have the Scent of Wood Smoke." *Washington Post*, November 10, 2021, https://www.washingtonpost.com/climate-environment/2021/11/10/eu-cop26-biomass-wood-emissions/.

19. Climate Action Tracker, "Glasgow's 2030 Credibility Gap: Net Zero's Lip Service to Climate Action," Warming Projections Global Update, November 2021, https://climateactiontracker.org/documents/997/CAT_2021-11-09_Briefing_Global-Update_Glasgow2030CredibilityGap.pdf.

20. Matthew Fitzpatrick and Robert Dunn, "Contemporary Climate Analogs for 540 North American Urban Areas in the Late 21st Century." *Nature Communications 10, no. 614 (2019): 1–7, https://www.nature.com/articles/s41467-019-08540-3/,*

21. Mark Lynas, *Our Final Warning: Six Degrees of Climate Emergency* (London: 4th Estate, 2020), pp. 85–86.

22. Users can find the climate analog to their home city using the mapping site established from Fitzpatrick and Dunn's calculations at https://fitz lab.shinyapps.io/cityapp/.

23. Intergovernmental Panel on Climate Change, *Climate Change and Land: An IPCC Special Report on Climate Change, Desertification, Land Degradation, Sustainable Land Management, Food Security, and Greenhouse Gas Fluxes in Terrestrial Ecosystems. Summary for Policymakers* (2020), p. 7. Available at https://www.ipcc.ch/srccl/.

24. Tim Lenton, C. Xu, J. F. Abrams, et al. "Quantifying the Human Cost of Global Warming," *Nature Sustainability* (2023), https://doi.org/10.1038/ s41893-023-01132-6.

25. See https://www.oecd.org/agriculture/topics/water-and-agriculture/.

26. IPCC, "Summary for Policymakers," in *Climate Change and Land: An IPCC Special Report on Climate Change, Desertification, Land Degradation, Sustainable Land Management, Food Security, and Greenhouse Gas Fluxes in Terrestrial Ecosystems* (2019), https://www.ipcc.ch/srccl/cite-report/.

27. Jo Handelsman, *A World Without Soil* (New Haven, CT: Yale University Press, 2021).

28. Ibid, p. 7.

29. Jack Nicas, "A Slow-Motion Climate Disaster: The Spread of Barren Land," *New York Times*, December 3, 2021, https://www.nytimes.com/ 2021/12/03/world/americas/brazil-climate-change-barren-land.html.

30. Chi Xu, Timothy A. Kohler, Timothy M. Lenton, Jens-Christian Svenning, and Marten Scheffer, "Future of the Human Climate Niche," *PNAS* 117 (2020): 11350–11355.

31. The niche identification here was subsequently revised with new data.

32. Xu et al., "Future of the Human Climate Niche," p. 11352.

33. Lenton et al., "Quantifying the Human Cost of Global Warming."

34. Ibid., p. 2.

35. Gaia Vince, *Nomad Century: How Climate Migration Will Reshape Our World* (New York: Flatiron Books, 2022).

36. Lenton et al., "Quantifying," p. 6.

37. Laurie Pearson, *Carbon Colonialism How Rich Countries Export Climate Breakdown* (Manchester: Manchester University Press, 2023); Farhana Sultana, "The Unbearable Heaviness of Climate Coloniality," *Political Geography* 99 (2022): 102638, https://doi.org/10.1016/j.pol geo.2022.102638.

38. Johan Rockström, J. Gupta, D Qin, et al., "Safe and Just Earth System Boundaries," *Nature* 619 (2023): 102–111, https://doi.org/10.1038/s41 586-023-06083-8

39. Henry Shu, *Climate Justice* (New York: Oxford University Press, 2014); Mary Robinson and Caitriona Palmer, *Climate Justice* (New York: Bloomsbery, 2018); Olúfẹ́mi O. Táíwò, *Reconsidering Reparations* (New York: Oxford University Press, 2022).

40. Achille Mbembe, *Necropolitics* (Durham, NC: Duke University Press, 2019).

41. White House, Remarks by President Biden at the COP26 Leaders Statement, November 1, 2022, https://www.whitehouse.gov/briefing-room/speeches-remarks/2021/11/01/remarks-by-president-biden-at-the-cop26-leaders-statement/.

42. White House, *National Security Strategy*, October 2022, https://www.whitehouse.gov/wp-content/uploads/2022/10/Biden-Harris-Admi nistrations-National-Security-Strategy-10.2022.pdf.

43. Rush Doshi, *The Long Game: China's Strategy to Displace American Order* (New York: Oxford University Press, 2021).

44. Julie Michelle Klinger, *Rare Earth Frontiers* (Ithaca, NY: Cornell University Press, 2017).

45. See White House, "Remarks by National Security Advisor Jake Sullivan on Renewing American Economic Leadership at the Brookings Institution," April 27, 2023, https://www.whitehouse.gov/briefing-room/speeches-remarks/2023/04/27/remarks-by-national-secur ity-advisor-jake-sullivan-on-renewing-american-economic-leaders hip-at-the-brookings-institution/. On the term "de-risking," see Damien Cave, "How 'Decoupling' from China Became 'De-risking,'" *New York Times*, May 20, 2023, https://www.nytimes.com/2023/05/20/world/decoupling-china-de-risking.html.

46. A critical mineral is any mineral, element, substance, or material that the US Secretary of the Interior or Energy deems at high risk of supply chain disruption and that serves an essential function in energy technologies.

47. Agathe Demartis, "How Climate Change Will Reshape Economic Statecraft," Carnegie Research, June 2023, https://carnegieendowm ent.org/2023/06/20/how-climate-change-will-reshape-economic-sta tecraft-pub-89978.

48. National Intelligence Council, *National Intelligence Estimate: Climate Change and International Responses Increasing Challenges to US National Security through 2040.* October 2021, https://www.dni.gov/files/ODNI/documents/assessments/NIE_Climate_Change_and_National_Secur ity.pdf.

49. See https://ourworldindata.org/annual-co2-emissions.

50. See https://ourworldindata.org/world-population-growth.

51. Hannah Ellis-Petersen, "India's Energy Conundrum: Committed to Renewables but Still Expanding Coal," *The Guardian*, November 15, 2022, https://www.theguardian.com/world/2022/nov/15/india-committed-to-clean-energy-but-continues-to-boost-coal-production.

52. Tim Gore, *Carbon Inequality in 2030: Per Capita Consumption Emissions and the 1.5°C Goal*, Institute for European Environmental Policy, Oxfam, June 11, 2021.

53. "China's Solar Boom Is Already Accelerating Past Last Year's Record Surge," *Bloomberg News*, May 22, 2023, https://www.bloomberg.com/news/articles/2023-05-22/china-s-solar-power-boom-is-accelerating-past-last-year-s-record-surge.

54. Aroush Kondal, "Is India on Track to Achieve 40 GW Annual Solar Capacity Addition to Meet 2030 Target?" *India Times*, May 29, 2023, https://energy.economictimes.indiatimes.com/news/renewable/is-india-on-track-to-achieve-40-gw-annual-solar-capacity-addition-to-meet-2030-target/100574366.

55. Lisa Friedman, "China and U.S., at Odds on Many Issues, Agree on a Surprise Climate Deal," *New York Times*, November 10, 2021, https://www.nytimes.com/2021/11/10/climate/china-us-climate-deal-kerry-xie.html.

56. Brad Plumer and Lisa Friedman, "Negotiators Strike a Climate Deal, but World Remains Far from Limiting Warming," *New York Times*, November 13, 2021, https://www.nytimes.com/2021/11/13/climate/cop26-glasgow-climate-agreement.html.

57. John Foster, "The Weasel Words of Cop28 Can Be Easily Twisted," *The Guardian*, letters, 25 December 2023, https://www.theguardian.com/environment/2023/dec/25/the-weasel-words-of-cop28-can-be-easily-twisted.

58. Clive Hamilton, *Defiant Earth* (Cambridge: Polity, 2017), pp. 84–85.

59. Latour, *Down to Earth*.

60. Rubenstein, *Astrotopia*, p. 96.

61. Oreskes and Conway, *The Collapse of Western Civilization*.

62. Amitav Ghosh, *The Great Derangement: Climate Change and the Unthinkable* (Chicago: University of Chicago Press, 2016); David Pilling, "Calls for a Just Energy Transition in Africa Carry Echoes of Elite Panic," *Financial Times*, July 11, 2022, https://www.ft.com/content/817a5868-872d-401a-802a-ce7ef3465e0c.

63. Naomi Oreskes and Erik M. Conway, *Merchants of Doubt* (New York: Bloomsbury, 2011).

64. Michael Mann, *The New Climate Wars* (New York: Public Affairs, 2022).

65. Malm, *How to Blow Up a Pipeline.*

66. Anatol Lieven, *Climate Change and the Nation State: The Realist Case* (London: Penguin, 2021).

67. Christian Parenti, *Tropic of Chaos: Climate Change and the New Geography of Violence* (New York: Nation Books, 2011).

68. For a version of such a dystopia, see John Lanchester, *The Wall* (New York: Norton, 2020).

69. Mbembe, *Necropolitics*, p. 27.

CONCLUSION

1. Lori Montgomery, "In Norfolk, Evidence of Climate Change Is in the Streets at High Tide," *Washington Post*, May 31, 2014, https://www. washingtonpost.com/business/economy/in-norfolk-evidence-of-clim ate-change-is-in-the-streets-at-high-tide/2014/05/31/fe3ae860-e71f-11e3-8f90-73e071f3d637_story.html.

2. The Virginia Institute of Marine Sciences projects that by 2050, Norfolk at Sewell's Point will see 1.32 feet of sea level rise. There will likely be a massive sea wall project undertaken in the area to try to prevent this.

3. United Nations Framework Convention on Climate Change, *Technical Dialogue of the First Global Stocktake: Synthesis Report by the Co-facilitators on the Technical Dialogue*, September 8, 2023, p. 5, https://unfccc.int/ sites/default/files/resource/sb2023_09_adv.pdf.

4. Given his position Guterres has to chose his words carefully. See Somini Sengupta, "U.N. Chief's Test: Shaming without Naming the World's Climate Delinquents," *New York Times*, September 19, 2023, https://www.nytimes.com/2023/09/19/climate/guterres-climate-sum mit.html.

5. Romain Ioualalen and Kelly Trout, *Planet Wreckers: How 20 Countries' Oil and Gas Extraction Plans Risk Locking in Climate Chaos*, Oil Change International Report, September 2023, p. 4, https://priceofoil.org/cont ent/uploads/2023/09/OCI-Planet-Wreckers-Report-Final.pdf.

6. Damien Carrington, "We're in Uncharted Territory for the World's Climate, UN Says," *The Guardian*, October 31, 2021, https://www. theguardian.com/environment/2021/oct/31/were-in-uncharted-territ ory-for-the-worlds-climate-un-says; Fiona Harvey, "World Likely to Breach 1.5C Climate Threshold by 2027, Scientists Warn," *The Guardian*, May 17, 2023, https://www.theguardian.com/environment/2023/may/ 17/global-heating-climate-crisis-record-temperatures-wmo-research.

7. Bruno Latour, "Seven Objections against Landing on Earth," in Bruno Latour and Peter Weibel, *Critical Zones: The Science and Politics of Landing on Earth*. (Cambridge, MA: MIT Press, 2020).

8. The welcome critique of the discipline of Economics for its abject failure to allow real ecological costing of economic activities can be applied to the subfield of International Relations, which also has excluded discussion of the broader geo-ecological costs of grand strategies, great power rivalries, and wars.

9. It is a prevailing conceit in US geopolitical culture that the United States does not have territorial ambitions. But the liberal world order that it defends and expands through extended alliance systems is a territorial order, one that has made exhaustive demands on the common geo-ecological territories of the planet.

10. Tim Jackson, *Post Growth: Life after Capitalism* (Cambridge: Polity, 2021); Jason Hickel, *Less Is More: How Degrowth Will Save the World* (London: Penguin, 2020); Samuel Alexander, Sangeetha Chandrashekeran, and Brendan Gleeson, eds., *Post-Capitalist Futures: Paradigms, Politics, and Prospects* (Singapore: Palgrave Macmillan, 2022).

11. Roy Scranton, *Learning to Die in the Anthropocene* (San Francisco: City Lights, 2015).

12. International Energy Agency, *World Energy Investment 2023*, May 2023.

Index

For the benefit of digital users, indexed terms that span two pages (e.g., 52–53) may, on occasion, appear on only one of those pages.